literary
dublin

Books by Herbert A. Kenny

A CATHOLIC QUIZ BOOK

SONNETS TO THE MOTHER OF CHRIST (*poetry*)

TWELVE BIRDS (*poetry*)

SUBURBAN MAN (*poetry*)

CAPE ANN: CAPE AMERICA

LITERARY DUBLIN: A HISTORY

for children

DEAR DOLPHIN

ALISTARE OWL

Herbert A. Kenny

literary dublin

A HISTORY

WITH ILLUSTRATIONS BY

Charles Carroll

820
9941
KEN

TAPLINGER PUBLISHING COMPANY / NEW YORK

GILL & MACMILLAN / DUBLIN

75-22038

First Edition

Published in the United States in 1974 by
TAPLINGER PUBLISHING CO., INC.
New York, New York

Also published in 1974 by
Gill and Macmillan Ltd
2 Belvedere Place
Dublin 1
and in London through association
with the
Macmillan Publishers Group

Grateful acknowledgment is made to Devin-Adair Company and to
Mrs. Patrick Kavanagh for permission to quote "Who Killed James
Joyce" by Patrick Kavanagh. From *Collected Poems of Patrick
Kavanagh*, Copyright © 1964 by Patrick Kavanagh. The lines "Old
Woman in Front of the Abbey Theatre," by L. A. G. Strong are re-
printed by permission of A. D. Peters and Company.

Published simultaneously in the Dominion of Canada by
Burns & MacEachern, Ltd., Ontario

Library of Congress Catalog Card Number: 72–6626

Taplinger ISBN 0–8008–4921–3

Gill and Macmillan ISBN 0 7171 0702 7

Designed by Mollie M. Torras

To Teresa

and

all our Irish forebears

ACKNOWLEDGMENTS

Any number of persons on both sides of the Atlantic have been helpful and encouraging to me: Sybil Lebrocquy, John V. Kelleher, John Philip Cohane, Mr. and Mrs. Sean Donlon, Stephen Preston, Sr. M. James, S.N.D., Evelyn Crowell, Philip Driscoll, Robert Taylor, Seamus O'Neill, Terence De Vere White, Walter M. Whitehill, and the staff of the Boston Atheneum, Philip J. McNiff and the Boston Public Library, Cornelius Howard, Mary Baker, Michael Heaney, John Armstrong, David Marcus, George Gloss, Bobs Pinkerton, and Terry Lent. I thank them again.

For permission to quote L. A. G. Strong, I thank A. D. Peters, the London Literary Agency, and for permission to quote from his own work, I thank Micheál MacLiammóir, whose letters are as gracious as his stage presence. I thank Professor David Greene for permission to quote from his translations from the Irish, and I thank the National Library in Ireland for permission to quote from the diary of Joseph Holloway.

So personal is the city of Dublin that there is an inclination to thank it.

HERBERT A. KENNY

CONTENTS

ILLUSTRATIONS

I believe profoundly, with the most extreme of Nationalists in the future of Ireland, and in the vision of light seen by Bridget which she saw and confessed between hopes and tears to Patrick, and that this is the Isle of Destiny and the destiny will be glorious and not ignoble, and when our hour is come we will have something to give the world, and we will be proud to give rather than to grasp.

AE (GEORGE RUSSELL)

(Quoted by President John F. Kennedy before the Dail Eireann, June, 1963)

BENDACT FOR CECH N-OEN LEGFAS

.

INTRODUCTION

Let us begin with some vignettes, for the Irish and all Dubliners are storytellers, and stories can tell us a good deal, for they are parables or allegories or fables or instructive tales that have insights, if we but find them, and profound truths if we can seize their essences.

Once upon a time, a wandering minstrel, a poet, a bard, came into the town called Dublin and sang his love lyrics in the thin mists that rose from the Liffey where the long boats of the Vikings raised their graceful prows. The year was perhaps A.D. 950 and the Vikings had been there for two hundred years, which is the age of the United States of America. The poet sang in Irish, for it is the language of love and the language of song, and the Vikings by that time had learned to listen and to understand and even to speak it, for it was a language superior to their own.

Our poet was not the first who had sung to them in the hopes of a copper or iron coin, and he was angry when they paid him no attention. He turned on them in his anger, struck fire from his harp, and threatened them with satire. Today we do not feel satire to be much of a threat—the magic has gone out of it unless we hold political office and the satirist is a political cartoonist. This could be, of course, because we are less literate than those people were in A.D. 950 and not because we are wiser. More than that, at that time in that barricaded town in that country of poets, satire had not merely an element of magic, it had an element of voodoo.

The simple fact was that a satire could be an evil thing and that a man could die from a satire made against him. Thus when our poet found himself neglected to the point of insult, he threatened the Vikings with satires but agreed to let them buy themselves off, two pence from good Vikings, one pence from bad Vikings. Each Viking gave him two pence lest he be thought a bad Viking and hence just maybe more suitable to a satire. To this day in Dublin, satire is no laughing matter.

Four hundred years before our wandering minstrel challenged the Vikings in their Dublin stronghold—and he must have been a poor poet indeed since the best of them were singing in the lush barbaric courts of the Irish kings and feudal lords—the greatest of the Irish pagan poets, Oisin or Ossian, returned to Ireland from the magic land of Tir-na-nOg. Where is Tir-na-nOg? Alas, we have lost its location. It is the holy land where men never grow old and women are eternally beautiful. Oisin had been taken there three hundred years before by a fairy queen who came riding one day on a white horse over the scruff of the sea. She had come from Tir-na-nOg looking for a human bridegroom and was struck by his beauty, for he was the son of a king as well as a poet. She took him back and the three hundred years he lived with her seemed to him but a day. When he became lonesome for the Fianna, the giant warriors who had served his king, she allowed him to return under certain conditions. Thus it was that Oisin, who should have died centuries before Christianity came to Ireland, nevertheless was privileged to meet Saint Patrick, or should it be the other way around?

The saint and his followers met the poet and his companion, and the poet charmed the saint with his stories of Fionn Mac-Cumhaill (pronounced Finn McCool), one of Ireland's great folk heroes, leader of the Fianna, a king's guard, who hundreds of years earlier had exulted in heroic deeds on behalf of the

High King of Ireland. After the intoxication of the hours of
storytelling, the saint was shaken by his conscience and worried
that he had betrayed his mission, which was to preach the doc-
trine of Christ Crucified and not to listen to the pagan stories
of pagan poets. As a result he slept that night uneasily, but as
he slept his two guardian angels told him not only had he done
well to listen to the stories, but that he would do even better
if he saw that they were recorded for posterity, because Ossian,
of course, had no alphabet or writing. The saint put his scriptors
to work and the course of Irish literature was altered, and today
we have such marvelous stories as the following:

When Mis, the only daughter of Daire Daoidgheal, saw the
body of her father slain in battle, she went mad, drank blood
from the wounds, and fled into the wilds of a mountain near
Tralee. For one hundred to three hundred years she lived like
a beast, killing and eating people and animals alike, and growing
in appearance more savage than the beasts she killed. Hair
spread all over her body, and her nails on hand and foot became
claws with which she would kill and rend her victims. She was
a nuisance to the countryside, but the insane are sacred and
the king would not have her killed, but offered large rewards
for whoever would take her alive. Many failed fatally. Duv
Ruis, a poet and harper, offered to try to capture her with
his harp. The king was skeptical but agreed and even provided
gold and silver coins the youth requested.

The youth's plan was simple. He thought if he could lie with
her he could cure her of her madness. So he went to the mountain, spread his cloak, placed gold and silver around, lay with
his harp on his chest and with his whole body exposed. He
caught her attention, first with his music, and then with the
sight of him.

Professor David Greene translates their first meeting thus:

"Aren't you a man?" she said. "I am," said he. "What is this?"
said she, putting her hand on the harp. "A harp," said he. "Ho,
ho!" said she, "I remember the harp; my father had one like it.

Play it for me." "I will," said he, "but don't do me any damage
or harm." "I won't," said she. Then she looked at the gold and
silver and said, "What are these?" "Gold and silver," said he.
"I remember," said she, "my father had gold. Och, ochone!"

As she looked at him, she caught sight of his nakedness and
his members of pleasure. "What are those?" said she, pointing
to his bag or his eggs—and he told her. "What is this?" said she,
about the other thing that she saw. "That is the wand of the
great feat," said he. "I do not remember that," said she, "my
father hadn't anything like that. The wand of the feat; what is
the feat?" "Sit beside me," said he, "and I will do the feat of
the wand for you." "I will," said she, "and stay you with me."
"I will," said he, and he lay with her and knew her, and she
said, "Ha, ba, ba, that was a good feat; do it again." "I will,"
said he; "however, I will play the harp for you first." "Don't
mind the harp," said she, "but do the feat."

For two months he stayed with her, cooking the food she
caught, and scouring her with animal fats and washing her in
the brook, and at the end of that time, the hair had fallen away
and rationality returned.

They were happily married and she bore him four children
and, as the story concludes, she was one of the loveliest and
most talented women in all Munster in her day.

The story was found preserved in the library of the famous
Irish seminary, St. Patrick's College in Maynooth, having been
written down in the eighteenth century in modern Gaelic. The
story and the incident point up a paradox in the Irish people
that is perhaps no paradox at all, except to an Anglo-Saxon
society; they are a puritanical people but they have a natural-
ness of expression that would silence an English drawing room.
Yet, as we see in the story of Duv Ruis and Mis, delicacy and
forthrightness go hand in hand.

Part of the explanation lies in the failure of Victorian prudery
to touch the Irish-speaking people, cut off as they were from
the hypocrisies of that period and, instead, fed by the natural
innocence of the countryside. Although an American reader

will find it hard to believe, the average Dubliner is much more rational in his approach to sexuality than the average New Yorker saturated by sex-keyed advertising and the lure of amorality. It is well to remember that the Comstockian laws on obscenity that prevailed in the United States were breached by the book of a Dubliner, James Joyce, who, in his own speech, interestingly enough, in his mature years never used profanity of any sort, sacrilegious or sexual.

The notion that sex is a necessary physical therapy for the young, the old, and the indifferent, and that the sublimation of it a menace to mental health, is a superstition of the affluent, sensate, and materialistic society, and deemed absurd in the Far East and Ireland. Men and women concerned with survival, or men and women with enough spiritual sense to guess at the depths of human psychology—they too know better.

This does not mean that the Irish do not have their Bowdlerizers, their bluenoses, their fanatics, and, notoriously, their censorship, once so irritating but now fast fading. For the puritan element is ever so slowly ceding to the strain of Catholicism that sparkles in Chaucer and in early Irish literature, that has marked Latin Catholicism, and which, as a result of Vatican Council II, despite the resistance of the conservative Irish bishops, will restore the balance in Ireland. That will profoundly affect the future development of Irish literature and Dublin's litterateurs.

The other vital factor so far as the future of Dublin's literary history is concerned is a resolution of the political problem. The isolated counties of the north must inevitably be returned to the Republic of Ireland and this will come about only with great travail and great travail will follow their return. Nevertheless, it will be, and it will be a good thing too for Ireland and for England because it will enable them to breed more of the literary giants who take their strength from the two cultures, men like Edmund Burke and Jonathan Swift, who benefited one way; men like Bernard Shaw and Sean O'Casey and Samuel Beckett, who benefited in another.

The rigorousness of Irish Catholicism is a posture that was demanded by history if the Irish nation was to survive as a nation. The violence that desecrates the north today is a measure of the distortion of that nationalism. Once the nation's integrity is guaranteed, the violence will disappear and the religious rigorousness modulate to a true spirituality. Dublin's greatest days lie ahead.

This is a lighthearted book but nonetheless serious for that. It is lighthearted because it removes as much emphasis as possible from the violence and tragedy, the bitterness and the bloodshed, the political crimes and international cruelties that have marked Dublin's history from its beginnings. Much art if not most art has roots in suffering, deprivation, and conflict, nor are the literary arts an exception, but it is on achievement rather than on causes that we will lean, and on persons rather than their works, for these should be read for themselves.

To write the literary history of Dublin will, at times, seem tantamount to writing the literary history of Ireland, but we will endeavor to keep the city in focus and if our animadversions wander from that base we ask the reader to keep one foot in the city, and, to make an Irish bull of it, both feet well in hand. At the end, we hope that he will be reluctant to leave Dublin, for it is an extraordinary and lovable city with a distinct personality. Many have called it "dear old dirty Dublin." Dear it remains, but as the years turn, it is cleaner today than Boston or New York, although like them threatened by an insensate industrialism.

Over those cities and over London, Dublin has a curious advantage that has played its part and still plays its part in advancing its extraordinary literary tradition. Dublin is not only the capital of the Republic of Ireland, it was once the second city of the British empire. Not only is it the political capital of the young republic, and a city of ancient architectural charm, it is the literary capital, the financial capital, the artistic capital, the industrial capital, the musical capital, and the educational capital, for it has at its very heart one of the preeminent universities of the Western world.

More than that, all these qualities stand in excellent equilibrium. The city has internally and externally that mysterious quality called scale, a property that leaves a man his dignity when he stands beside a monument or walks along a thoroughfare. We might put it this way: Dublin is a very human city and no man is lost within it as he is lost in New York or London. If Washington, New York City, and Boston were miniaturized and melded into one city, then you would have Dublin. It is a city where you can find the wife of the prime minister shopping beside you, see Samuel Beckett, a Dublin-born Nobel prize winner, hurrying from his Parisian exile to a recording session on O'Connell Street, listen to the nation's foremost poets reciting in a pub, walk among eighteenth-century buildings redolent with charm and history, marked by bullet holes but also by a muted grace.

Here is a city a man can stride the length and breadth of and not be exhausted; a city where the students of Trinity College can cross the block to Leinster House and observe the sessions of the Dail, their national parliament; a city where a householder can walk down from Belvedere Place through layers of history to pay a tax bill in Dublin Castle, once the stronghold of English dominance, among the ghosts of the most literate and articulate patriot-martyrs ever to die for a seemingly hopeless cause.

Jorge Luis Borges, the Argentine writer, conceived of a magic crystal ball called an Aleph in which the human eye could catch all geographical space in a miraculous condensation. That is the quality in Dublin which I would emphasize, for nowhere else can one find such an *omnium gatherum* of elements calculated to heighten one's intellectual, imaginative, and intuitive faculties by a perpetual and electric mutuality of exchange. It is a special dimension—let us call it the Dublin Dimension. Against such a claim, a skeptical reader might suggest, say,

Budapest. Dublin has another superiority to mark it off from such rivals: because the English language is the language of the overwhelming mass of the people of Ireland (only a handful still speak only Irish) the residents of Dublin are, in turn, members of the globe-encircling, English-speaking community which, at the moment, dominates the world, and yet they have the additional resource of another language, their aboriginal Gaelic, which has a splendid literature of its own. They are happily placed in time, the Dubliners, for they are politically a young people, looking eagerly forward, unlike the English, who are faced with reflecting on lost glory and fearful of a diminution of identity and force as they merge with the European Economic Community. Dublin then is unique and we should expect from it unique achievement. That we find can be documented.

A propagandist could make the case that Dublin has produced the greatest novelist of the twentieth century (James Joyce), the greatest poet of the twentieth century (William Butler Yeats), the greatest playwrights of the English stage in this century (Bernard Shaw and Sean O'Casey), the greatest modern national theater (the Abbey with John M. Synge, Yeats, T. C. Murray, Lady Gregory, Padraic Colum, Sean O'Casey, Brendan Behan), the greatest English playwrights since Shakespeare (William Congreve, Richard Brinsley Sheridan, Thomas Southerne, Oliver Goldsmith, Oscar Wilde), the greatest orator of the English tongue (Edmund Burke), the greatest satirist the language has known (Jonathan Swift), three Nobel prize winners (Shaw, Yeats, and Beckett), and the foremost short-story writers of the age (Liam O'Flaherty, Mary Lavin, Frank O'Connor, and Sean O'Faolain).

Such a catalogue, gratuitously indited, can be gratuitously challenged but only in its parts. Someone might well say, thinking of vocal effects, that Burke was not the greatest orator in the history of the House of Commons; that he doesn't care for Joyce; or that designating any poet as "the greatest" is nonsense. The fact is that more critics will muster to the side of

Yeats than to the side of any other twentieth-century poet; that Joyce's achievement is so formidable that it doesn't matter much how one classifies it; and that, if Burke was not pre-eminent orator, Dublin has produced more distinguished orators than any city three times its size. Such a catalogue demonstrates simply that an account of Dublin as a mother of literature is amply justified, and to subsume it under the heading of English literature has become a piece of critical nonsense. However much writers like Congreve, for example, rebelled against the place of their birth or education, they somehow absorbed whatever the alembic of the Dublin atmosphere distills, and so represent a fragment of the prodigious orality of Irish culture, which is, one of the major facets, if not the unique characteristic, of the literature and the daily life.

The Irish had no written literature until Palladius, or Patrick, brought them the alphabet along with Christianity. Before that, perhaps for two thousand years, their laws, songs, and sagas, and an intolerable number of genealogies, were committed to memory by scholars meticulously trained through years of apprenticeship. Incredible mnemonic strength is a peculiarly Celtic trait and tradition, like chess playing today among Russians. One does not need a degree in psychology or linguistics to recognize the obvious link between a tradition of interminable memorization and interminable talk.

Padraic Colum, one of Ireland's most famous authors of the twentieth century, poet, playwright, and historian, told me that when he was assigned, after Irish independence, to record folklore of the illiterate country people, lest it be lost forever, he learned that their ignorance of writing helped improve the memory (that physical muscle) so that the average illiterate Irishman had a speaking vocabulary of six thousand words while the average English factory worker, in part the victim of the dehumanization of mass-production lines, commanded in his speech only two thousand. These are unlikely figures. However, if we grant some force to the nominalistic theory that the concept is not in the mind until the term is, or, in brief, that words make the man, we can posit for the man with the larger vocabulary, all things being equal, an interior life of far more depth and vitality.

William Carleton, one of Dublin's greatest novelists in the nineteenth century, heard innumerable stories from his father, a man who Carleton said had committed to memory most of the Old and New Testaments. The winter nights in Ireland are long and the winter itself is long and the darkness is more tiresome than the cold and there is more of it. The shanachie, or Irish storyteller, was as traditional as the bard, and he had a magazine of stories, long and short, he could draw on endlessly. From Halloween—the best of nights for storytelling—until Saint Patrick's Feast in the middle of March, an expert shanachie could wear away the winter darkness (or at least the wakefulness of his audience) without repeating himself one night. One of them is reported to have discoursed half a million words of stories, sagas, and songs. The storytelling sessions, called *ceilidhe*, which is pronounced "kaylee," would bring half a dozen storytellers together in a sort of competition. Many of the stories were the same, of course, differing in the technique of telling, but not in words.

"And," writes William Butler Yeats, "if any had a different version from the others they would all recite theirs and vote and the man who had varied would have to abide by their verdict. In this way, stories have been handed down with great accuracy." The passion for accuracy was rooted in the Celts, for under their laws (which scholars had to commit to memory) much of a man's rights, privileges, and patrimony depended on his genealogy (with numerous kingships involved), so that everyone of sense held in his head, ready for immediate discharge, his family tree for generation on generation. That tradition, maintained even after writing came to the island, was then fortified or reinforced by foreign impositions that made Irish a forbidden language, and, hence, forced to hide in one's memory, and denied schooling to the people, who taught themselves. In brief, the history of Ireland is a history of an oral culture.

Such a culture would naturally lead its members to excel in certain types of literary forms, if "literary" under the circumstances does not seem a paradoxical term. To put it another way, people born to this culture, surrounded by this culture, or reared in it, should, it would seem, tend to excel in oratory, repartee, rhetoric, storytelling, song, witty exchange, lyric poetry, drama, and extemporaneity. And so they do and so they have.

We find the Irish in the forefront in drama and oratory; we find them noted for their storytelling and their wit; we hear them commended for their extemporaneous rhetoric and as masters of conversation. We have from them the word "blarney," and they themselves speak of their "gift of gab." Much of Irish prose is marked by a rocking rhetoric, a rolling rhetoric. At its worst, Irish oratory became too orotund and Irish poetry too musical. The Irish are weakest in analytical constructions. In modern times Bishop George Berkeley is their only philosopher of first rank. They are a highly critical people yet they have produced few preeminent critics. They are an extremely religious, even a pious people, but have produced no great theologians, or in modern times, no great saints, although their missionaries encircled the globe and still do. They have sent into the courtrooms of the world the outstanding forensic orators in history, but have made no major jurisprudential contributions. But they have produced a literature absolutely outsized for the dimensions of their capital city, and while it appears in great part to have been a cross-fertilization with the English culture, they are slowly showing the world what they themselves have known for a long time, that while their major and minor voices may use the English tongue they do not use the English mind.

Anyone setting out to write a history of literary Dublin is immediately at a loss as to where to start. The city has never been an Irish-speaking city. For the eight hundred years it was under English rule, the seats of Irish learning lay elsewhere. Douglas Hyde, the first president of the Republic of Ireland, a Protestant, a poet, and a scholar, wrote a *Literary History of Ireland* and never mentioned anyone who wrote in English. Given the title of the book, it was a curious piece of mistitling and should have borne the title *History of Literature in Irish*. This points up the problem. In the history of literary Dublin there are two languages involved, Irish and English, and perhaps a third, for there is a style, Anglo-Irish, so individual, so vital, so readily distinguishable that it is almost a language of its own. Perhaps it would be better to designate it Irish-English, for the adjective Anglo-Irish is reserved in Ireland's history for something other.

Although Dublin sits at the center of Irish history today it was not founded by the Irish but by the Norsemen, those incredible mariners who scourged the civilized world from the Black Sea to the extremities of Ireland, sending their fleets up the Liffey river and the Shannon, where the airport spreads today, to put a Viking king on the throne of Limerick, and into the great loughs of the land. Nothing is known of any pre-Viking settlement where Dublin smokes today, although it seems likely that a salient Celtic center must have grown at the site, for the harbor is capacious and the landscape so benign as to be irresistible. The Vikings gave it the name Dubhlinn, which is, nevertheless, an Irish word meaning Blackpool, while the Irish called it, or something near it, Baile Atha Cliath, which means the town of the hurdle ford. While none of the more extreme enthusiasts for the revival of the native language would drop the name Dublin altogether, among Gaelic speakers the city is most commonly called Baile Atha Cliath.

Baile Atha Cliath was evidently farther up the Liffey from the sea than the pre-medieval bastion mounted by the Norse raiders, the sort of heathen that made the Dark Ages dark. The Norsemen brought no literature to Ireland when they came at the end of the eighth century, and they usually destroyed what they found. They established Dublin as the military base from which various invaders set out to conquer the whole of Ireland. Such was the dream of Turgesius, also called Thorgestr, a bold commander of the savage searovers, who arrived in the early eighth century, about half a century after the first Vikings came, when gold was still mined in Ireland. The Vikings, at first, despoiled everything, rape and rapine being the rule, and fought among themselves over women and loot. They took over all the ports, launched fleets on the shining loughs, and destroyed such strongholds of civilization as they came across, which meant, for the most part, monasteries. God knows how many early magnificent manuscripts were lost to us as a result. Some of the monks, however, fled to the continent, to which, two hundred years earlier, they had gone as missionaries to restore learning and replenish Christianity. The Ireland which the Vikings overran in the ninth century was for three hundred years the foremost center of Christian studies in Europe, having escaped Roman rule and the rapacity of the Goths. Because of the Viking scourge, many monks who fled took with them their illuminated manuscripts and other books so that today a number of treasures of Irish literature are to be found only outside Ireland. Despite the Viking depredations, many inland monasteries survived.

The raids began about 350 years after Saint Patrick, called Padraig MacCalpruinn in modern Irish, a name which makes him as real as the man next door, but for all that he remains a shadowy figure. However insubstantial the historical details about his person, the results of his missionary expedition to Ireland became the core of the country and the pulse of the people. He brought Latin learning with him, poor scholar though he was himself, and he encouraged the monasteries, although he was no monk. It was these monks who spread the use of the Latin alphabet and Latin culture and turned the chanting Celtic druids into earnest Christian scholars.

The Irish monks by the close of the sixth century were the foremost calligraphers in the world, created majuscule lettering, and, just before the Vikings arrived, had developed the art of illuminating manuscripts to its apogee. The Book of Kells, which is now exhibited in the library of Trinity College Dublin and a page of which is turned each day for the edification of visitors, has been called the most beautiful book in the world. It was not the only such book to survive the Viking terror, for, as was to happen again and again throughout the centuries, with marauders such as the Vikings, they did not conquer the whole of Ireland. They held the ports and the waterways but in the interior life went on much the same, and during the years of Norse ascendancy, many monasteries continued to flourish, and, indeed, many Vikings embraced the religion and spoke the language of the people they had pillaged and subdued.

Before the tenth century arrived, the Irish had begun to weaken the hold of the Vikings on the country, and, by the end of it, Brian Boru, the High King of Ireland, had unseated them at Limerick. In A.D. 1014, on Good Friday, he defeated the Viking king of Dublin and his allies, some of whom, to meet the Irish challenge, were drawn from Norway, Sweden, and the Orkney and Shetland islands.

The Irish victory, known as the Battle of Clontarf, was decisive, although Brian Boru, his son, and his grandson were slain. While the victory marked the end of the Viking hegemony, it meant no peace for Ireland, for the petty kings quarreled among themselves for prime sovereignty, and the issue was not settled until 1166, one hundred years after the Norman conquest of England, and too late to give Ireland the unity it needed against a new impending invasion.

No sooner had Turloch O'Conor been crowned High King of Ireland, than Diarmuit MacMurrough, who had made himself King of Dublin and Leinster, was deposed in an ancillary struggle by an outraged king of Brefni, Tiernan O'Ruairc, whose wife he had stolen. MacMurrough fled to England to petition the English king, Henry II, for permission to seek allies among the Anglo-Norman feudal barons in Wales. In 1170, with such adventurers, he returned to Ireland and marched on Dublin.

King O'Conor massed the Irish for the defense of the city, with some Norsemen fighting beside him. They were defeated by the invaders. The poet chroniclers tell us that the Irish fought wearing linen shirts against invaders clothed in armor. After the defeat of the Irish, King Henry II came to Ireland to receive the homage of both sides. O'Conor and the Ulster chieftains refused to pledge fealty and fled north.

What the Viking invasion and occupation of the ports had done was to establish Dublin as the capital of Ireland and it was to that city, in 1172, that Henry came to assert his kingship, having the encouragement of Pope Adrian IV, who, as it happens, was the only Englishman to become Pope. From that day to this, Dublin has been the capital of the island and the seat of power, however disputed. From that day until the year 1922—750 years—it remained under English control. What had been the Norse kingdom of Dublin, after little more than a century of Irish kingship, became the headquarters of the English Pale (the word derives from the word paling or fence), from which we get the popular expression "beyond the pale," for until well into the sixteenth century, English rule did not extend beyond that strip of coastline the Vikings had originally occupied. The history of literary Dublin could well begin with the poet we found singing his Irish songs for the Viking warriors and terrorizing them with his wit.

On the other hand, a history of literature in Dublin might well begin with the arrival in Ireland of Saint Patrick (who never that we know of saw the pre-Viking settlement) in the fifth century, and with his own writings, his "Confessio" done in crude Latin, more an apologia than an autobiography, and his "Epistle to Coroticus," also in Latin, in which he denounces the Christian soldier Coroticus for enslaving fellow Christians. Before Patrick nothing in Irish was written down, and after him the transcription of Gaelic literature began.

Gaelic is the Celtic language that was spoken throughout Ireland (today with four dialects) when Patrick arrived. All in all, it is a more difficult language than Latin and equally as expressive, yet until the monks came it had no practical alphabet and was not recorded except in funerary notices by an odd script called Ogham. Despite that, it had a vast oral literature and subsequently developed, under Latin monastic stimulus, a highly complicated prosody and a lively and vivid prose. The pre-Christian material was carried in the heads and distilled by the memory of scholars. These were of three grades, all deemed a learned caste. The most important personages were the poets, or *fili*, a generic term for an order with nine classes, one of which demanded an apprenticeship of twelve to twenty years. The other grades were the druids, who were pagan philosophers and something close to priests, and the bards, who were evidently minstrels, eulogists, and perhaps court jesters as well.

Under the intellectual pressures of Christianity, the druids disappeared but the *fili* persisted, incorporating into their techniques something of the services of lawyers, and like the latter, prone to overcharge for their work. This prompted a movement against them which might have led to their banishment had not Saint Columcille, the second giant figure in Irish literature, come to their defense and brought about a reform of their order and a regulation of their fees. An upshot of this was that one of the first poems written in Gaelic is a eulogy of Columcille. The author was Dallan Forgaill, an *ollav* (one of the nine types of *fili*). Columcille had made his defense of these *fili* in A.D. 574 and the poem exists only in an eighth-century version, but it is believed to have been composed at the time. The sad fact is, of course, that all early Gaelic writings exist only in latter-day manuscripts, a result of the repeated invasions, sackings, and spoliations.

Dallan Forgaill was succeeded as *ard-ollav*, or top dog of the poets of Ireland, by Senchan Torpeist, whose chief distinction is his discovery or recovery of the famous pagan Gaelic epic the *Tain Bo Cuailnge*, "The Cattle Raid of Cooley." The legend runs that Torpeist raised from the dead the Ulster hero Fergus MacRoigh, who then recited the saga to him so that he could memorize it, the whole having long been lost. What the legend indicates is that the pagan *fili* had adjusted themselves to Christianity and the Christian sages to the pagan poets. Indeed, the reconciliation of the Latin culture to the pagan tongue is also evident in the seventh-century work of Cormac Mac Cullenain, King of Cashel but a bishop as well, who wrote the book *Saltair Chaisil*, which incorporates the first comparative dictionary in Europe, and Cenn Faelad, a layman and a *fili* who wrote a treatise on Gaelic grammar about the same time. From those writings, many scholars date the birth of Irish letters, and it might be argued that the story of literature in Dublin could begin there.

By the year A.D. 900 Gaelic began to replace Latin in the monasteries and after a hundred years, a golden era of Irish literature began, encouraged by Brian Boru, and moved into a classical period that stretched from A.D. 1200 to 1600. In brief, the most glorious centuries of Irish literature began just about the time that King Henry II brought the English royal presence to Dublin, a presence that was to doom and destroy the Gaelic culture.

If we look for one of the first poems written in English by a Dubliner, we can turn to Richard Stanyhurst (1547–1618), who was born in Dublin, where his father was the Speaker of the Irish House. Thoroughly English, a foe of the Gaelic tongue, Stanyhurst was a Catholic, who died in Brussels, in exile, a Jesuit, although he had been married somewhere along the line. His book of English verse was published in 1582. One of the better-known poems from it reads:

A Prayer to the Holy Trinity

Trinitee blessed, deitee coequal,
Unitee sacred, God one eeke in essence,
Yeeld toe they servaunt, pitifullye calling
    Merciful hyring.

Vertuus living dyd I long relinquish,
Thy wyl and precepts miserablye scorning,
Granut toe mee, sinful pacient, repenting,
    Helthful amendment.

Blessed I judge hym, that in hert is healed:
Cursed I know hym, that in helth is harmed:
Thy physick therefore, toe me, wretch unhappye,
    Send, mye Reddemer.

Glorye too God, the father, and his onlye
Son, the protectoure of us earthly sinners,
Thee sacred spirit, laborers refreshing,
    Still be renowned.   Amen

The conflict between the English and Irish tongues is reflected in his life, for he was outraged that "the Irish tongue shall be so universally gaggled in the English Pale." He was not the only one to make such a complaint.

The Irish culture developed outside Dublin. That military base for foreigners, who were regarded by the monastic Irish and Irish aristocrats, of course, as barbarians (although some Irish feudal chieftains were as rude), heard many tongues—English and Norman-French, much Irish, to be sure, and some Welsh and Flemish, but with English slowly but finally becoming predominant, although not without moments of recession when Irish asserted itself. For centuries, the area where English rule prevailed was extremely limited. A strip of the eastern coast around Dublin, fifty miles in length, and of varying depth, say thirty miles, such was the Pale, fenced by towers, walls, and palings. There and there only were the English supreme and secure.

Beyond that uneasy enclave, the Anglo-Norman feudal lords and the Irish kings held sway, a few towns only remaining English in loyalty. During the fifteenth century, the Pale was at its most diminished but the Battle of Bosworth in 1485 was to be as fateful for Ireland as it was for England, for it brought the Tudors to the English throne, and it was they who were to impose the beginnings of the most terrible tyranny on the Irish people, a tyranny that finally determined not merely on hegemony, but on extermination and extirpation.

The change began slowly. The feudal baronies that covered Ireland outside the Pale—Anglo-Norman or Irish—were technically in fealty to the English crown. The Anglo-Normans, of course, felt more so; the Irish less so, and some of the Irish deemed themselves in quiescent revolt. There was a parliament in Dublin but it was subject to Westminster. Whatever cultural or linguistic differences obtained at the time, the quarrels were not exacerbated by any religious test, for all were Catholics. Indeed, it must be remembered that the English presence had the tacit approval (there is a disputed Papal bull involved) of the Pope of Rome. The crunch came when Henry VIII, troubled over a woman, as even earlier King Diarmuit MacMurrough had been, proclaimed himself head of the Catholic church in England.

The Act of Supremacy was passed by the English parliament in 1534 and a few years later and very reluctantly by the Irish parliament. Henry VIII was also proclaimed King of Ireland, the first Englishman who dared take the title. The action further alienated the Anglo-Normans as well as the Irish, for the former had already taken on the coloration of their indigenous neighbors. The two peoples, who had lived as prickly neighbors or in sporadic skirmishings, were drawn closer together, particularly by the Anglo-Norman adoption of the Irish language. Now also, Irish resistance to English impositions was strengthened by the sympathy of Rome, which had earlier favored English sovereignty.

The Tudors, however, were not to be turned back. Under the brief reign of Henry's son, Edward, the religious policy of England was Protestantized. Under Mary Tudor, who was a Catholic, a mild reaction removed Protestant bishops from Irish sees and installed English Catholic bishops, but nevertheless it was under her that the insidious business of the "plantations" began, an infection that still sickens the island. English settlers were brought into Ireland and Irish landowners dispossessed of their properties. This was only one method chosen by the Tudors to compel the loyalty of Ireland, as they had compelled the Scots and the Welsh. Earlier, they had sought to Anglicize the Irish by educating some of the sons of the Irish feudal families at the English court and giving them English titles. Because of the religious issue, resistance was growing among the feudal lords of Ireland, and when one of them at length disavowed his English title, he was imprisoned in Dublin. He was an O'Neill of Ulster, the proudest Irish house, and it was that house that would lead a protracted war against Queen Elizabeth which was to end at the Battle of Kinsale in 1601 with the subjugation of Ireland.

The Beginnings

The history of literary Dublin might well begin with the accession of Elizabeth to the throne, for it was she (or Cecil directing her) who in 1592 established Trinity College and had ordered there the first book printed in Ireland and that book in Irish. All the major countries of Europe, because of the influence of Latin Christianity, had had universities much earlier, but Irish efforts to establish one had failed, in great part because of the concentration of learning in the monasteries (it is difficult not to think of the monastery at Armagh as a university since very early only its graduates might teach, or of many an Irish monastery as a college) but also because of the recurrent invasions and the absence of cities. Irish society clustered around the monasteries rather than any commercial core. The Irish system of government, traditionally loose, pulled against centralizations.

Universities are focal points for the collection and collation of knowledge and learning, and the foundation of Trinity College, which was to produce such an inordinate number of brilliant scholars and preeminent writers, could be a good starting point for a history of literary Dublin. Unfortunately, the case with Ireland is not that simple because when Trinity College was founded, Ireland already had a distinguished literature of which the ruling English, the Ascendancy, knew nothing and which, very humanly, to explain their ignorance to themselves, they dismissed as trivial or even barbaric.

"Cut off by its position, but even more by the relapse of

the greater part of its inhabitants into a state of semi-barbarism, from the general currents of European development, Ireland, which despite its insularity had done so much in the past for European civilization, was to most Englishmen at the beginning of the 16th century, a mere terra incognita," writes an English historian, Robert Dunlop, in the Cambridge Modern History series. The statement is interesting because it demonstrates that even today the average English scholar, possessed of goodwill, does not understand the situation that existed in Ireland at the beginning of the sixteenth century. The phrase "the relapse of the greater part of its inhabitants into a state of semi-barbarism" implies a decay of Gaelic learning and culture that had not then taken place. Not until the seventeeth century was the deterioration at all widespread. Indeed, the Irish language and culture, which had engulfed the Anglo-Normans, was threatening to engulf the Pale, and that two hundred years after the Statutes of Kilkenny forbidding the Anglo-Normans the Irish language. In the early half of the sixteenth century, Henry VIII had to seek again to enforce by law the use of English, while his daughter, Elizabeth, came close to surrendering and sought to proselytize the Irish away from their Catholic faith to loyalty to the crown by naming Irish-speaking bishops and having the New Testament translated into Gaelic. This, and her Irish catechism, were the first books published in Gaelic in Dublin.

Before these books were published, before Trinity College was founded, men of English birth and men of Irish birth were writing in English in Dublin. One of the first was James Yonge, who wrote an English translation of a work called *Secret des Secrets* by Jofroi of Waterford, written in Norman French, for it must not be forgotten that there was in Ireland a Norman-French literature (very meager) and a Latin literature (very clerical) as well as an Irish and an English literature. Yonge wrote in Latin as well as English, the former still at that time the language of scholars.

The lure that Gaelic had for invaders is an interesting matter and can perhaps be explained thus. When the Norman barons brought the Latin order, which was superior, to England at Hastings, they imposed the Norman idiom on the court and the bureaucracy. During that century from 1066 to 1166 which was to end with the invasion of Ireland by the Anglo-Norman lords, the English language was in an inchoate stage. Irish, on the other hand, not troubled by such a riptide as occurred by the meeting of Norman-French and Anglo-Saxon, was well-ordered, expressive, and profitable. If the natives were to be exploited, Gaelic was a practical vehicle, and on adoption proved a pleasant one. For the natives, one can sense, the unsettled jargon spoken by the Anglo-Norman invaders was harsh and uncertain. Before long, the Anglo-Norman barons were speaking Irish. The same thing happened to many English settlers.

Whatever the superiority of Gaelic to Anglo-Norman in the twelfth century, and in the thirteenth, the great days of English lay ahead, and the penalties imposed on an Englishman speaking Irish became so severe that the changeover was hastened. The watershed can pretty much be placed at the Battle of Kinsale, when the O'Neills were at last defeated.

Hugh O'Neill was an Ulster feudal lord reared at the English court, who on his return to Ireland in 1563 fought for the Queen's Lord Deputy and was awarded an English title, Earl of Tyrone. In Ulster, however, traditionally independent, the title Earl of Tyrone, so far as the Irish natives were concerned, was as nothing before the title *The O'Neill*. In 1593 Hugh O'Neill became *The O'Neill*. But even before that he had begun to plan a rebellion against the English throne, and patiently and shrewdly prepared.

He was the most perceptive and farsighted of the Irish chieftains, a man of intellect and vision, and a statesman before the word was devised. He sensed the need for Irish unity if the English shackles were to be shed, and he promptly allied himself with Red Hugh O'Donnell, another feudal chieftain in the north. By treaty, O'Neill was allowed, as Earl of Tyrone, six hundred men-at-arms, but, to develop an army, he changed the six hundred each year and trained another levee. Each year he amassed and stored arms, and in 1594, provoked by attacks made on a neighbor by an English high sheriff, he launched what came to be called the Nine Years War. With his allies, he met with success after success at Clonibrat, the Yellow Ford, and elsewhere. At the Battle of the Yellow Ford he inflicted heavy losses on the crown's forces.

Had his campaign gone according to his plan, the history of Ireland might have been altered but when Spanish auxiliaries arrived at Kinsale in the south, near Cork, instead of Ulster, as O'Neill had requested, he had to march his forces the length of Ireland. On December 24, 1601, he and his Spanish allies suffered a decisive defeat, a defeat that ended in rout. He was forced to surrender his title *The O'Neill* and his authority over vassals, but was allowed to keep his earldom and his lands. Sensing, however, that an English plot against him would finally end with his assassination, he sailed with one hundred friends and followers and left Ireland forever. Misfortune dogged his departure, and the ship ran into stormy weather. When they trailed behind them in the turbulent waters a relic of the True Cross, the seas calmed. As Tadhg o Cianain, the author of *The Flight of the Earls* (1609), recounted in Irish, "After that they were on the sea for 13 days with excessive storm and dangerous bad weather. A cross of gold which O'Neill had, and which contained a portion of the Cross of Crucifixion and many other relics, being put by them in the sea, trailing after the ship, gave them great relief. At the end of that time, much to their surprise, they met in the middle of the sea two small hawks, merlins, which alighted on the ship. The hawks were caught and fed afterwards."

O'Neill unsuccessfully sought aid all over Europe in the hope of returning to Ireland but died in Rome in 1616, the year of Shakespeare's death, a pensioner of the King of Spain. His will was written in Irish and bequeathed what little he had left to his wife and children. It is fair to say that with him the last hope of Gaelic culture died and with him died the aristocracy of Irish-speaking Ireland, Irish court life, and its Maecenas-like patronage of Irish literature, such patronage as alone keeps a literature alive. From that moment on, Gaelic, which had subdued Norman-French and had threatened to subdue English, succumbed to the sword.

In 1641, the speech of the Speaker of the House in the Irish Parliament had to be translated into Irish so the Gaelic chieftains and the Anglo-Norman lords might understand, but the famous Patriots Parliament in 1689, not half a century later—convoked by James II in Dublin in his last bid for the reclaim of his throne—was conducted entirely in English. Less than a century had made the transformation.

Yet we can read in Douglas Hyde's *Literary History of Ireland*:

> The absorbing power of Irish nationality continued so strong all through the 17th century that according to Prendergast many of the children of Oliver Cromwell's soldiers who had settled in Ireland could not speak a word of English. It was the same all over the country. In 1760 Irish was so universally spoken in the regiments of the Irish Brigade [on the continent] that Dick Hennessy, Edmund Burke's cousin, learnt it on foreign service. Still later, during the Peninsular War, the English officer in one of the Highland regiments attempted to abolish the speaking of Gaelic at the mess table, but the Gaelic-speaking officers completely out-voted the others. Irish was spoken at this time by all the Milesian families, those who held their ancestry ran to Mildeh, except when they wished to deliberately Anglicize themselves. Michael Kelly, the musical composer and vocalist, who was born in Dublin in 1764, tells us in his *Reminiscences*:
> "I procured an audience of the Emperor of Germany at Schoenbrunn and found him with a half-dozen of general officers, among whom were Generals O'Donnell and Kavanagh, my gallant countrymen. The latter said something to me in Irish which I did not understand, consequently made him no answer. The Emperor turned quickly on me and said, 'What! O'Kelly, don't you speak the language of your own country?' I replied, 'Please, your Majesty, none but the lower orders of the Irish people speak Irish.' The Emperor laughed loudly. The impro-

priety of the remark made before two Milesian generals flashed into my mind in an instant, and I could have bitten off my tongue. They luckily did not, or pretended not to hear."

It is from the middle of the 18th century onward that the Irish language begins to die out.

Thus it is no surprise that Irish literature was still being written in the seventeenth century, as Dr. Geoffrey Keating's history of Ireland—*Forus Feasa ar Eirinn*—testifies, a scholarly work, partisan but charming, written while he was on the run, an outlaw priest. Besides writing the history, Dr. Keating, regarded as a master of modern Irish prose, was the author of a variety of peoms in traditional and experimental meters, and of devotional works. One of his poems merits quotation here, brought over from the Irish by Patrick Pearse:

> O woman full of wile,
> Keep from me thy hand:
> I am not a man of the flesh,
> Tho' thou be sick for my love.
>
> See how my hair is gray!
> See how my body is powerless!
> See how my blood hath ebbed!
> For what is thy desire?
>
> Do not think me besotted:
> Bend not again thy head,
> Let our love be without act
> Forever, slender witch.
>
> Take thy mouth from my mouth,
> Graver the matter so;
> Let us not be skin to skin:
> From heat cometh will.
>
> 'Tis thy curling ringleted hair,
> Thy gray eye bright as dew,
> Thy lovely round white breast,
> That draw the desire of eyes.

Every deed but the deed of flesh
And to lie in thy bed of sleep
Would I do for thy love,
O woman full of wile!

Keating's history of Ireland was completed about 1650, half a century after the Battle of Kinsale and two years before the birth of Nahum Tate in Dublin, who was to become poet laureate of England, and who was one of the first dramatists and poets out of the Pale. Keating's work was a climax to the long history of Irish writing; it was after him that the slow reduction to semi-barbarism and worse began.

The years from 1014, the year of the Battle of Clontarf, to 1250, when the Anglo-Norman power took hold, were the most creative in the history of Irish literature. With the Anglo-Norman invasion, the monasteries began to decline because the Irish-speaking abbots were displaced and Irish literature began to calcify into a classicism that became sterile chiefly because travel to the continent was denied Irish-speaking scholars.

When the defeat at Kinsale and the Flight of the Earls brought an end to Irish court life, the traditional role of the court poet, often a hereditary title held by noble families, passed to folk poets, and the complicated order of poets compressed into the narrow bardic family. The bards caught up much of the authority of the monasteries which, after the invasions, began slowly to cede to lay scholars, and it was they and the bards who produced the salient Irish grammars.

Queen Elizabeth died before *The O'Neill*, and James I, son of Mary Queen of Scots, took the English throne. Despite his Catholic ancestry, the Catholics of Ireland were granted little respite in the persecutions laid on them, and the Presbyterians in Ireland suffered likewise. Catholic education was proscribed and the oath of supremacy prevented Catholics from serving in the government or entering the professions or bearing arms. Trinity College, also, was closed to them and would remain so until 1793.

Under Charles I, the diligence of his Lord Deputy, Thomas Wentworth, who was to become Earl of Strafford, prevented Charles's tolerance for Catholics in England from easing the plight of the Irish. The darkest days lay ahead. The Flight of the Earls had been followed by the Plantation of Ulster, the ulcer which to this day troubles Ireland. The land was divided into lots of two thousand acres or less and English and Scottish Protestants were brought in, and they, as might be expected, of a poor sort. The entrepreneurs, who maintained their own troops, managed the lots, rented to tenants (Catholic tenants were allowed only on thousand-acre lots and paid higher rents), were called "undertakers," a name which today has a sort of gallows humor about it. Besides Ulster, other plantations arose under James I.

The plantations, Catholic disabilities, and other grievances provoked a rebellion against English rule in 1641, a rebellion led by another O'Neill, Phelim, who routed the settlers of Ulster, killing some four thousand of them (the figure is in dispute), some, no doubt, the victims of butchery. This rebellion raged while Charles I was slowly succumbing to the Roundhead Parliament and was still in progress when Oliver Cromwell in 1649 took charge in England, decapitated the king, established the Commonwealth, and brought his army to Dublin. Three months after his arrival, Owen Roe O'Neill, a distinguished soldier and a foremost Irish leader, died. Cromwell arrived in August and with his usual dispatch (he was a genius at warfare) in a month's time had besieged Drogheda, seized the town, and massacred the inhabitants, 3,500 men, women, and children. He went on to Wexford and butchered the inhabitants there, so ferociously and effectively that New Ross surrendered without a struggle. In 1650, Kilkenny, which had been a headquarters for the Irish patriots, capitulated and after that Clonmel, where Owen Roe O'Neill's nephew, Hugh Duff O'Neill, held out for several weeks but finally had to quit. Cromwell then went back to England; the war was won. Limerick surrendered to his son-in-law, Ireton; Ulster was brought to heel; and in 1652 Galway capitulated to end all the fighting.

After that, conditions in Ireland from a mere physical stand-point were· grim indeed and worsened drastically for the Catholics of the country because of the Cromwellian settlement which deprived almost all Catholic aristocrats of their land and sent them "to hell or Connacht." With few exceptions, they were driven west of the Shannon and had to resettle there. The Cromwellian settlement was the most extensive of the "plantations." During this time, of course, the bulk of the land came into Protestant hands.

In 1660, Charles II was proclaimed King of England and Anglicanism was again declared the state religion in Ireland. Administrative machinery was set up to recover some of the Irish lands from the Cromwellian settlers but it was ineffective. A measure of tolerance for the Catholic population was permitted, but the laws against Catholics remained on the statute books, and when the Popish Plot was discovered, the purpose of which (it never existed) was said to be to unseat Charles and put his Catholic brother, James II, on the throne, a wave of hysteria rolled over England and spread to Ireland with consequent enforcement of all anti-Catholic laws and the enactment of new ones. In a while the pressure eased a bit and what has been called "connived toleration" obtained.

With the accession of James II to the throne of England, the situation for Catholics in Ireland bettered considerably, but James's policy was actually ineffective. Moreover, the English parliament was still Protestant and Puritan, and before the Catholic position in Ireland had been generally improved the Protestant parliament invited William of Orange, husband of James's Protestant daughter, Mary, to rule England; in 1689, shortly after the Dutchman William arrived in England at the head of a large army, King James fled to France.

Irish politics now became merely part of continental politics. Ireland, in short, became a pawn in a titanic chess game. England was part of the Grand Alliance organized against France, and France saw James as a cat's-paw. Within Ireland there was a maelstrom of conflicting emotions and contrary allegiances. Richard Talbot, Earl of Tyrconnel and leader of the Anglo-Irish Catholics, had been put in charge of the army in Ireland by James. He was a loyal Jacobite. Before he could act however, the northeast corner of the country, forecasting the divisiveness of today, declared for William and Mary, England's joint rulers. Even as France was interested in James Stuart only as a tool in its campaign against England, so he was interested in Ireland only as a means of regaining his crown. William in turn was intent on a quick victory in Ireland so he could turn his attention to the continent, where lay the main battlefields.

James came to Dublin with ten thousand troops and in 1689 convened the Patriot Parliament, composed mostly of Anglo-Irish Catholics, and made generous promises to the nation. William mustered his forces, mostly Danish and German mercenaries, and faced James's army, reinforced by seven thousand French soldiers, at the Boyne river. The Stuart army was vastly outnumbered and was beaten. Not realizing how lucky he was to extricate his troops with relatively small losses, James fled the battlefield and went to France. For this piece of bad judgment, seen as cowardice, he won from the Irish the name Seamus A'chaca, which means, in vulgar English, James the Shit-Ass. The Williamites took Dublin and pushed west, and by the fall of 1691 were victorious despite the heroism of General Patrick Sarsfield and other Irish soldiers. The war ended with the Treaty of Limerick, the principal terms of which were most conciliatory.

Whatever were the intentions of King Billy, the Protestant parliament interpreted the terms of the treaty so viciously for the Catholics that in 1695 all but 10 percent of the land in Ireland was in Protestant hands, although the population remained overwhelmingly Catholic. To keep their supremacy, to make it perdurable, the Irish parliament (no Catholics admitted) passed a succession of acts known as the penal laws which have been described as the cruelest ever imposed on a subject people. It was after this and not before that the conditions described by Robert Dunlop came into being: the Irish people (save those who apostatized to Protestantism) were reduced to an unparalleled servitude, and they entered the eighteenth century with few more rights than animals and what amounted to no legal existence.

The penal laws prevented Catholics from voting or holding office, from schooling or from the professions, including teaching. The Catholic clergy were outlawed, and Catholics were forbidden to bear arms. Their property rights were reduced to an unassertable minimum. Large Catholic estates were broken up. If a Protestant offered a Catholic five pounds for his horse, the Catholic was compelled to sell. The laws were not always rigorously enforced because it would have been impossible to do so, and a Catholic gentry survived. Designed for the extermination of the Catholic religion, these laws were soon recognized as a political instrument quite perfect for keeping the Protestant minority (which held the land) in its blissful Ascendancy.

Even as the Vikings began to speak Irish and practice the Christian faith, and even as the Anglo-Normans became more Irish than the Irish, and even as the first English began to "gaggle" in Gaelic, so too the Protestant Ascendancy became infected with the thing called Ireland, even as they fought against it, proclaimed their Englishness, and condemned the destitute, semi-serfs around them.

This subtle transformation can be seen very clearly in the life of Jonathan Swift, known the world over as the author of *Gulliver's Travels*, and so, by an irony he would have relished, remembered as a storyteller for children, whom he could not bear, instead of what he was and is, the greatest satirist to write in English, an Anglican clergyman who moved for a while among statesmen as their peer, and who felt himself in exile as dean of St. Patrick's Cathedral in Dublin, the city of his birth.

Consequently, by a very logical sense of procedure, a history of literary Dublin may well begin with Dean Swift, who was born in 1667 and died in 1745, the year before Henry Grattan was born, another Dubliner and an incomparable statesman who was to win for Ireland parliamentary independence from Westminster only to have it taken away by subornation and bribery masterminded by another Dublin-educated statesman, Lord Castlereagh. Grattan died in 1820, and with him died the dream of an independent Irish parliament co-equal with Westminster under the aegis of a common crown. Within the lifetimes of those two men that dream was born, achieved, and crushed. It began, and so does the story of literary Dublin, with Swift.

Over the centuries the Irish have observed a great deal of death and of dying. With Italians, they say, the prime domestic ceremony is baptism; with the French, it is marriage; and with the Irish, the wake. The Irish seem to have given that custom to the world. They have seen a great deal also of those smaller, second deaths, emigration and exile, the journey to a foreign land with little hope of return, and banishment and permanent expatriation. They have developed, thus, a critical taste for the last words of dying men, speeches from the scaffold, songs on the way to the gallows or to lifelong separation from one's beloved, lyrics of farewell and good-bye, laments, and lastly, epitaphs.

The most famous epitaph in Ireland is one that has not yet been written, that of Robert Emmet, who, before he was hanged as a revolutionary (the English said "traitor"), enunciated the most often quoted speech in the English language, except, perhaps, for the Gettysburg Address. He made it in the dock before the court after having initiated the most quixotic rebellion Ireland has ever known, with his personal fortune spent on weapons and organization.

> Let no man write my epitaph [he said in his peroration] for as no man, who knows my motives, dares now vindicate them, let not prejudice or ignorance asperse them. Let them rest in obscurity and peace! Let my memory be left in oblivion, and my tomb remain uninscribed, until other times and other men can

45

do justice to my character. When my country takes her place among the nations of the earth, then, and not till then, let my epitaph be written. I have done.

The most famous epitaph in Ireland written in English is that of William Butler Yeats, taken from his poem *Under Ben Bulben* and inscribed over his grave:

> Cast a cold eye
> On life, on death:
> Horseman, pass by.

These lines of Yeats's have been read one way and another by critics and have offended some of his admirers as expressing far too cynical a sentiment for a man who was far from cynical. The eighteenth century was much given to moralizing in epitaphs, most of which suggested, to whoever were to read them, that life was transient and the reader should remember this and so mend his life. Yeats, some would have it, set out to moralize to the effect that one should not moralize, that one should be preoccupied neither by the meaning of life nor the certainty of death. To press this lesson on aristocrats, one critic suggests, would be condescending since they know it already, and so Yeats concludes "Horseman, pass by." Horseman, by this dispensation, is the equivalent of aristocrat, since only the affluent would not be afoot. This is a sense that strains when there is a simple meaning to recommend itself. "Horseman" is rather someone with something to do. Go do what you have to do, Yeats tells him; do not be diverted by the vanities of life or the terror of death.

So by a mild digression, we come to the most famous Latin epitaph in Ireland, that of Dean Swift. He composed it himself, and he carried the sentiments beyond a mere minatory reflection on the transience of life. He urged on viewers that they carry on the struggle for liberty. Swift wrote it in Latin, and it is carved into the black stone over his tomb in St. Patrick's Cathedral.

> Hic depositum est corpus
> Jonathan Swift, S.T.D.
> Hujus Ecclesiae Cathedralis
> Decani
> Ubi saeva idignatio
> Ulterius
> Cor lacerare nequit.
> Abi Viator
> Et imitare, si poteris,
> Strenuum pro virili
> Libertatis vindictatorem.
> Oblit 19 die mensis Octobris
> A.D. 1745.   Anno Aetatis 78

The crisp Latin phrases have been translated many times, and can be rendered:

> Here lies the body of Jonathan Swift, S.T.D.
> dean of this cathedral, where savage indignation
> can no longer lacerate his heart. Go, traveler,
> and emulate, if you can, the heroic exertions of
> this champion of liberty.

What happened to Swift was to happen to other members of the Protestant Ascendancy: he became outraged at the injustices he saw about him, injustices perpetrated and perpetuated by greed riding the twin horses of bigotry and political jobbery. His vision was limited at first but later was broad, generous, and bold. He did not come to his position immediately; but when he grew concerned, when savage indignation did lacerate his heart, he wrote brilliantly and effectively, and his gift for acid satire served him and Ireland well.

Swift was not the first literary man to rankle under the indignities the Protestant Ascendancy felt imposed on it by the English parliament at Westminster. That honor falls to William Molyneux, like Swift Dublin-born, and like Swift a graduate of Trinity College. Molyneux has been hailed by more than one Irish patriot as "the father of our modern struggle for Parliamentary Independence." In 1698, when he was a member of the Irish parliament sitting for the University of Dublin, he was a minority of one when the vote was taken that destroyed Irish world trade. Later he edited an inflammatory pamphlet entitled *The Case of Ireland's Being Bound by Acts of Parliament in England, stated by William Molyneux of Dublin, Esquire* and dedicated it to King William. Obsequious in tone, nevertheless it uttered powerful statements particularly when they are appraised in terms of their times and the Irish political scene.

"If a villain with a pistol at my breast," he wrote, "makes me convey my estate to him, no one will say that this gives him any right, and yet just such a title as this has an unjust conqueror." Although he insisted he spoke only on behalf of the Protestant interest, he was impelled to declare, "All men are by nature in a State of Equality, in respect of Jurisdiction or Dominion: this I take to be a principle in itself so evident that it stands in need of little proof. . . . On this equality in Nature is founded that Right which all men claim, of being free from all subjection to positive laws, till by their own consent they give up that freedom by entering into civil societies for the common benefit of all members thereof." Small wonder the English House of Commons found the book "of dangerous consequence to the Crown and Parliament of England." They ordered it burned by the common hangman. The sentiments expressed were to plague the British crown from another quarter, however, for they were incorporated into the American Declaration of Independence. In 1765, Charles Thompson, an Irish immigrant, had Molyneux's book in his possession when he joined the American patriots in Philadelphia and later when he served as secretary to the American Congress, and no doubt it was familiar to the Founding Fathers.

Other writers, some older than Swift, some his contemporaries, were born within the Dublin Pale. Nahum Tate, the son of Dr. Faithful Tate and a graduate of Trinity, is an example, who with his fellow Irishman Nicholas Brady composed a metrical translation of the Psalms, which is not as idle or pietistic an accomplishment as it sounds. W. H. Auden has written, "It would be difficult to overestimate the debt which the technique of English verse owes to the exercise of making rhymed versions of the Psalms and translating Virgil and Ovid." Tate was well rewarded and became poet laureate of England, succeeding Thomas Shadwell. He is illustrative for more reasons than one: he was a prototype of the Dubliner going to London to make his fortune, or at least a living, and he shared the traditional Irish conviviality apparently, for he was described as a "fuddlin' companion." He was not the first of the Irish playwrights to adorn the London stage. That honor probably goes to Ludovick Barry, a native of Cork, whose play *Ram Alley* was performed in 1610. Tate had several plays performed, and rewrote *King Lear* to give it a happy ending!

In an age when other profitable avenues might be closed, the London stage in the seventeeth and eighteenth centuries offered opportunities to young men of talent, a situation that has prevailed from that day to this. Tate was among the first to seek a livelihood with plays. Four Dublin dramatists who won greater fame than he (although his hymn "While Shepherds Watched Their Flocks by Night" may well be sung forever) were Thomas Southerne (1660–1746), born near Dublin; Richard Steele (1672–1729); George Farquhar (1677–1707); and William Congreve (1670–1729). Steele, born in Dublin and educated in England; Congreve, born in Yorkshire but educated at Trinity; Farquhar, born in Ireland and thrown out of Trinity.

They were all in London at the same time, in those brilliant years when John Dryden (1631–1700) was the chief man of letters. Besides Ludovick Barry, two other Irishmen had been before them. One was Sir John Denham (1615–1668), a native of Dublin, sometimes described as the first Irishmen to write in English, a tall pockmarked man, long-legged and stooping, with "goose-grey" eyes that could see through you. His best poem is perhaps *Cooper's Hill*, which the historian David Hume said had a "loftiness and vision which had not before him been attained by any English poet who wrote in rhyme." Denham also had a play, *The Sophy*, performed in 1640. The other was Roger Boyle (1621–1679), who fought for Charles I and II, as well as Cromwell, and wrote poetry, prose, and plays, and bore the title Earl of Orrery.

To be sure, fame and fortune lay in London, which long has been to Dublin as Broadway is to Boston, but Dublin was not without its theater. When the plague swept London in 1636, the theaters there were closed and James Shirley (1596–1666) and other playwrights and actors came to Dublin. Shirley became the playwright for St. Werburgh's Theatre and during his sojourn in Dublin wrote one of his best plays, *St. Patrick for Ireland*.

That these playwrights had some place to flee the plague was due to one of Ireland's preeminent viceroys, Sir Thomas Wentworth, the Earl of Strafford, who in 1633 brought John Ogilby (1600–1676), a Scot, a dancing master, a printer and pioneer of atlases, to Dublin as a Master of the Revels, and a Theatre Royal was established. The English Civil War sent Ogilby back to London but he returned to Dublin to continue his theater. Still, it was not until 1662 that the first permanent theater was established in Dublin in Smock Alley.

The Smock Alley theater had its greatest days under an extraordinary member of an extraordinary Dublin family, Thomas Sheridan II (1719–1788), whose remarkable career has been eclipsed by the genius of his son, Richard Brinsley Sheridan (1751–1816). His own father, Thomas Sheridan, D.D., was born in Cavan of ancient Irish stock and became the clerical intimate of Dean Swift, who wrote most of *Gulliver's Travels* in Sheridan's home. Sheridan's large family and his wife's numerous relatives were his financial undoing. Swift, ever the misogynist, referred to Mrs. Sheridan as "the greatest beast in Europe." They began a literary dynasty, however, which included their son, Thomas II, actor, author, and lexicographer, who married Frances Chamberlaine, herself a playwright. Among the children of this marriage was Richard Brinsley Sheridan, who became one of the brightest ornaments of the

English theater. His son, Thomas III, was a poet and father of Mrs. Caroline Norton, also a poet. Other writers boasted collateral relationships.

Thomas Sheridan II became an actor after attending Westminster School in London and Trinity College. In 1742 David Garrick came to act in Dublin and Sheridan's course was set. He turned actor with astonishing success, became manager of the Smock Alley theater while still in his twenties, and was deemed by some (although not the discerning) as a peer of Garrick. He, more than anyone else, rid the theater of the dreadful practice of having members of the audience wander or charge onto the stage. Such reform was not achieved without disturbance and riots that wrecked the theater. He too went to England, where he became an intimate of Dr. Samuel Johnson, wrote a rival dictionary, and received a pension from the crown for that work, even as Dr. Johnson did, and much to Johnson's annoyance. He also wrote a life of Dean Swift, his father's friend and his own idol. After he and Johnson had a falling out, he returned to the theater in Dublin, where his success prompted a fellow Dubliner, Spranger Barry, to start a rival theater on Crowe Street. From Ogilby's day on, Dublin was never without a theater, and Smock Alley lasted a century before it was turned into a warehouse. It was on the Smock Alley stage that Farquhar forswore acting and turned playwright, and it was in the audience there that Congreve and other Dublin playwrights learned stagecraft.

The Restoration of the monarchy in England with Charles II's arrival in 1660 ended the intellectual and artistic bankruptcy that existed under the Cromwells and the Commonwealth. The stage and the arts came alive again, and the momentum of this, like a strong current, drew talented Dubliners to England.

Farquhar and Congreve lit up the stage, as also did Steele, although his true talent lay in journalism and essays, including the famous Sir Roger de Coverley papers, the product of his friendship with Joseph Addison, formed when they were at the Charterhouse School in London together. Southerne's forte was tragedy and a keen business sense. The four of them had in common geniality as well as wit, traits certainly not foreign to the Irish, and missing, for example, in Addison. There were minor parallels in their lives: Farquhar, expelled from Trinity (for referring to Christ flippantly, the legend runs, as a "man born to be hanged"), turned to acting. By accident in a dueling scene at the Smock Alley theater he gave another actor a near-mortal wound and forswore acting forever. For a while he was in the English army, as were Southerne and Steele. The last while in uniform wounded another man seriously in a very real duel. While Farquhar was thrown out of Trinity, Steele quit Oxford and Congreve abandoned the law. Congreve and Southerne became the most financially secure. The former, who remains the outstanding writer of the comedy of manners, found political favor and became the lover of the Duchess of Marlborough, who bore him a child. He had, among other political jobs, the post of Commissioner of Wines, so it is no surprise, he could, though myopic, read a label and so suffered from gout and grew corpulent, deposing that he had been born with a "round-belly." Southerne, it seems, found financial security through innate business sense. Both Swift, politically, and Dryden, literarily, befriended Congreve, who as critics said, if he was not quite Molière, was England's closest approach. Congreve resented being called Irish but never forgot his lowly Dublin acquaintances. Leigh Hunt said of Congreve that he had "the solid reputation of never having forgotten anyone who did him a service." He seems to have drifted from woman to woman until his last days with Henrietta, Duchess of Marlborough. She, after his death, had a statue made of him in ivory and used to talk to it daily and nod back as if she heard it speaking. His charms of conversation, Thomas Davies wrote in his *Dramatic Miscellanies*, "must have been very powerful."

Steele had to work a good deal harder and won the reputation of being an ingrate. While he was in the army, his poem on the death of Queen Mary won him a promotion and place.

By 1705 he had had three plays produced. These, like an earlier book, *Christian Hero*, were marked by high-minded moralism. When *Lying Lovers* folded after few performances, he declared it had been "damned for its piety." His literary efforts, however, having won him political preferment (he became Commissioner of Stamps, among other things) he turned to making journalistic history. On April 12, 1709, he published the first issue of *The Tatler* because he preferred looking to the public for support than "gambling for the patronage of men in high office." *The Tatler* ran for two years, enjoying significant influence during that time. Steele then brought out *The Spectator*, in which he and Addison achieved immortal collaboration. It was Steele who created the character of Sir Roger de Coverley. His political writings brought about his expulsion from the House of Commons and lost him the friendship of Swift, to whom he had owed initial advancement and with whom he shared the pen name Isaac Bickerstaff (all the more confusing since there was a real Isaac Bickerstaff, a Dublin writer). His friendship with Addison also cooled.

In 1706 Steele's first wife, Margaret Stretch, died, leaving him a legacy that proved somewhat disappointing, for he was constantly in debt, finding it much easier to earn money than to keep it. His second wife was Mary Scurlock and his letters to her make delightful reading. Like Congreve, he suffered from gout. In the collaboration that made him and Addison immortal (since his plays today are not performed), he did the bulk of the work. He was knighted in April, 1715, by King George I and died on September 1, 1729, aided in his last days by the estate of his second wife.

Like Steele, Farquhar was tormented by penury and constant indebtedness. Of the four Irishmen mentioned above, his life was the shortest (he died at thirty) and one that was ill-starred. His plays failed to support him, although managers grew rich off them. A womanizer, like Congreve, he was lured into marriage by a lady who pretended a fortune to win him. Win him she did, but he forgave her deception. Through his last years, his constant friend was Robert Wilks, the actor. Colley Cibber's account of the provenance of Farquhar's most famous play, *The Beaux' Stratagem*, is poignant:

> Wilks . . . found him in a most miserable situation, lodged in a back garret, and under the greatest agitation of mind . . . Wilks advised him to write a play. "Write!," says Farquhar, "it is impossible that a man can write common sense who is heartless, and has not a shilling in his pocket." "Come, George," replied Wilks, "banish melancholy, draw your drama, and I will call on you this day week to see it; but as an empty pocket may cramp your genius, I desire you will accept my mite,"—and gave him twenty guineas. Mr. Farquhar immediately drew up the drama of *The Beaux' Stratagem*, which he delivered to Mr. Wilks, and it was approved by him, and finished in six weeks. Mr. Farquhar, during the writing of this play, had a settled sickness on him, and most of it he wrote in his bed, and before he had finished the second act he perceived the approaches of death.

One tradition is that he died on the third night of its performance, which, was, as was frequently the case, for the benefit of the author.

Swift was born before any of these playwrights, except Southerne, and only Southerne outlived him. The contrast between each of them and him is remarkable. Steele he despised for what he deemed a betrayal. He remained Congreve's friend to the end of the wit's days. Their paths had first crossed at Kilkenny College, which was to Protestant Ireland what Eton was to England. In his *Journal to Stella*, Swift reports, "I was today to see Mr. Congreve, who is almost blind with cataracts growing on his eyes . . . and besides he is never rid of the gout, yet he looks young and fresh, and is as cheerful as ever. He is younger by three years or more than I, and I am twenty years younger than he."

Congreve was one of the leading wits of a day when wit was highly valued. His friend Steele said of him, "The uncommon praise of a man of wit, always to please and never to offend. No one, after a joyful evening, can reflect upon an expression of Mr. Congreve's that dwells upon him with pain." Farquhar also was noted for his wit, which William Hazlitt said was "easy and spontaneous; his style animated, unembarrassed and free-flowing; his characters full of life and spirit." Both he and Congreve were deemed licentious in their day, and Jeremy Collier, an English clergyman, charged the older man with making vice attractive. Steele had lost popularity with his moralizing, but in the gift of wit and humor he resembled the others. Geniality marked his essays, and his reputation for being an ingrate contrasts strangely with his acknowledged amiability.

No one ever accused Swift of geniality, but the major contrast between him and them is more significant to the history of Dublin's literary life and the history of Ireland, for, while they went off to England to make their literary reputations, Swift came from England to Ireland with his literary reputation made. Although he, like Congreve, did not care to be called an Irishman, the city of his birth and Trinity College, and the intellectual intensity generated by them, had put its mark on him, as it had on them.

Much as Swift protested, much as he resented returning to Dublin, it was his rallying to the cause of a nationalist Ireland that would establish his reputation as the greatest satirist in English literature.

He was born in Hoey's Court in Dublin, a stone's throw from the cathedral where he would end his days as dean. The date was November 30, 1667, and there is the possibility that he was illegitimate. That is of little interest perhaps except to those who cherish the notion that children born of illicit passions are often brighter than the average. In any event, Swift is said to have been able by the age of three to read any verse in the Bible. More excitement attaches to his having been kidnapped by his nurse, if kidnapped is the word (the episode is scarved in mystery), and held by her until he was six, so it must have been she who taught him his letters.

At the age of six, he was sent to Kilkenny College, seventy-three miles southeast of Dublin, and there had as a fellow student the famous Irish philosopher George Berkeley, as well as Congreve. He remained at Kilkenny College for eight years and on April 24, 1682, entered Trinity College, Dublin. He didn't do brilliantly. He read what he chose rather than what was assigned. Sometime later, Daniel Defoe, the author of *Robinson Crusoe*, would say of him—"a walking index of books who has all the libraries of Europe in his head . . ." The turbulence in Ireland following the usurpation of William of Orange in the Revolution of 1688 drove Swift to England, where he found employment as an amanuensis with Sir William Temple, at Moor Park, Surrey. Sir William was a man of broad cultivation, a statesman and a diplomat, who was, when Swift arrived, intent on writing his memoirs, and indeed, it is said his prose style influenced that of Swift. His library and acquaintance certainly furthered Swift's education. Above all, it was here that Swift's future was pledged both as to a career and as to romance, for it was Temple who induced him to enter the priesthood, and it was at Temple's home that he met Esther Johnson, or Hester. The daughter of a woman in Temple's household (and at times hinted to have been his daughter, as it was hinted that Swift was his son), Miss Johnson was to be Swift's pupil and companion for thirty years, his beloved Stella. Swift is in many ways a sphinx, and scholars have worried the question since 1784, when Thomas Sheridan (1721–1788) brought out a life of Swift and an eighteen-volume edition of his work! Did Swift and Stella marry? Certainly they never lived together as man and wife, but they may have been married secretly, as some scholars believe. There are, however, no records, no proof, and there is reason to think otherwise. In any event she was only eight years old when Swift came to Moor Park.

In 1690 Temple confided to a friend, "He has latin and greek, some french, and writes a very good and current hand, is very honest and diligent." Swift, a tall man, with blue eyes and aquiline nose, was doubled-chinned but possessed a dimple not emphasized in the portraits. Dr. Samuel Johnson in his *Lives of the Poets* describes him as having a muddy complexion. His forehead was high, and they say he never laughed, or if he did, his face cracked into a sardonic smile. Yet his conversation could keep everyone else in the room rocking with laughter.

When he arrived at Moor Park he was not yet the sort of person who could dominate a room or a circle of wits. He was an insecure man of twenty-two years, as gauche, no doubt, as his future conduct was to be eccentric, giving no sign of the genius that would make him preeminent in English letters. Indeed, his life for the next ten years would center on Temple, and although much was written perhaps while Temple was alive, he published no major prose until after Temple's death in 1699. He had taken a master's degree at Oxford to prepare himself for an ecclesiastical career, and on October 28, 1694, he was ordained a deacon in Ireland and the next January ordained a priest.

During these years Swift was back and forth between Ireland and England several times. Despite one alienation from Temple, Moor Park remained his base. In 1695 we find him prebend at Kilroot near Belfast, a period marked by his unhappy romance with a Jane Waring, to whom he proposed and by whom he was refused. Returning to Moor Park, he found Stella grown to womanhood, and though he never offered her his manhood as he had Miss Waring, she became the central woman in his life from then on.

He looked to Temple to get him a benefice in England, but perhaps from fear of losing so good a secretary, Temple procrastinated until it was too late. The diplomat's death in 1699 came as a surprise and Swift, although named as literary executor, lacked means and found it expedient to take a temporary post as secretary to the Lord Justice of Ireland. In 1700 he was installed as prebend at St. Patrick's Cathedral. He was by nature and tradition a Whig and his first political tract, published in 1701, was a defense of impeached Whig statesmen. He was by that year of sufficient fame and importance to win a doctor's degree from his old university, but real distinction came with the publication of *The Battle of the Books* and *A*

Tale of a Tub, both of which had undoubtedly circulated in manuscript at the Temple household before the diplomat's death. *The Battle of the Books* took its rise from a response made by scholars to an essay of Temple's. It was not merely a reply to them but a jeu d'esprit on the part of Swift. *A Tale of a Tub* was something more serious, a comic masterpiece. Where *The Battle of the Books* was a mock-heroic piece with various books battling like Homeric warriors, *A Tale of a Tub* was a satire against the theological opponents of Anglicanism. Chief among them were the Roman Catholics, of course, and the Presbyterians, or Dissenters. Swift was confirmed in his conviction that the via media of Anglicanism and an established Church was essential to the well-being of England, and indeed of mankind. While he scoffed at Catholics, he reserved his detestation for Presbyterians, evangelicals and enthusiasts, and Scots generally. He had had experience of them when he served in Ulster a century after Plantation and that was enough for him.

While *A Tale of a Tub* and a succession of political pamphlets made his reputation and he basked in a circle of wits that included Congreve, Addison, Steele, and Prior, the book probably, as much as anything else, cost him the English bishopric he so desired, because Queen Anne, that dull and unfortunate woman (she had fourteen conceptions but left no heir), found the diction of it vulgar and offensive, and would never receive Swift even when his political activity brought him to eminence and power in her antechambers. The year before she died, he was installed as dean of the Dublin cathedral, disgruntled, and in his own eyes, in exile.

He did not himself understand what was happening to him. He was slowly turning from an Englishman to an Irishman; from a Whig to a Tory; from a dependent, seeking preferment from his social or financial superiors, to an independent scholar and writer, a polemicist, if you will, as much sought after as self-seeking. Then, too, Stella had come to Ireland to be near him and had made it her home, and indeed for the last twenty years of her life (she was to die in 1728) never returned to England. What must be remembered, to understand the political atmosphere of the time, is that so far as Ireland was concerned the Tories were the liberals and the Whigs the oppressors. From 1710 to 1714 Swift was active as a political journalist. It was during this period that he wrote his famous *Journal to Stella*, composed of the letters he sent from London to her in Ireland. Ireland, even as he was then away from it (1710–1713), had become his home. He edited *The Examiner*, a Tory journal, and, if his friendship with Steele and Addison chilled somewhat, he came closer to Pope, Congreve, and Sir John Arbuthnot (1667–1735), physician to Queen Anne, who was also a witty political polemicist. Most important, at this time he met Esther Van Homrigh, who under the name of "Vanessa" was to figure large in his life.

When the Tory cabinet fell in the summer of 1714 and Queen Anne died, the Whigs were assured of control. Swift returned to Ireland, and took up his sacerdotal duties at Dublin. Despite his protests, Esther Van Homrigh, whose letters reveal her depth of passion for him, followed him to Dublin and took up residence. Assuredly he had encouraged her too much, and he was to break her heart, for his treatment of her contributed to her death, and liquor may have played its part. It certainly played a part in the death of the Reverend Thomas Parnell (1679–1718), archdeacon of Clogher, and another Dublin-born poet, and a friend of Swift, Pope, and the other literary men of his age. Parnell's brother, Judge John Parnell, by the way, was the forebear of the nineteenth-century statesman Charles Stewart Parnell. The introduction of his name here is not a digression. He was one of the circle of friends that Swift built while dean of St. Patrick's. Others were Patrick Delaney and Thomas Sheridan, both Protestant parsons, both Trinity men, both younger than he, and, like Parnell, thoroughly Irish. For seven years, Swift, one might say, lay low. He had reason to do so. The power-hungry Whigs were as vengeful as they were greedy, and some Tories even took flight to the continent.

One could say also that the seven years were literarily fallow
(he tried his hand at some history of his times but did poorly)
because he was ordering things at the Deanery to his satisfac-
tion. He did that job and very well. One could also say that
the seven years were a period of incubation (if that's the time
it takes all our cells to change) for out of the cocoon came not
a butterfly resigned to placid rustication, but a green wasp filled
with an anti-Whig venom. In those seven years, the dean, who
never forget that he was also a priest, observed the inhuman
destitution around him and was appalled.

It is at this time that Swift grows into the monumental and
grotesque figure that history shows, a monster crashing open
a massive iron gate, breathing fire, the pyrotechnic satire that
can melt chains, depose tyrants, and remold a world. He was
learned, cantankerous, scatological, odd to the nth degree, not
exceptionally perspicacious, ambitious, loving and religious, at
once caustic, insulting, and kind, the sort of man who snarled
at his neighbors and gave surreptitiously to the poor. He had
little use for children. Someone has said that one cannot find a
line in all his writings that shows affection for them. Thus the
great irony is that his *Gulliver's Travels* has become a children's
classic, and his fiercest satire, *A Modest Proposal*, centers on
starving children. Although his literary reputation was established before he settled down as dean of St. Patrick's Cathedral,
it was what he wrote after 1713 that forever linked him with
Irish letters and the Irish nation, for he was perhaps the first
man to use that phrase—"Irish nation"—in the English language.

In 1720, he emerged on the Dublin scene with his *Proposal
for the Universal Use of Irish Manufactures*, in which, by in-
direction, he recommended that the Irish burn everything from
England except the coal. The tract was inflammatory, but it
made Swift extremely popular since the interests of his Protestant church and the Catholic Irish at that instant were allied.
It was, of course, unsigned, and the printer was brought to trial.
The petit jury refused to convict, and the charges were later
dropped. Although Swift, with an anonymous ballad, let it be

known that he was the author of the seditious pamphlet, the rabid resentment of the judiciary frightened him off, and, once again, he laid low. Soon, however, a fascinating manifestation of political corruption aroused him to his famous *Drapier's Letters.*

The occasion for the letters was this: the Duchess of Kendal, a former mistress of King George I, although a German already receiving a pension out of Irish taxes, won from the king a patent to coin 100,800 of halfpence and farthings in Ireland. She sold it to William Wood (1671–1730), who hoped to make 40,000 pounds on the deal, part of which (one historian writes) would go to this "disgusting harpy." The coins bore the laurel-crowned head of George I on the obverse and Hibernia with a harp on the reverse. Wood debased the coins from the beginning and when challenged by the Irish said he "would cram his brass down their throats in spite of them." Then came *Drapier's Letters.* Swift interrupted the composition of *Gulliver's Travels* to write them. The traditionally obsequious Irish parliament had surprisingly roused against Wood's halfpence, and Swift's letters, signed "M. B. Drapier," stiffened its resolve and caught the public mood.

The Speaker of the House in the Irish parliament at this time was William Conolly, who was also Chief Commissioner of the Irish Revenue and then deemed the richest man in Ireland. His lasting monument is Castletown, called the "greatest house in Ireland," located in County Kildare. (The house today is being preserved through the generosity and enterprise of the members of the Georgian Society and has nowhere near the number of visitors it deserves.) Conolly may be used here as a symbol of the growing affluence and influence of the Protestant nation within a nation, which was feeling its oats, and for which Swift spoke out loud and clear. Like Molyneux before him, Swift protested great devotion to the king, suggesting that the patent had been gained by chicanery.

Therefore, my friends, stand to it one and all, refuse this filthy trash. It is no treason to rebel against Mr. Wood. His Majesty in his patent obliges nobody to take these halfpence, our gracious prince hath no so ill advisers about him; or if he had, yet you see the laws have not left it in the King's power, to force us to take any coin but what is lawful, of right standard gold and silver. Therefore you have nothing to fear.

Wood was coining copper, but he had lost the fight. M. B. Drapier was to win the day: a humble shopkeeper speaking to humble shopkeepers. But the row went on for three years. Once again there was the threat of prosecution. The printer was arrested as a result of the fourth letter, and Swift was at pains of cost to see to his defense.

Other Drapier letters followed and letters under his own name, defending Drapier. At length the English Privy Council capitulated. But English opposition to any Irish autonomy was rising. Swift prepared an *Address to Both Houses of Parliament* but didn't publish it until much later. He was seeking to rouse a spirit of nationalism. He was seeking to appeal not merely to the parliament, not merely to the Protestant nation within a nation, but to the whole people of Ireland. By assuming the role of Drapier he appealed to those middle-class Catholics who, debarred from landowning and public office, were allowed to trade, many of them quite successfully.

> The *Address to Both Houses of Parliament* justified the conviction that the apparent narrowness of his Irish patriotism, its apparent restriction to the Protestant Irish, was an appearance only. For, if the Irish parliament could have had the moral courage to follow Swift's lead, nothing could have prevented it from becoming the representative of the Papists as well as the Protestants.

The quotation above is from J. Middleton Murry's *Jonathan Swift: A Critical Biography*. He continues: "Swift may have closed his conscious mind to that inevitability; but it was inherent in his proposals. It is not a paradox that the people salute in him the prophet of an independent Ireland."

In 1726, *Gulliver's Travels* appeared. *"Travels into Several*

Remote Nations of the World: In Four Parts, by Lemuel Gulliver, First a Surgeon and then a Captain of Several Ships" reads the title page. Benjamin Motte in Fleet Street, London, published it. The very real experiences of Alexander Selkirk, who was a castaway on an island and later rescued, had inspired Daniel Defoe to write *Robinson Crusoe,* and some critics would have it that *Robinson Crusoe* inspired *Gulliver's Travels,* to give the book its popular name. Indeed, say some, it is a rebuttal to the mercantile tone of *Robinson Crusoe.* We know Swift had told the love-sick Vanessa that he was reading every book on travel he could put his hands on, but it is more likely that *Gulliver's Travels* took rise from the Irish *immrama,* or from the Irish tale, Eisirt, a story of little people in a land of giants. Swift had no Gaelic, although it must be remembered that at this time the vast majority of the people in the country spoke only Gaelic, but among his Irish acquaintances was the poet Hugh McGauran, who is credited with giving him a translation of a Gaelic poem which Swift rewrote, entitling it *The Description of an Irish-Feast, translated almost literally out of the Original Irish.* If McGauran gave him that at a time when he was devouring books on travel, without doubt McGauran translated for him the Aided Fergusa, the Irish story about a voyage. More than a word, of course, must go to Thomas More's *Utopia.*

Gulliver's Travels begins in Lilliput and Brobdingnag, with such innocent mirth and charming wit as mark many tales by Irish shanachies, but in the last two books the fancy becomes savage as the dean's misogyny takes over and scatology and venom flow from his pen. The first two remain, of course, the favorites of children. Bulwer Lytton said of them:

> And lo! the book from all its end beguiled
> A harmless wonder to some happy child.

The third book is a failure. The fourth, despite the scatology and the venom, rises to heights of moral grandeur in its denunciation of war and other sins of man. Corruption in political life, if common now, was the rule then. Swift's satirization of the follies of the human race and its grosser foibles was linked, of course, with his political pressure for an Irish parliament independent of England. To make this campaign even more offensive to the Whigs it came not too long after the union of England and Scotland, achieved by threats and bribery, in 1707. England was now Great Britain; the Scots had been broken. Consequently, the movement toward a truly independent Irish parliament, begun by Molyneux and Swift, came at an inappropriate time.

The year after *Gulliver's Travels* appeared was the year Swift made his last visit to England, and the next year, 1728, his beloved Stella died. Vanessa had died two years before, but whereas he was happily rid of her, the loss of Stella (whom he never saw without her companion Rebecca Dingley being present) reduced him. She had been a restraint on the scatological side of his nature, which now worsened, and his anal neurosis, which it surely was, intensified. Yet, in 1729, he composed and published *A Modest Proposal*, which Frank O'Connor has called the first great masterpiece written in English in Ireland. The full title of the work is *A Modest Proposal for Preventing the Children of the Poor People in Ireland from being a Burden to their Parents or Country, and for making them beneficial to their Publick*. The pamphlet, of less than five thousand words, purported to be a letter from a public-spirited citizen pointing out that conditions in the country could benefit if the children were taken at the right age and eaten, first choice among them being given to the landlords "who . . . have already devoured their parents." It is a devastating document, blazing with all the genius that made him the outstanding political pamphleteer of his age. (The perpetual appeal of the piece can be gauged by a reproduction in my hands by Leonard Baskin, the distinguished Massachusetts artist, who calligraphed and illustrated *A Modest Proposal* with his cruel, thundering ink drawings on the 240th anniversary of its appearance.)

After that Swift was to write *The Legion Club*, a violent attack on the Irish House of Commons, and the famous *Verses on the Death of Dr. Swift*, where the old charm of the *Journal to Stella* comes through again. Although he wrote poetry all his life, and displayed in it his incisive political wit and his acid satirical gift, he has not been highly regarded as a poet. Recent criticism is lifting that reputation to new levels of appreciation, for it is evident on sympathetic reading that his passionate concern for human suffering comes through to move the reader. His scatological poetry can be offensive and reveals the deterioration that set in after the death of Stella.

"Everyman desires to live long," he once wrote, "but no man would be old," and on another occasion, pointing to a withering tree, he said that, like it, he would die from the top down. He did. Arteriosclerosis was added to his symptoms of Ménière's disease and both turned him into a madman; in 1742 he was declared to be of "unsound mind and memory." He was on hand, however, to hear Handel's *Messiah* performed for the first time in the new Music Hall, a historic event in Dublin. Dr. Patrick Delaney that day rose in his seat and cried, "for this be all thy sins forgiven." Swift's physical torment was on occasion severe. A doctor lived with him for much of his last days. He died on October 19, 1745, and was buried at midnight beside his beloved Stella in the cathedral he had served as priest. Later, their bones were dug up and their skulls handed around among the curious in Dublin drawing rooms but they were returned to the tomb, this time mingled together. Swift remains, as more than one critic has written, the sphinx of his age. His role in Anglo-Irish literature, however, is clear. He had awakened the Protestant conscience and had begun the movement for Irish unity and nationalism that has yet to win its ultimate goal.

To him and his straightforward, disciplined prose, we owe a hundred phrases in the language, which, for the most part, he took from the common talk about him, Dublin talk he loved to listen to: "You must eat a peck of dirt before you die," "Wait till the cows come home," "Your barking curs will never bite," "You are a sight for sore eyes," "Hail fellow well met," "Fingers were made before forks," "A penny for your thoughts," and the often quoted, garbled, or polished lines:

> So nat'ralists observe, a flea
> Hath smaller fleas that on him prey;
> And these have smaller fleas to bite 'em
> And so proceed ad infinitum

That he rhymed "flea" with "prey" is an additional clue, perhaps, that the dean was enough of an Irishman to speak with a brogue.

The movement Swift began reached its apex in the life of Henry Grattan, who was born the year after Swift died. If Dublin had just given the English-speaking world its greatest satirist, it was about to sire its greatest orators, men who were to enjoy a memorable role in literary Dublin. No account of Dublin's literary heritage can omit its early orators.

The culture of Ireland was oral when Saint Patrick arrived, and it has continued mainly oral to this day. The men of Ireland have excelled at poetry, song, and drama, and equally at oratory. England's only right in Ireland, Dean Swift said, was the right of an armed grenadier over a naked man. All that is left to the naked man is speech. During the life of Dean Swift, the Catholics of Ireland were not permitted to speak, and since most of them spoke only Gaelic they wouldn't have been understood by the English anyway. But the Anglo-Irish Protestant nation within the Irish nation did have a parliament, and there the first great Irish orators spoke out. No nation has produced a more eloquent clutch of speech-makers.

No doubt Saint Patrick brought to Ireland in his person a remarkable gift for preaching, for persuasion, and, when necessary, blistering invective. No doubt the Irish monks who carried the ancient learning, the *philosophia perennis*, back to the European continent after it had been brutalized by the Visigoths and Vandals had books on rhetoric in their saddlebags and the native gift for silver speech on their tongues. All oratory is at best an evanescent art, except with men like Cicero who recorded their speeches post factum. Most speeches, recorded before or after delivery, lacking the personal presence, the inflections, the tones, the emphases, the gestures, the pauses, the accelerations, do not read as convincingly as they are reported to have sounded. None strikes us as they are said to have struck auditors. Not least of all, the nuances of irony are lost. Irish oratory is no exception. Indeed, it took its rise at a time, and in a community, when the periodic sentence was preferred to the conversational style; when rhetorical rhythms were appreciated (in the English House of Commons Pitt kept time with his head to the metronomic measures of Henry Grattan and turned and whispered, "By God, that's oratory!"); when fustian was looked for and rodomontade forgiven, but most of all, when the average literate man was sufficiently disciplined to use and to follow an extended abstract thought. The orators of the eighteenth century fulminated, and they fulminated at length. They were the heirs to Demosthenes and looked to him as a model. Of these men, Dublin bred the best. Their speeches—many of them—are literary masterpieces.

Chief among them was Henry Grattan (1764–1820) so far as parliamentary speech-making was concerned; John Philpot Curran (1750–1817) for advocacy at the bar; and Daniel O'Connell (1775–1847) for haranguing multitudes. These are three among many who distinguished themselves in Ireland.

Edmund Burke (1729–1797), Dublin-born and Trinity-educated, is said to have been the greatest orator ever to sit in the British House of Commons. His speech "On Moving His Resolutions for Conciliation with America" (1775) was once the staple of every American schoolboy and remains his most masterful presentation. No one, it has been said, used the English language more majestically than Burke, and no parliament has ever harbored a more high-minded man. He comes as close to being a true philosopher as anyone who sat in the House of Commons, and is today a rallying figure for the politically conservative.

A compliment from such a man, an accolade from his critical judgment commending another orator might well be enough to raise the other man among the oratorical immortals. That accolade fell on his fellow Irishman, Richard Brinsley Sheridan (1751–1816), also Dublin-born, who delivered a five-hour speech in the House of Commons on Warren Hastings, whose impeachment Burke had moved. Burke described the speech as the "most astonishing effort of eloquence, argument, and wit, united, of which there is any record or tradition." So affected was parliament that the members adjourned until they calmed their emotion. Yet, Sheridan is remembered as a playwright.

Grattan, like Burke, was a Trinity man. He was born of well-to-do parents who were not aristocrats, although his grand-father became chief justice. He became a lawyer, was given a seat in the Irish parliament under the peculiar English political system of the day, and was soon involved in the political fight for Irish independence and free trade. The leader of the faction pressing for independence at this time was Henry Flood (1732–1791), himself an orator close to the stature that Grattan was to achieve.

We must first understand the nature of the society and its parliament in which Grattan moved. If, in America, the Irish have been associated with the political corruption of city machines, one has to consider the tradition the immigrants of the eighteenth and nineteenth centuries inherited from the Anglo-Irish houses of Grattan's day. It is no exaggeration to say that no more corrupt parliament, no more corrupt judiciary, has been known in any English-speaking land. The phrase "conflict of interest," so common today, was unknown, nor would its principle have been understood, as it was not understood, say, even by Daniel Webster. Most of the members of the Irish House of Commons were pensioners, grafters, or hirelings of one sort or another. Most of the judges were professional hang-men. Most of the juries were bought by favor, prejudice, or intimidation before a trial began. To stand in the opposition took courage, physical courage, and there is no question that

Grattan and others of his prominence were stalked by assassins when they could not be framed by perjured informers. Cicero prepared his Pro Milone speech but never dared deliver it. Grattan never funked, nor did Flood before him, although Flood was accused of selling out. Perhaps the most courageous of all was Curran, who fought the case of Irish independence in the perfervid arena of the courtroom. Once when confronted by the implied threat of soldiers rattling their muskets before him as they stood guard in the courtroom while he addressed a jury, Curran paused long enough to stalk over to them and cry out, "You may assassinate, you will not intimidate me." The verdicts against his clients were usually foregone conclusions, but he used the courtroom as a platform to denounce the ignominy and corruption of the government and to seek, in vain, to touch the English conscience. No doubt the viceroy in Ireland would gladly have let any number of alleged traitors go free if he could have silenced Curran, but Curran was incorruptible, and his pilloried opponents, as a result, must bear the condemnation of history and the contumely of posterity.

Flood and Grattan in their youth were friends. They acted together in amateur Shakespearean productions when they were young men. They were united in their desire for an independent Ireland; they differed on means. Flood, like the majority of the Anglo-Irish, was opposed to Catholic emancipation. With the vast majority of the country reduced to a sort of slavery, the Protestant rulers had a nice thing going, and Flood, the illegitimate son of a chief justice, wanted no change. He feared, as many did, that any concession to the Catholics would lead only to further demands and ultimate equality. Such would have been the end of the Protestant sleigh ride. Grattan was moved by no such mean motives. He saw Catholic emancipation as a major step toward an independent Ireland. "The question is now," he said in 1782, "whether we shall be a Protestant settlement or an Irish nation."

With Great Britain warring, off and on, with France, and simultaneously engaged in battle with the American colonies, the nationalist Anglo-Irish saw their chance. In 1778, declaring they feared an invasion by France, and with only a handful of English troops (5,000) in Ireland, the Anglo-Irish organized the Volunteers (100,000), replete with splendid uniforms and sufficient arms. Catholics, forbidden to carry arms but with a prosperous middle class, supported Grattan and his volunteers; Presbyterians also were behind him. In 1780, Grattan called for the repeal of legislation that had made all acts of the Irish parliament subject to approval by the English parliament and sent England what amounted to an ultimatum. The English parliament capitulated.

When the message from the lunatic and bigoted King George III was read, and a motion of thanks passed, Grattan moved his Declaration of Rights for the third time and won. Exhausted from his efforts (having been twice defeated) and not then in robust health, he said:

> I am now to address a free people; ages have passed away, and this is the first moment in which you could be distinguished by that appellation.
>
> I have spoken on the subject of your liberty so often that I have nothing to add, and have only to admire by what heaven-directed steps you have proceeded until the whole faculty of the nation is braced up to the act of her own deliverance.
>
> I found Ireland on her knees, I watched over her with eternal solicitude; I have traced her progress from injury to arms, from arms to liberty. Spirit of Swift, spirit of Molyneux, your genius has prevailed. Ireland is now a nation. In that new character I hail her, and bowing to her august presence, I say, esto perpetuus.
>
> She is no longer a wretched colony, returning thanks to her governor for his rapine, and to her king for his oppression; nor is she now a squabbling, fretful sectary, perplexing her wits, and firing her furious statutes with bigotry, sophistries, disabilities and death, to transmit to posterity insignficance and war.

The Declaration of Rights passed without a dissenting vote. It was April, 1782. The year before, Lord Cornwallis, who later would come to Ireland to serve the crown there, had surrendered at Yorktown (on October 19) and, the next year, came recognition of the independence of the American colonies. During the intervening time, England was at war with Holland, Spain, and France. By February, 1782, England's fortunes were at their lowest ebb; Ireland, the cat's-paw in that international game, had scratched at the right time. The Treaty of Paris of September 3, 1783, ended the American Revolution.

Grattan's joy was short-lived. The villain in the disillusion was Robert Stewart, the second Marquis of Londonderry, Viscount Castlereagh (1769–1822), himself Dublin-born, surely one of the most unprincipled statesmen in history, and the man responsible for the English policy in the peace settlement at the close of the Napoleonic Wars. His father had been a landowner in Donegal and Down. Castlereagh was educated at Armagh and in England and became a member of the Irish parliament in 1790. In the 1790 parliament with Robert Stewart, as he was then called, was Arthur Wellesley, later to be Duke of Wellington, and Lord Edward Fitzgerald, the brother of the Duke of Leinster, who would die for his loyalty to Ireland, even as Stewart would become one of the most hated men in Irish history—hated even by himself, for he was to die by his own hand, his throat slashed. Grattan, too, was in the 1790 parliament, elected for the city of Dublin, but he was now aware that the legislative independence he had won was being frustrated by the English control of the executive. His former friend Flood, now his foe, was protesting that Grattan had not wrung enough from the British parliament, had disbanded the Volunteers too soon, and was wrong about Catholic emancipation. In 1791 Grattan cried out that "the Irish government in its perverted state is composed of responsible officers who are not resident and resident officers who are not responsible." Someone else said that Ireland was the victim of "the deputies of deputies of deputies." His achievement was undone by Castlereagh who, in one of the most sordid bits of jobbery in legislative history, bought up the Irish parliament and had it, in 1801, vote union with Westminster and dissolve itself. Grattan's oratory had not prevailed, and subsequently in the House of Commons in London, while acclaimed, it accomplished little more. He died fighting for minority rights. Before his death an even more powerful voice was heard, no Trinity man, but a scholar from St. Omer's College in Belgium, an Irish aristocrat from the old Gaelic tradition, Daniel O'Connell, whom the King of England would irritably call the King of Ireland.

While Grattan was orating in the parliament on behalf of liberty, Curran, who had quit parliament to devote himself entirely to the law, was achieving an unparalleled reputation. Born on July 24, 1750, of humble parents in Newmarket, County Cork, he went to Trinity bent on an ecclesiastical career, but determined instead on the law. As a student, he was already famous as a wit, a mimic, a raconteur, and a genial companion. He went on to the Middle Temple in London, where his easy habits with money, having left him one day broke, he sat on a park bench, disconsolately whistling an Irish air. A stranger, apologizing, asked Curran where he had learned the tune. Curran said he had learned it in his native Ireland.

"But how comes it, sir, at this hour when other people are dining, you remain here whistling old Irish airs?"

"Alas, sir, I too have been in the habit of dining, but today, my money gone, my credit not yet arrived, I am even forced to come and dine upon a whistle in the park."

The stranger was Charles Macklin (1690–1747), who was born McLaughlin, the Irish actor and playwright, and that night Curran was his dinner guest. They would meet again when Curran was as famous as Macklin.

Fame did not come easy to Curran. Naturally eloquent, he was not because of that a born orator. A contemporary has described him thus: "His person was mean and decrepit, very slight, very shapeless—spindle legs, a shambling gait, one hand imperfect, and a face yellow and furrowed, rather flat, and thoroughly ordinary." But he goes on to say, "Yet I never was so happy in the company of any man as in Curran's for many years." Yet in the portrait of him by Thomas Laurence, his large lustrous eyes are striking and must have been a force when he addressed a jury. Lord Byron was astonished by him:

> Such imagination! There never was anything like it that ever I saw or heard of. His published life, his published speeches, give you no idea of the man—none at all. He was wonderful, even to me, who had seen many remarkable men of the time. The riches of his Irish imagination were exhaustless. I heard him speak more poetry than I have ever seen written. I saw him presented to Madame de Stael, and they were both so ugly that I could not help wondering how the best intellects of France and Ireland, could have taken up respectively such residences.

Curran's greatest fame was earned by his defense of the men taken in the rebellion of 1798. Lord Brougham, no mean orator himself, thought Curran's speech in defense of A. Hamilton Rowan, "the greatest speech of an advocate in ancient or modern times." He was the barrister for Theobald Wolfe Tone (1763–1798), the second charismatic Irish patriot, who was made an adjutant general in the French army to lead French troops on a raid on Donegal.

If the Irish courts were at that time mere instruments for the imposition of bloody injustice, Curran used them as a sounding board to denounce English misrule in Ireland. His speeches to this day remain an indictment of the depravity of the English control at the time. The key man in the conviction of one Irish patriot after another was that horror figure in Irish history, the informer, almost always a professional perjurer.

Although most of the verdicts were prearranged, the genius of Curran occasionally triumphed. Patrick Finney and fifteen others were charged with treason in January, 1798. The informer was a James O'Brien, but Curran in cross-examination destroyed the man. In his speech to the jury, his denunciation was overwhelming:

> Have you any doubt that it is the object of O'Brien to take down the prisoner for the reward that follows? Have you not

seen with what more than instinctive keenness this bloodhound has pursued his victim? How he has kept him in view from place to place until he hunts him through the avenues of the court, to where the unhappy man stands now, hopeless of all succor save that which your verdict shall afford? I have heard of assassination by sword, by pistol and by dagger, but here is a wretch who would dip the Evangelists in blood. If he thinks he has not sworn his victim to death, he is ready to swear without mercy and without end; but oh, do not, I conjure you, suffer him to take an oath; the arm of the murderer should not pollute the purity of the gospel; and if he will swear, let it be on the knife, the proper symbol of his profession.

In an interesting aftermath, O'Brien was hanged for murder. Curran's client was found not guilty. On one occasion the crowd outside the courthouse boosted Curran to their shoulders and bore him through the streets cheering. Those in the Castle —symbol of the English executive rule—considered bringing legal action against Curran in order to be rid of him but his fame was by then international and they did not dare.

Curran's most famous clients both died in jail. They had been inspired by the French Revolution and the American Revolution before it. Both had visited America. Both were associated with the Insurrection of 1798. Tone was tried and found guilty of treason. Curran fought courageously for him to the very end, and on the day that he won a habeas corpus to bring Tone to court for a new hearing, the young patriot, who was unaware of the appeal, cut his throat with a penknife and died a few days later. Lord Edward Fitzgerald, who had been cashiered from the British army when he renounced his title and declared his republican principles, died from a gunshot wound received when he was captured. After his death, the relentless Castlereagh sought to make beggars of his children and Curran defended them.

Tone himself was an able orator and spoke from the dock. His writings are of a very literate order. He had left Trinity and eloped with Matilda Witherington, but returned to study law and was called to the bar in 1789, the year of the French Revolution. He joined a literary club in Belfast, and although a Protestant, like Grattan and Curran, and indeed, quite anticlerical, wrote his *An Argument on Behalf of the Catholics of Ireland*. He then organized the Society of United Irishmen, conspired with the French, and had to flee Ireland. He might have become a farmer in America, but his patriotism brought him back to Ireland and his death. His journal is engrossing reading still.

The Catholic emancipation for which, along with Irish independence, Tone and Fitzgerald gave their lives was not to be achieved until thirty-one years after their deaths. It was achieved by an orator who was, given the occasion, worthy of the company of Burke, Curran, Grattan, or Plunkett. He was Daniel O'Connell (1775–1847), not a Trinity man, nor a Dubliner by birth, although in 1841 he was elected Lord Mayor of Dublin. O'Connell was known variously as King Dan and, more correctly, The Great Liberator, because of his achievements on behalf of religious liberty. His speeches, however, do not match in literary elegance those of Curran, Grattan, or Burke, nor do they have the magic of Burke's. O'Connell's mastery was in his presence and his delivery. What man today, without microphones, could address a crowd of one hundred thousand and be heard? No more moving picture of O'Connell can be drawn from history than that of his release from imprisonment for his endeavors to effect an end to the reunion and a reestablishment of the Irish parliament which Castlereagh had suborned to its destruction. Hundreds of thousands of the Irish lined the street as he was driven by carriage from the jail to his home. On passing the abandoned House of Parliament, he stood in his carriage and dramatically, without words, pointed to it. The Irish crowd roared with understanding and determination.

I V

Before we turn to Burke, we must remark that the orators we have chosen were only the most eminent. There were others in the Dublin scene, some earlier than Grattan and Flood, men like Anthony Malone; some contemporaries of O'Connell, for example, Richard Lalor Sheil, who, like Sheridan, was a playwright turned politician, and Charles Phillips (1787–1859), like Curran, a barrister, but whose floridity disqualified him from greatness; and some who came after, like Thomas Meagher, who became a general in the Northern army during the American Civil War, and even when necessary Charles Stewart Parnell, whose mother was an American whose father, Admiral Charles Stewart, had commanded Old Ironsides; and before Parnell, Isaac Butt, who began as an Orange man and ended a nationalist patriot, too convivial for life itself, and certainly for political life. (Parnell in 1880, incidentally, addressed the House of Representatives in Washington, D.C.)

Religion has played such a central part in the history of Ireland that it is well to remember that the men most distinguished as patriots during the eighteenth and nineteenth centuries were Protestants: Grattan, Tone, Curran, Flood, Butt, Parnell, Fitzgerald, and others. The same is true of Robert Emmet, whose fame as an orator rests on his one speech and that made from the dock. In 1803, he launched the most quixotic of revolutions, and his romantic story has been told ten thousand times. Earlier we quoted the peroration of that speech, which has given him literary immortality. We have only to add here that he had been known for his speeches before student groups at Trinity College and elsewhere in Dublin and it was no mere accident of genius that his speech from the dock is a classic. He was captured by the English when he returned, unnecessarily, to bid farewell to his sweetheart, who was Sarah Curran, daughter of the famous advocate. The romance, his pathetic rebellion, his beloved figure, have been more in Irish minds symbolic of the heroic struggle for liberty than the deeds of any other man in Irish history, including O'Connell. If O'Connell could be thought of as an uncrowned king of Ireland, Emmet is certainly the crown prince.

While Grattan and O'Connell sat in the British House of Commons, their oratorical triumphs were scored elsewhere. Burke's took place in that House of Commons, and he stands unrivaled by the other orators that have spoken within those walls. He was, like Grattan, Dublin-born; like Curran, supreme in debate; but beyond them he had a mind that dealt with profundities, that rose above the quiddities of partisanship to philosophic planes, although this did not save him from the brawls and buffets that attend on politics.

As a boy he was of sickly constitution and so driven to reading. His father was a Protestant and his mother a Catholic, and as a child he was educated at the hedge classes and a Quaker school. At fourteen he entered Trinity, where he evidently read as Swift did, that is to say, what he pleased, but with wide-ranging taste. In 1747 he organized the Historical Society, where students addressed each other on subjects that interested them. He went to England to study for the law but spent his time listening to debates in the House of Commons and was never admitted to the bar. He had begun to write by that time and sell to periodicals. When his health was impaired, he moved into the home of his doctor and married that good man's daughter, like his mother, a Catholic. His first essay was his *Vindication of Natural Society*, which was a defense of organized religion, but what caught the eye of Dr. Samuel Johnson and won Burke fame was *A Philosophical Inquiry Into the Origin of Our Ideas of the Sublime and the Beautiful.* With Robert Didsley, a publisher, he launched *The Annual Register*, a survey of the year's events, which first appeared in 1759 and to which he contributed for thirty years. Burke remained throughout his life a member of the Anglican Church but because of his Catholic connections was often depicted by cartoonists in the garb of a Jesuit. Charles Watson-Wentworth (1730–1782), who became the Second Marquess of Rockingham, took on Burke as his secretary and brought him into the House of Commons. He was the leader of a group called the Rockingham Whigs and it was they alone who had vision regarding the American colonies. Burke became his secretary in 1765, when Watson-Wentworth was head of the government. The next year the government fell and from then until his death late in 1782 Watson-Wentworth was in opposition, although in March of that year he was again called on to form a government. He began negotiations for peace with the colonies and began a program of reform of royal patronage and spending. During these years, Burke became the most distinguished orator in the House and exerted immense influence on his patron, who was not, however, an exceedingly forceful man.

In many ways, Burke's political life was a failure. Although he was once elected to parliament from Bristol the voters there turned him out when he stood for economic rights. He was thereafter maintained in office by a pocket borough owned by his patron. His speech *Conciliation with the American Colonies* failed of its purpose.

Two of his best speeches were made in support of a bill to reorder the method by which England ruled India. The bill did not pass. He then became the central prosecutor in the impeachment of Warren Hastings, the first governor-general of India. The trial dragged on for eight years and ended with Hastings's acquittal. Burke bought an estate that was too big for his purse and kept him in debt. He labored on behalf of Catholic rights in Ireland and got nowhere on that score. As a result of his prosecution of Hastings his popularity diminished, even though the whole affair led to the reform of Britain's operations in India. His son succeeded him in parliament but died young in office. When Burke accepted a pension from the king (after his denunciation of the regicidal French Revolution) he was violently attacked. His last concern was for his native land.

Wherein lay Burke's greatness? Certainly in his majestic prose. Lord Macaulay said of him that he was "in aptitude of comprehension and richness of imagination superior to every orator, ancient or modern." He had not Curran's disadvantages. He stood about five feet ten inches in height, one biographer tells us, and was erect and well-formed, and women esteemed him as handsome. He was never robust in health and wore eyeglasses. His manner was courtly and unaffected. His wife survived him and when she died, their home, on which he had spent so much energy and money, burned down. The great barrier to complete success as a politician lay in his poverty, for in England, in those days, money and family had to be weighed in the scales with ability. None matched Burke in ability; the testimony of his contemporaries is uniform. Fox claimed he learned more from Burke than from the classics. Many have said since that he was a philosopher who wasted his time as a politician, but as others have pointed out, his role was that of an educator. He instructed not only his colleagues and his party; he instructed a nation and taught politics as a science to half a world. However, Burke's genius was in many ways wasted on the House of Commons at the time, and late in his career, when his popularity had waned, he was called the "dinner-bell of the House" and the benches would empty when he rose to talk. Woodrow Wilson, a historian before he was President of the United States, thought him a genius, and while preeminent as an orator, above all, a man, and he was captivated by Burke's *Letter to a Noble Lord*, in which he defended himself for having accepted a pension.

To list other Irish orators could occupy many more pages.

The Reverend Thomas N. Burke, O.P., who was born in County Dublin, became head of the Irish Dominican College in Rome and one of that ancient city's most celebrated preachers. He was in great demand for the pulpits of Ireland, and in the United States he gave a series of polemical lectures to answer the anti-Irish historical lectures of James Froude, who, whatever his misjudgments on Ireland's history, loved the summers there and wrote a novel about the country still worth reading.

The Reverend Theobald Matthew, a Capuchin (1790–1856), who completed his studies in Dublin, became the greatest temperance preacher of his age and one of the first Catholic ecumenists. Father Matthew Total Abstinence Societies were formed all over Ireland and in the United States, where at least one still survives. They are but two of the eminent clerical orators of the country.

Lest it be thought that all Irishmen were orators or inherited in their genes the gift for talking, let us remember Burke's contemporary and friend Oliver Goldsmith (1728–1774), poet, playwright, novelist, and essayist, another Irishman, and one who was at Trinity College with Burke in the 1740s. Goldsmith it was who "wrote like an angel, but talked like poor poll." He too had come to London to seek his fortune, and he would have suffered more indignities than he did if it were not for the friendship of Dr. Samuel Johnson, whose circle Burke and Goldsmith both shared. It was Johnson who took from Goldsmith the manuscript of *The Vicar of Wakefield* and sold it while the bailiff was sitting in Goldsmith's parlor for unpaid debts.

Goldsmith was a lovable man, whose epitaph testified that he touched nothing that he did not adorn. Good humor, grace, and ebullience bubble up in all that he wrote; his spirit was marked by compassion and affection. Like Steele before him, he went to England to seek his fortune and wrote essays. His *Vicar of Wakefield* appeared in 1766, seven years after that eccentric masterpiece *Tristram Shandy*, by another Irish-born genius, Laurence Sterne, whose career, however, does not touch

Dublin. In 1773, *She Stoops to Conquer* took the stage and endured as one of the finest comedies in English. If Goldsmith could talk only like a poll parrot (so far as David Garrick was concerned) he could write captivating dialogue.

The foremost playwright of the era was another Dubliner, Richard Brinsley Sheridan (1751–1816), a friend of Burke's also and a fellow M.P. We have quoted Burke's opinion of Sheridan as an orator. We have only to consider him as a playwright. His *The School for Scandal* has been hailed as the brightest comedy on the English stage since Shakespeare. It was first played in 1777, only four years after Goldsmith's masterpiece. Two years before, *The Rivals* had taken London by storm. Within the past ten years, his *St. Patrick's Day* was performed by a Boston troupe on a national United States television network. Its vitality is unabated. We will remember his grandfather as Swift's friend and his actor-father as the biographer of Swift. Unlike Congreve and Southerne, Sheridan died in poverty.

An examination of an era that opened with Jonathan Swift might well close with his fellow collegian Bishop George Berkeley, the most distinguished philosopher Ireland has produced. As relentlessly as Swift pursued his role of misogynist and crosspatch, so Berkeley persisted in benignity, irenicism, and good works. Where Swift was concerned with the manners and mores of men, Berkeley, although not above satire, was concerned with man on a more profound level—his religious convictions and the extent to which they were based on correct philosophical premises. It was with the intention of combating the materialism of the scientists and the atheism of the freethinkers that Berkeley addressed himself to philosophy. His thesis, to hint at it with ridiculous brevity, was this: matter does not exist in the way scientists believe but, corporeal though it is, takes on its nature only from our perception of it, and all causal connections posited in nature exist only in our minds; and secondly, general or universal ideas are terms only; thirdly, the whole is demonstrably contingent since there is not chaos but order in nature and a predictable succession of phenomena (although causality is a matter of faith) and hence must be the work of a Divine Intellect.

Berkeley was born in Dysert, County Kilkenny, in 1685, and attended the college there shortly after Swift. He entered Trinity College in 1700, and in 1707 was named a fellow, teaching Greek, Hebrew, and divinity, and in 1709 brought out his first philosophic work, *An Essay Towards a New Theory of Vision*, a study in psychology. In 1710 his *Treatise Concerning the Principles of Human Knowledge* won him international notice, and he followed it in 1713 with *Three Dialogues Between Hylas and Philonous*, a felicitous explication of his imaginative theory. At this time, he made the acquaintance of Swift, Addison, Pope, Steele, and others, and through Swift became secretary and chaplain to Lord Peterborough and traveled to Italy and Sicily. On his return he became tutor to the son of the Bishop of Clogher and toured Europe, returning to England during the South Sea Bubble scandal. The South Sea Bubble was the name given to the financial disaster that followed an attempt by the ministry of Robert Walpole to manage the national debt of Great Britain by paying off the creditors in part through the South Sea Company, a crown-chartered company, formed in anticipation (that proved illusory) of trade with the Spanish colonies after the treaty that was to conclude the War of the Spanish Succession. The stock leaped from 175 to 1,000 (with German-speaking George I as head of the company), and Walpole, who was in on the ground floor, sold out at the top of the boom. Thousands were ruined; many committed suicide; and a scapegoat was jailed. The scandal prompted Berkeley to write his *Essay Towards Preventing the Ruin of Great Britain*. Later he would write an inscription for a statue of George I (a strange man who had the body of his wife's lover burned in an oven, alive, some whispered).

After the scandal and that essay (which first brought Berkeley into public affairs) he took off for America and stopped at Whitehall, near Newport, Rhode Island, where he continued his philosophical studies while waiting a promised grant from Prime Minister Walpole with which he hoped to found a college in the "vexed Bermoothes" for the education of the heathen aborigines. Walpole failed to come through and Berkeley went home. As a result of his stay in America, his influence was transmitted to the great American theologian Jonathan Edwards through Samuel Johnson (1696–1772), a New Englander who met and corresponded with Berkeley during the Newport period.

On his return from America, Berkeley brought with him the manuscript of *Alciphron or the Minute Philosopher*, another dialogue directed specifically against free-thinkers, considered by many to be his finest work. Two years after his return, in 1734, he was made Bishop of Cloyne near Cork and began his pastoral duties. His return to his native land brought a recrudescence of affection for it.

From 1735 to 1737 he published in three parts *The Querist*, a series of tracts containing more than eight hundred questions, all dealing with Irish economic and social conditions. He spoke, of course, for the Anglo-Irish nation within the Irish nation, but his work was seminal to the future of an independent Ireland. He urged relaxation of the dread penal laws and argued for religious tolerance. Of the eight hundred questions the most celebrated was 134, "Whether, if there was a Wall of Brass, a Thousand Cubits high, round this Kingdom, our Natives might not nevertheless live cleanly and comfortably, till the Land and reap the Fruits of it?" In the United States, nothing in his writings is more quoted than the first line of the last quatrain of his poem *On the Prospect of Planting Arts and Learning in America*.

> Westward the course of empire takes its way,
> The first four acts already past;
> A fifth shall close the drama with the day—
> Time's noblest offspring is the last.

With Maria Edgeworth (1767–1849) and her novella *Castle Rackrent*, which appeared in 1800, the Irish novel has its beginning. To give the lady her due, the Waverley novels have their beginning there as well, for Sir Walter Scott acknowledged that it was her pioneer work that turned him to writing about medieval Scotland. Maria was born in Oxfordshire, England, on January 1, 1767, the eldest daughter of Richard Lovell Edgeworth (1744–1817), a graduate of Trinity College, who had twenty-two children by four wives and whose own memoirs are part of the Dublin literary heritage. His family had been in Ireland since the time of Queen Elizabeth, and in 1773, the year Robert Emmet was born, he brought his wife and children there for good. Maria would remain at Edgeworthstown in County Longford, an admired and beloved woman, until her death in 1849.

Her father was an industrious eccentric who installed the first telegraph in England, tinkered with other inventions, wrote *Roads and Carriages*, anticipating macadam, and deemed himself a writer and critic and, above all, an educator. He was determined to reform the landlord system in Ireland by dealing fairly with his Catholic tenants. One result of this was that during a minor rebellion in the district, the Edgeworth house was not looted by rebels as others were.

Edgeworth père instructed his daughter in bookkeeping and had her run his estate while he indulged his enthusiasms, in which she also shared. Under such forced steam, Maria became a scholar and in 1798 collaborated with him on *A Treatise on Practical Education*, and together they compiled an *Essay on Irish Bulls*, those peculiarly Irish malapropisms, not the animals. Despite these extensive activities, she managed to write her historic book *Castle Rackrent*.

Four years earlier she had published her first literary effort, *The Parent's Assistant*, stories which she had devised to entertain her numerous siblings and half-siblings on the estate, filling six volumes. *Castle Rackrent* is still read today and its satire and storytelling triumph over its moralism. The book recounts the deterioration and ruin of an Ascendancy family as seen by an old retainer, Thady O'Quirk, through whose eyes we observe the Rackrents, originally O'Shaughlins, for four generations. It was the first novel in English to range over a hundred years or more of one family. The name Rackrent was taken from an exorbitant rental practice thrust on the Irish peasantry. Six years later she wrote a sequel of sorts, *The Absentee.*

This book was followed by a profusion of novels and tales, until the diminutive, plain-Jane transplant from England—but now as Irish to her fingertips as the Ascendancy mind permitted—had a worldwide reputation. A meticulous manner of dressing accented no doubt the tininess and tidiness of her figure and her pale face shone with lustrous eyes and an exuberant intelligence. Her exquisite manners and natural address made her an impressive person. In 1832, when she visited Walter Scott at Abbotsford, she delighted him. The death of her father in 1817 was a blow despite the intensity with which he had overborne her at times. She said of him, "Few, I believe, have ever enjoyed such happiness, or such advantages, as I have had in the instruction, society and unbounded confidence and affection of such a father and such a friend."

Maria had been to Dublin with her father many times when he was sitting in that corrupt parliament of which he was one of the incorruptible members although a Unionist at heart. She had also traveled to the continent. Her novel *Ormond* was published in the year of his death and he is said to have dictated several passages in it on his deathbed. His influence may have diluted her artistry, but she declared that if it had not been for him she would not have written at all. *The Absentee*, in which she showed the destructiveness to Irish society of absentee landlordism, is deemed by some her best work. Despite her sympathies for the impoverished and penalized Catholics, she never identified with them in her writings, and the terrorism of the Whiteboys and the Ribbonmen, violence-prone secret societies representing the more rambunctious among the peasants, frightened her off. In 1834, she published *Helen*, a novel with an English setting, and after that a children's story, but her reputation rests on her Irish novels, and the innovative use of the economic aspects of social life.

For the last fifteen years of her life Maria wrote nothing. Throughout the famine years, 1845 until her death, she strove mightily with her little frame and waning strength to feed her tenants and, indeed, probably died of the strain put upon her by the burden. Her literary heritage was great and Scott was not the only writer she influenced. Jane Austen admired (and then overshadowed) her. The nineteenth-century realists on the continent owe her a debt. Her collaborative work with her father has a place in the history of education.

The year *Castle Rackrent* appeared a six-year-old, ragged, barefoot, Irish-speaking gossoon, the youngest boy among fourteen children, was helping his father on a fourteen-acre farm in County Tyrone, a boy whom King Daniel O'Connell would call the "Walter Scott of Ireland." He was William Carleton (1794–1869), one of the most enigmatic, talented, curious writers ever to walk the streets of Dublin to sell his pen to the highest bidder. Miss Edgeworth came to say that not until she read Carleton did she really know Irish life, and subsequent critics have said that from him alone do we have the true picture of the pre-famine and famine-ravaged Irish peasantry. He was the physical opposite of Miss Edgeworth, a large muscular man, an athlete, a heavy drinker, a womanizer, and a man with no loyalty except to his pen, which he put at the service of one faction and then another. Born a Catholic and trained for the priesthood, he abandoned the faith of his fathers and became a Protestant, a conversion that later hurt his reputation.

Carleton was launched on his writing career by the Reverend Caesar Otway (1768–1842), a native of Tipperary, a graduate of Dublin University, and the founder of *The Christian Examiner*, Dublin's first religious magazine. Otway was a cleric with talent whose mind was malformed by a maniacal hatred of Catholicism. His own book, *Sketches in Ireland, Descriptive and Interesting*, composed of material he had written for his magazine, appeared in 1827 to limited popularity, and Otway became for a while the center of Dublin's literary world. Carleton, commenting to him on his essay on Lough Derg, told of his own pilgrimage to that lake and was asked to put the tale in writing. He did so and his pen from that day never stopped until death stopped it.

Carleton had come to Dublin with two shillings and nine pence in his pocket and a copy of *Gil Blas*, the book that, more than any other, lured him away from County Tyrone to literary Dublin. Before going down to Dublin, he had taken a job as a tutor but his spirit yearned for a larger arena. His change of religion, while momentarily furthering his literary career, entangled it in political polemics that ravaged him and left his reputation overshadowed by a bigoted backwash. The Protestants wanted him to write exposés of the Catholic causes and to denounce the church he had abandoned. To an extent he did this, but it is obvious from his writings that he loved the Catholic peasantry which he wrote about as no one else did, and that affection shines through his work.

The power of Carleton's talent is recognized by all. Yeats was to say of him that modern Irish literature began with him, and others would give him the title of the greatest of Irish novelists, although his work is marred by the literary conventions of his day.

In 1818 Carleton came into Dublin, a twenty-four-year-old wandering schoolmaster, married a Protestant girl, and took a job teaching. Not until 1825 did he meet Otway; but in fifteen years' time he was the most famous of Irish writers. Before he was done, the *Edinburgh Review* would rightly say of him, "It is in his pages, and in his alone, that future generations must look for the truest and fullest, though still far from complete, picture of those who ere long will have passed away from that troubled land, from the records of history, and from the memory of man forever."

His first work that showed his genius was *Traits and Stories of the Irish Peasantry*, which came in 1830 and drew on what he knew, indeed, on what was to remain his forte, his single but fecund source. Others of his works followed: *The Poor Scholar, Valentine McClutchy*, and *William Reilly* and his *Dear Colleen Bawn*. The last two give the most vivid pictures of the horrors of landlordism and the tragic condition of the peasantry under the penal laws. His autobiography, which he didn't live to finish, is one of his most fascinating creations.

While he did not have the techniques of structuring a novel which are the passing talent of every hack today, he had a retentive ear for the lilting, racy speech of the countrymen, a keen eye for their mores and manners, and profound sympathy with the human condition in its distraught aspects. His instability affected his work as much as his style. While in *Parra Sastha* and *Rody the Rover* he could depict the peasants in their most brutal moments, or ridicule their organization against the landlords, his *Valentine McClutchy* was, in turn, a most virulent attack upon the landlords themselves. He was the most perceptive writer during Ireland's most awful hours, for he was born well before the famine and lived long after it. He saw it all and told it as no one else did or could, for he understood the peasantry and its oral tradition better than any other Irish novelist including James Joyce, who knew them not at all. He had within him the contradictory elements that have made Irish literature great, and the tensions of his heart put passion into his prose. He had a love-hate affair with the Catholic church and the hedge priests he had known and who had taught him; he was to a degree a "spoiled priest," to use the Irish expression, and a gypsy fortune-teller had predicted his fate. "He will never be a priest," the prophecy ran, "he will love the girls too well. But when he grows up he will go to Dublin and become a great man." So he did; and later fell from grace, a fate which the gypsy had not predicted.

While Miss Edgeworth is a beginning, William Carleton is a culmination and the end of a literary movement. The contrast between them is a key to the understanding of the whole period, a whole half century, for the story of the Irish novel dealing with landlordism begins in 1800 and by 1850 had pretty well run its course. Carleton said it would be fifty years after him before his equal would come, and his prediction was true.

Innumerable literary figures were coeval with him and Maria

Edgeworth but they never surpassed either in the writing of fiction. There was, for instance, Lady Morgan (1785–1859), who began life as Sydney Owenson, the daughter of an impoverished actor who had Anglicized his Irish name, Sydney Mac-Owen. She started her career as a domestic but rose to keep the most fashionable literary salon in Dublin and play host to the leading literary figures of her day. Thomas Moore (1779–1852) came to sing at her parties, and her novels were read all over England. Her novel *The Wild Irish Girl* came out in 1806 and was prodigiously popular. Her success was a benison to her aging father, who, weary with debts, and having lost the theater of which he had been manager, had been on the road staging performances for barracked soldiers throughout Ireland. In 1809, he performed in a play of his daughter's, *An Irishman All the World Over*, in which the shillelagh and caubeen, the perdurable properties of the stage Irishman, were much in evidence. Like Maria Edgeworth, Lady Morgan was a chronicler of the Ascendancy.

V

Charles Lever (1806–1872) and Samuel Lover (1797–1868), forever the source of a schoolboy joke about love'r and leave'er, sought to portray an Irish peasantry they really didn't understand. What they brought to the superficial portrayal was ebullient humor; Lever, more robust, and riotous; Lover, as befitted his name, more kindly, and not as impressive. Both were Dublin-born; both died elsewhere, Lover in England, Lever in Trieste, where an ever more distinguished Irish novelist, James Joyce, would later live in elected exile.

Lover was the son of a stockbroker but left home in his teens to begin life as an artist. His marine paintings and more particularly his miniatures brought him fame and a measure of fortune. His portrait of Paganini was hung in London and that of the Duke of Wellington was so well done he narrowly missed being named painter to the royal family. In 1828, he became secretary to the Royal Hibernian Society in Dublin. From an early age he had mixed writing and music with the practice of painting, and, while still quite young, was called upon to sing one of his own compositions at a Dublin dinner for Thomas Moore (1779–1852), the greatest songwriter of the day. Moore alone as a songwriter exceeds Samuel Lover in enduring popularity. Lover's novels are still read, but it is his songs that remain a staple of Irish drawing rooms and, indeed, of drawing rooms wherever the English language is spoken. "The Low-Backed Car" is perhaps the most popular.

Nathaniel Hawthorne delighted to hear Lover sing his songs and found the performance of "rich and humorous effect, to which the comicality of his face contributed almost as much as the voice and the words." His stage productions, the musical comedies of their day, were produced at the Haymarket Theatre in London, but it was his three-volume novel, *Rory O'Moore, A National Romance*, written at the request of Lady Morgan, that is his fictional masterpiece. *Handy Andy* is perhaps his most humorous and most popular. He adapted it from a ballad he had written, and then adapted a stage play from the novel. The first Tyrone Power, a distinguished Irish actor, performed in the premiere in 1837. Lover wrote more than three hundred songs and poems, enjoyed performing them, and was very popular. "Little Lover" was the nickname his friends gave him, and the sparking wit of his verse was manifest in his person. His visit to the United States, where he performed in one of his own plays, was marred by the news of the death of his wife, and he hastened back to England. He married again but the death of a beloved daughter saddened his last years.

Lover's depiction of the Irish was gentler than the portrayals by Charles Lever (1806–1872), Dublin-born son of an English carpenter and an Irish mother. Lever senior worked on the construction of the splendid Custom House that is such an architectural ornament of Dublin, and it must be remembered that it was during the reigns of the Georges that the city took on the charming architectural aspect that it has today, and retains, because it escaped the industrial revolution. When Grattan's parliament collapsed and vanished, Dublin became a backwash, diverted from the mainstream. Lever went to Trinity College and there joined the more riotous students in their horseplay and outrageous roughhouse. He elected medicine and the pursuit of its arcane knowledge took him to the continent, where he met Goethe and traveled widely. In his youth he visited the United States and actually lived with an Indian tribe. One of his major experiences after he returned to Dublin and set up his office in Talbot Street was fighting a cholera plague in the west of Ireland. Only his robust constitution saved him from the disease, and only his jolly nature kept him from fleeing. His writing career began relatively late. When the *Dublin University Magazine* was founded in 1833, he began to write seriously. *The Confessions of Harry Lorrequer*, which appeared in it in 1837, brought him critical attention. Indeed, it brought him a job, and in January, 1842, he became the magazine's editor. His home became a watering-hole and the bibulous Isaac Butt and William Makepeace Thackeray were among the visitors. Lever's reckless nature, his gambling and extravagant life, kept him financially pressed despite his income and a legacy.

Lever had an itchy foot, and in 1845 left the magazine, after a near duel with S. C. Hall, another Dublin editor, whose wife's book, *Popular Tales*, was of sufficient merit to win her a state pension. On the continent, Lever continued to write and his novels tumbled on each other's heels. Like Lover, he was a man of charming personality. Elizabeth Barrett Browning, writing to a friend, found he had "a most cordial vivacious manner, a glowing countenance, with animal spirits somewhat predominant over the intellect, yet the intellect by no means default." In his *Book of Snobs*, Thackeray accused him of "lordolatry," and there is no question he liked to live well, but the distinguished critic George Saintsbury dismissed the charge. Lever loved life more than work, and his books, if marred by slovenly writing, are redeemed by the full comedy, the practical jokes, the roughhouse humor of hard-drinking Irish squires. He lacks the more sentimental drollery of Lover. William Ellery Channing, the famous Boston divine and a contemporary, was quite right when he said of *Charles O'Malley*, perhaps Lever's best novel, that it was "a strange mixture of gay conviviality, recklessness and bloodshed," that did not go "very far into human nature." Despite his love of a life of ease his novels fill thirty-seven volumes.

William Hamilton Maxwell (1794–1850), an Ulsterman educated at Trinity College and a distinguished author, was the discoverer of Lever. Maxwell was induced to take holy orders

by an aunt who promised to make him her heir, but his dis-
position ran mostly to the sporting life. His first novel, *O'Hara*,
was written in a hunting lodge rather than a parsonage. His
Wild Sports of the West (1832) set a literary fashion on which
Lover and Lever both drew. Together they created the stage
Irishmen, the uncouth buffoon whose sole access to wit was the
practical joke and the pratfall.

For eccentricity matched with a literary gift, the Reverend
Charles Robert Maturin (1782–1824), a Dublin native, and like
Lover and Lever a graduate of Trinity, is a unique figure. Like
Swift, he was shocked by the poverty around his church, St.
Peter's, in Dublin, but his own financial condition was not too
solid. To supplement his clerical income he first tutored students
and then took to writing, using the pseudonym Dennis Jasper
Murphy. His first novel, *The Fatal Revenge*, was admired by
Scott, and his *The Milesian Chief*, which appeared in 1812,
was said to have inspired Scott's *The Bride of Lammermoor*.

By 1812 Maturin had won a reputation for eccentricity. Besides combining his clerical career with the writing of stage
plays and Gothic novels, he was a dandy in dress, who had
such a passion for dancing that he drew the curtains of his
drawing room during the day so he could prance safe from
prying eyes. Better than that, he used to stick a white wafer
of unleavened bread on his forehead as a signal to his household that he sensed "the estro of composition coming on him,"
and so was not to be disturbed. Another report is recorded
that he sealed his mouth with a paste of flour and water when
he sat and wrote in company. Like every other literate Irishman of his day who needed money, he tried writing for the stage,
and Lord Byron saw to it that his tragedy *Bertram* was produced, but his next work, *Manuel*, Byron called "the absurd
work of a clever man." He returned to the novel and let his
horrific imagination have full sway in *Melmoth the Wanderer*.
This appeared in 1820, was admired by Balzac, and to this day
remains a favorite with lovers of the macabre. In 1824, he forswore writing to give himself full time for his pastoral duties,

but his eccentricity increased and his clothes became sloppily fantastic.

If he didn't influence Edgar Allan Poe, as he may well have, Maturin certainly influenced his fellow Dubliner Joseph Sheridan Le Fanu (1814–1873) who, to aficionados of Gothic tales, remains a master. Le Fanu was the grandson of Richard Brinsley Sheridan's sister Alicia and proud of the connection. His numerous novels are overshadowed in popularity by the superb vampire tale *Dracula*, written by his contemporary Bram Stoker (1847–1912). (Abraham) Bram Stoker was born in Dublin and educated at Trinity, and began, like Le Fanu, as a journalist. He gave up his role as drama critic and editor to become private secretary to Sir Henry Irving, the great actor. *Dracula* remains the most celebrated of vampire stories, as a novel, a play, and a movie.

Le Fanu, a professional journalist who founded and edited several Dublin journals, was so saddened by the death of his wife he became all but a recluse in his home in Merrion Square (which looked much the same in his day as it does today). In that setting he turned out his celebrated ghost stories. Le Fanu had a brother, William Robert Le Fanu (1816–1894), whose *Seventy Years of Irish Life* is a compilation of Anglo-Irish humor. He treated Irish life with the same sort of levity that marks Lever's work.

If these writers—Lover, Lever, Maxwell, Le Fanu, and others —attempted to bring the Irish peasantry to paper, they created types that the Catholics found offensive. The Banim brothers, John (1798–1842) and Michael (1796–1874), one of Ireland's most famous collaborative teams, set out to present the true picture, which could be a very violent one indeed. Their significance lay in their Catholicism, for they were the first Catholic novelists in Ireland and so in sympathy with the peasants rather than with the Ascendancy. Their determination was to correct the ludicrous portraits of the Irish peasants limned by Lever and others. In 1820, John was teaching art in Dublin, far from his native Kilkenny, but gave up art to try his hand at literature.

O'Connell's oratory was shaking the land and his gallowglass
was Richard Lalor Sheil (1791–1850), himself a distinguished
orator, and it was he whom John Banim had for a friend and
patron. His recommendation of Banim's tragedy *Damon and
Pythias* had it produced at Covent Garden, London, in 1821.
The next year, Banim and his brother Michael planned their
Tales of the O'Hara Family, a collaborative work. Michael's
talent was at its best in the vital, brutal story *Crohoore of the
Billhook*. John's novel *The Boyne Water* was Ireland's first historical novel. By 1830, John, stricken by a wasting disease,
was an invalid and had to retreat to Kilkenny, where the presence of Michael and visits from Gerald Griffin (1803–1840),
the Limerick novelist, brightened his last days.

Griffin's novel *The Collegians* is deemed one of the best of
the period and, as *The Colleen Bawn*, became one of the most
popular dramatic productions of the century, both as a play
and an opera. Among Griffin's other works were *Holland-Tide
Tales, Tales of the Munster Festivals,* and *Tales of My Neighborhood*. He wrote for the most part in London, and it was
late in his life that he came to Dublin and then under strange
circumstances. He became convinced that the fiction writer
could not truly portray life without conniving with sin, and
that, indeed, all literature was a vanity. Thus motivated, he
burned his papers, including an unpublished tragedy, distributed
his property among his brothers, and became a member of the
religious community of the Christian Brothers, working as a
menial in Dublin and later in Cork, where his extreme asceticism
more than likely contributed to his death. He was twenty-five
when he wrote *The Collegians*, which more than one nineteenth-
century critic called best of the Irish novels.

The development of the Irish novel during the first half of
the nineteenth century in Ireland saw the emphasis shift from
the Protestant Ascendancy and its dream of independence to
a more native literature taking its strength from the subdued
aboriginal people, the difference, in brief, between Maria Edgeworth and Charles Kickham. For English Dublin was begin-

ning to discover the Irish nation that toiled beyond the Pale and to interest itself in that great body of Irish literature, folklore, legends, tales, and history that constituted old Ireland.

Between the birth of Maria Edgeworth in 1767 and the death of William Carleton in 1869 lies a century rich in history. In both the squalor of the boglands and the splendor of the great houses of Ireland, Irish nationalism was beginning to fester and it is interesting to reflect that the British empire was to die of the disease, for in the twentieth century Ireland was the first colony to break away.

In 1767 everyone in London and Dublin was reading *The Vicar of Wakefield* by Oliver Goldsmith, whose inspiration for the story lay in his childhood days in Ireland, as did that of *The Deserted Village*, which was soon to follow. It was the age of Sheridan and Burke and Grattan and of the American Declaration of Independence (signed by more Irishmen than any other foreign-born signers). Noah Webster was teaching Americans to spell; Goethe was writing and Mozart composing; and Edmund Malone (1741–1812), a Dublin man, published his edition of William Shakespeare, a landmark in the critical studies of our greatest poet. The year after the United States Constitution was ratified, the Bastille fell. In brief, it was the age of the Enlightenment, with national awakenings everywhere.

In Ireland the penal laws relaxed painfully slowly, and revolution was being preached in Dublin. The spirit of the French Revolution fired the hearts of Irish patriots and Wolfe Tone (1763–1798) and Robert Emmet (1778–1803) mounted their rebellions, and died: Tone by his own hand in prison, Emmet on the scaffold. Tone's autobiography, pamphlets, and letters would have won him a literary reputation if he had died in bed. Emmet's speech from the scaffold is a masterpiece of oratory, eternally quotable. Within a decade of their deaths, Daniel O'Connell had emerged as the Irish paladin.

Napoleon's star blazed over Europe and fell into the oblivion of St. Helena. The War of 1812 between England and the United States came and went. Queen Victoria was born in

1819, and ten years later, through O'Connell's genius, Catholic emancipation came to Ireland. In New England, the great American literary flowering was under way. In 1845 the Great Famine began in Ireland and, with only one brief respite, ran into 1848. Besides the political revolutions that were racking Europe, the industrial revolution was well under way. Crowns were falling on all sides. The French Commune frightened England and inspired Irish revolutionaries, but the people were too weak from starvation to fight. They assembled in revolutionary ranks only in the hope of a ration of bread from the leaders. The Young Ireland movement, which had begun under brillant leaders, petered out with their exile. Maria Edgeworth died in 1849 and although Carleton lived until 1869, his best work was done by the mid-century mark. The year before Miss Edgeworth died, John Henry Newman was received into the Catholic church and later came to Dublin in a disappointed effort to found a Catholic university there. Slavery was abolished first in the French colonies and then in the English colonies, but in the United States the end of slavery would come only through the terrible bloodletting of the Civil War. Carleton lived beyond all this, a pathetic figure cadging drinks in Dublin pubs when he wasn't in the bankruptcy courts for defaulted debts. To catch the continuity of Irish literature, the parallel persistence of its conflicting themes, one must observe that in the year Carleton died Oscar Wilde and Bernard Shaw were teenagers and William Butler Yeats a boy in the streets of Dublin.

In the year of Carleton's death, Charles Kickham (1828–1882) published *Sally Cavanagh*, a popular novel, and ten years later his more famous novel, *Knocknagow*, sprang to wider popularity with the Irish than anything by Carleton, for, while Kickham lacked Carleton's genius, he also lacked his ambivalence and took his stand four-square with his tormented countrymen. Despite his dates, he must be linked with Carleton, a pure stream petering out in desert sands momentarily, for the Irish stream was taking its strength elsewhere in the recovery or discovery of Gaelic literature.

It is the incredible irony of the century that only when the peasantry had lost its native tongue did the torrent of Gaelic literature pour into the literary stream of Dublin. The examination of that torrent may best begin with the familiar name Thomas Moore. Moore (1779–1852), the son of a Dublin shopkeeper, was one of the first Catholics admitted to Trinity College, and his place in the development of Irish literature is even more important than those of the Banim brothers and Gerald Griffin. Despite his failings as a poet, in the hearts of the people of Ireland and certainly to the Irish *in partibus infidelium* he holds a position akin to that held by Robert Burns in Scotland, although Moore was nowhere near as good a poet. What he did was make the world aware of the melancholy tragedy of Ireland and write some of the world's most popular songs. His own assessment of his achievement runs this way:

> Dear harp of my country, in darkness I found thee,
> The cold chain of silence had hung o'er thee long,
> When proudly, my own island harp, I unbound thee,
> And gave all thy chords to light, freedom, and song.

Moore's first literary endeavor appeared the same year as *Castle Rackrent*, and it is interesting to dwell on those two separate streams of literature, which would come to mingle in glory only three generations later. His first work was a translation of Anacreon, dedicated to the Prince Regent, a significant gesture if one accepts the criticism made of Moore that he debased the quality of true Irish poetry in order to win popularity in the salons of London. He suffered more truly than Lever from "lordolatry."

Not until 1803 did the first of his *Irish Melodies* appear and it was these that won him instant fame and fortune. He would continue to produce them until 1834. In between those two dates he had been appointed registrar of the Admiralty Court in Bermuda and had gone to visit that island as well as the continent of North America. In Bermuda he deputized a man to act for him, as was the practice with many such appointments, and then returned to Ireland. Later the deputy was charged with embezzlement to the profound embarrassment of Moore. Meanwhile he was singing his songs in the most elegant drawing rooms in Dublin and London—"Believe Me, If All Those Endearing Young Charms," "Oft in the Stilly Night," "The Minstrel Boy," "The Harp That Once Through Tara's Halls," and dozens of others. Financially, he was well rewarded for the rights to publish his songs.

His popularity was such that he was commissioned to write a major poem, and his publisher gave him $16,000 or thereabouts to do it. The advance was the largest ever given a poet up to that time, and I doubt if any poet has received so handsome a one since. The poem was *Lalla Rookh*, which was four years in the making, and if little read or regarded today, it was a triumph in his day. Within a short space of time it ran through six editions, and its Oriental flavor made it popular in Persia, where, some say, it was sung in the streets.

The financial difficulties arising from the embezzlement made Moore flee with his wife to the continent, and for three years he lived fashionably in Paris, writing busily. His prose deserves far more praise and attention then it gets. He wrote a life of Sheridan, as well as the life of Lord Edward Fitzgerald, which is accounted an excellent biography. When he paid off the obligations incurred by the embezzlement he returned to Great Britain, but his last days were overshadowed by tragedy. His five children died before him, and for several years before his death he was as senile as Swift. With his melodies he had made literary history, won the sympathy of the English-speaking world for a sentimental version of Ireland (still apparent in the popularity of St. Patrick's Day in the United States), and turned the attention of hundreds of other writers to the possibilities of poetic adaptations to be made of the unmined Irish literature.

As Moore was the son of a well-to-do Irish grocer and vintner, and was himself successful financially, his contemporary and fellow poet James Clarence Mangan (1803–1849), the tragedy of whose life contrasts sharply with the success of Moore's, was the son of a poor shopkeeper and died in poverty. He was born in 1803, the year Moore had set off for Bermuda and was destined to precede him in death. He received his education not at Trinity College but in the tutelage of a priest who made him something of a linguist, although Irish was not one of the languages. Yet his chief fame came from drawing upon the Irish heritage, even as Moore's did. In the year of the famine he published an anthology of German poetry and meanwhile his own poems began to appear. Unhappy at home where his family did not sympathize with his literary endeavors, he found likewise no intellectual stimulation at his work. He spent seven years toiling as a copyist for a scrivener and two years in an attorney's office before his poetry caught the eye of another distinguished Dublin litterateur, the artist George Petrie (1789–1866), president of the Royal Irish Academy, who had been placed in charge of the Dublin Ordnance office. To his side Petrie had gathered an erudite staff which included John O'Donovan (1809–1861), a master of Irish and a formidable scholar, and Eugene O'Curry (1796–1862), O'Donovan's brother-in-law, to collect and codify Irish-language manuscripts. O'Curry, awkward-looking, horse-faced, with a crop of white hair, although self-educated, was also an eminent scholar. He had learned Irish from his father, who, no scholar himself, possessed a number of old Irish manuscripts. These excited the imagination of his son, who, being slightly lame, found study more congenial than physical activity. The amount of work that the brothers-in-law managed under Petrie in the Ordnance Survey was prodigious. Before the budget was eliminated (the authorities feared the Irishness of it all) more than four hundred volumes had been collected of extracts from Irish manuscripts in various museums, all relating to Irish history, language, ancient customs, and the like. O'Curry went on to codify the Irish manuscripts in the British Museum. O'Donovan's work was equally extensive, and perhaps more solid, and the two names are forever linked in the history of literary Dublin and of Irish literature.

Sometime after Mangan's work caught Petrie's eye (the poet by then had a job in Trinity College library) the artist-scholar brought him to work with O'Curry and O'Donovan. They saw to it he was furnished with prose translations of Irish poems and from these he fashioned his own to win immortality. His most celebrated poem is "My Dark Rosaleen," a passionate hymn to his native Ireland in which he sees the country as a dark, sorrowful woman, a vision that has persisted in ten thousand poems and songs. When he went to work for the Ordnance Survey his health was already impaired by native indisposition aggravated by alcoholism and the use of opium. He depicted his own tragedy in his poem "The Nameless One." For several years he contributed articles to the *Irish Penny Journal* edited by Dr. Petrie and to *The Nation*, the journal of the Young Ireland movement that was to supersede O'Connell's leadership. What a strange figure he must have cut on the streets of Dublin, a man already showing the ravages of malnutrition, moving from his humble quarters off York Street to the offices of various periodicals, conspicuous with his flaxen wig, obtrusive false teeth, and outsized black hat. He died in the cholera epidemic of 1849 and it was not until a decade after his death that a collection of his poetry was published by John Mitchel.

The Nation, where Mangan placed some of his best work, was the work of literary men, one of them a poet of near-equal rank, Thomas Osborne Davis (1814–1845), who was reckoned more of a national clarion than Mangan. Davis's collaborators in the journal were Charles Gavan Duffy (1816–1903), who founded the journal, and John Blake Dillon (1816–1866). Their paper, with its political-literary interests, lent strength to the cultural revival of Irish literature and culture and is one of the significant forerunners of the great Irish literary renaissance that was to emerge late in the nineteenth century. O'Connell, having won political emancipation for the Catholics in 1829, had set the stage for a true development of nationhood (even as he helped destroy the Irish language), a concept that was foreign to the old Irish clans, and which, having surfaced in a glass darkly under Brian Boru, faded again and all but disappeared with the Flight of the Earls. We have already seen the seeds sown by Swift, Grattan, and others. Swift, as we said, was the first man to use the phrase "Irish nation."

To fan the spark of nationalism was the purpose of *The Nation*, for Davis was bent on creating a national literature. He was more a man of vision than he was a poet; and his influence was far-reaching. Unfortunately, neither he nor Mangan, nor a covey of poetasters who contributed to the papers of the day, were of sufficient stature to bear the burden of the vision that raised them. What Davis might have become had he lived is a lost question. In his brief career, he still managed to write the life of John Philpot Curran, and his essays became a wellspring of Irish nationalism. He died in 1845 and his Young Ireland movement collapsed in the ill-starred revolt of 1848. These were as well the years of the Great Famine when the Irish population dropped (from death and emigration) from eight million to six and a half million. By 1881 it was down to five million, the whole event a genocidal watershed in the history of the country.

At first, the Young Ireland group tried to work with O'Connell, the charismatic creator of an intense Irish national spirit. He and they were agreed that Union must go; but while O'Connell continued to insist on constitutional agitation, the Young Irelanders refused to bind themselves to a renunciation of force. O'Connell, moreover, had alienated the Protestants. The extremists among them hated him; the Liberals distrusted him. Davis was a Protestant and understood all this, and sought to achieve an irenic animus between the "two nations." He labored to enlist Protestants in the movement and while Gavan Duffy and John B. Dillon were Catholics, John Mitchel (1815–1875), a Unitarian, inspired by the Young Ireland daemon, succeeded Davis as editor of *The Nation*, but broke with Duffy and founded *The United Irishman*, only finally to get himself indicted for treason. None of them was ever far from this. Even Tom Moore, as a friend of Emmet's at Trinity, was gravely suspect when that young patriot made his bid for Irish freedom. The sentences of these leaders were commuted and they were shipped to antipodal imprisonment. These convictions, Davis's death, the whole abortive uprising, and the exile of the leaders ended the political thrust of the Young Ireland movement, although its offshoot, Fenianism, would revive the flame. The cultural thrust was something else again. It hadn't died and it wouldn't. In Davis's poetry, in Mangan's poetry, it moved onward. It moved onward in the drawings and writings of Dr. George Petrie, in the scholarship of O'Donovan and O'Curry, in the songs of Tom Moore, in the novels of Carleton, the Banims and Griffin, and later scholars, and in the translations of Edward Walsh, a schoolteacher at the heart of the movement, who was fired from his teaching post in a prison because he said good-bye to Mitchel being sent into exilic incarceration. The literary renaissance, the cultural revitalization that these men dreamed of, would not come until two generations later.

The movement survived and grew because of such men as Samuel Ferguson (1810–1886), a Belfast-born, Protestant scholar, who founded the Protestant Repeal Association, backing the Young Ireland movement, but who did not allow his political convictions to lure him from his literary and antiquarian activities. He clung to his center, prospered and propagated. In 1867 he was named deputy keeper of the public records in Dublin and in 1881 was elected president of the Royal Irish Academy. Three years earlier he had been knighted. He was a poet like Mangan and Moore—a more consistent poet than Moore, a less passionate poet than Mangan. An antiquarian like Petrie, he shared Petrie's interest in music, and his home, like Petrie's, was a literary salon. His commitment was to the old tradition.

If Ferguson, despite his sympathies, stood apart from the Young Ireland agitation, its leaders attracted to its journals a fluttering flock of poets and writers. Not least among them was Jane Francesca Elgee (1826–1896), daughter of an archdeacon of ancient Italian lineage. She contributed patriotic poems to

The Nation under the name of Speranza and, despite her detachment from political life (she watched the funeral of Thomas Davis not knowing who he was), achieved a name as Lady Jane Wilde, having married Dr. William Wilde, the president of the Irish Academy, in 1851. They became the parents of Oscar Fingal O'Flahertie Wills Wilde (1854–1900) but won literary distinction with their own work, he popularizing archaeology, she with her poems, collected in *Ancient Legends of Ireland* (1887) and *Men, Women and Books* (1891). In 1896, Lady Wilde died in poverty in London, the year of her son's imprisonment and disgrace. As with so many persons who die in exile, her obsequies were ill attended.

Those of another contributor to *The Nation*, John Keegan Casey (1848–1870), were something of a nationalistic demonstration. He had contributed his first poem to Davis's journal under the pen name Leo when he was only sixteen years of age. Subsequently imprisoned for his Fenian activities, he found his lungs impaired from incarceration and died young of a hemorrhage of the lungs. So popular was he for his verses and his patriotism that more than fifty thousand persons are said to have walked in his funeral procession.

Alexander Martin Sullivan (1830–1884) began to contribute to *The Nation* shortly after the mid-century mark along with his brother, the poet Timothy Daniel Sullivan, three years his senior. On the emigration of Charles Gavan Duffy, who in 1856 left Ireland in disgust to win fame, fortune, and a knighthood in Australia, A. M. Sullivan became editor of *The Nation*. On his retirement in 1876 his older brother took over. Sullivan, like some other Irish patriots, was sentenced to death by the Fenians because he did not see eye to eye with them on their methods or their objectives. He escaped assassination at their hands but was later jailed by the British for an editorial sympathetic to the Fenians! In 1857 he visited the United States and told of his trip in *A Visit to the Valley of Wyoming*. His literary reputation rests on *The Story of Ireland*, a popular history, and his memoirs, *New Ireland*.

The revolutionary violence that marked Sullivan for death but failed to bring him down did effect the assassination of a more distinguished literary man, Thomas D'Arcy McGee (1825–1868), journalist, poet, orator, and historian, who began as a boy editor and contributor to *The Nation* and ended a member of the Canadian parliament stabbed to death on the streets of Ottawa. His career is one of the most extraordinary among the extraordinary careers of Irish exiles. While in his teens he visited the United States and so impressed everyone with his oratorical and rhetorical powers that he was offered the editorship of the Boston *Pilot* at the age of nineteen. His oratory, which was praised by Daniel O'Connell, and his work on the *Pilot* won him a job on *Freeman's Journal* in Dublin and he returned there to work. He soon moved over to *The Nation* and into revolutionary activities. The abortive uprising of 1848 left him with a price on his head, and he fled to New York City disguised as a priest. He founded journals there and in Boston before settling in Canada, where his political acumen and speech-making ability earned him election to the Canadian parliament and the post of minister of agriculture.

Despite this peripatetic and crowded career he found time to write a volume of poetry, two biographies—*The Life of Art MacMurrough* and *The Life of Bishop Maginn—Irish Writers of the 17th Century*, a *History of the Irish Settlers in America*, and a *Catholic History of North America*.

All Irish revolutionaries had their literary side; it is the Dublin influence. William Smith O'Brien (1803–1864), who led the abortive and tragicomic uprising in 1848, was perhaps the last man in Great Britain to be sentenced to be hanged, drawn, and quartered—the customary English penalty for treason—but was transported to Tasmania instead. He was pardoned in 1854 and ultimately was able to return to Ireland but not to politics. Late in his life he wrote, in two volumes, *Principles of Government*, a worthy study.

Other literary men associated with *The Nation* were John Kells Ingram (1823–1907), who wrote "Who Fears to Speak of 'Ninety-Eight'!," a martial poem that was called the Irish Marseillaise; Denis Florence MacCarthy (1817–1871), Dublin-born, professor, poet, translator, chosen to give the memorial ode on the one-hundredth anniversary of the birth of Thomas Moore; and the Reverend Charles Patrick Meehan (1812–1890), a patriotic, polemical historian. This enumeration, of course, is far from exhaustive. The contributors were numerous but they were, with few exceptions, mediocre. Literary standards had been sacrificed to politics. Art cannot bear that sort of burden unless genius bears it; and genius, that is, literary genius, wasn't present. Incredible and ubiquitous talent, yes, but genius, no. That would come later.

For the transitional figure between the Young Ireland movement and the Fenian movement, there is no better writer to choose than John Mitchel (1815–1875), a Unitarian, an Ulster man, the son of a Presbyterian minister, a graduate of Trinity College, a solicitor, and a man with an extraordinary literary gift and a profound passion. He had contributed on numerous occasions to *The Nation*, and, on the death of Davis, Duffy asked him to take Davis's place. Mitchel did, and his prose was eloquent. In June, 1847, at the very depths of the famine, he wrote an article which the critic Aodh de Blacam concedes could be "the most terrific piece of writing ever done by an Irish pen." Rare praise indeed! Without question, he was a preeminent political writer. He was, however, a rash and reckless man; and his differences with Duffy led to their break and to Mitchel's founding of *The United Irishman*. He wanted more than militancy; he wanted revolution.

He was influenced, as others after him were, by James Fintan Lalor (1810–1849), a hunchback and autodidact, a contributor to *The Nation* and, subsequently, to *The United Irishman*. Lalor was devoted to the concept of the people and the land; the land belonged to the peasant, the artisan, the craftsman, the worker. Mitchel grew convinced; and the era of revolutions by the elite was over. As a consequence, Mitchel's periodical instructed the people in street fighting, in the fashion of the underground papers in America today, and urged them on to violent action. In a way, it is incredible that it lasted three months under English noses. In 1848, that fateful year for traditional authority, Mitchel was arrested, tried, and convicted, and quickly transported lest he be delivered. Lalor promptly published a paper called *The Irish Felon*—"Here, then, is the confession and faith of an Irish felon." He too was jailed and, half-deaf, half-blind, crippled in spine if not in spirit, died from the rigors of incarceration in 1849. Mitchel was moved from one prison ship to another, and finally to Van Diemen's Land in northern Australia, only to escape to New York and there blur his reputation and the dignity of his French motto, "Liberty, Equality and Fraternity," by opting for the Southern cause (for which two of his sons died), opposing abolition, and showing as well an ugly anti-Semitism. In Ireland his name remained that of a hero and he returned like a conquering champion, only to die literally from the very excitement. He wrote *The Life of Aodh O'Neill, Called by the English Hugh, Earl of Tyrone* and some other historical works, but his literary reputation turns on his *Jail Journal, or Five Years in British Prisons*.

Mitchel was the man who coined the phrase "the holy hatred of English rule," the fervor in which would mark the Fenians, breed the Easter Rebellion of 1916, and restore Ireland's independence. To understand the nineteenth century in Ireland one must understand Fenianism. First of all, to the Irish, the word Fenian has connotations of the most inspirational and romantic sort; the Fenians were heroes, and more than that, they were dashing heroes. They were, by nature or by force of circumstances, literary men, although they too were unable to carry both burdens and sacrificed preeminence in the arts in order to politick—but they would pass the literary baton on to the Irish renaissance.

V I

Just at the moment in Irish history when the general public was sick of political activity, disgruntled over what Catholic emancipation failed to bring or unfortunately entailed, and aggrieved over the collapse of the rebellion of 1848, Jeremiah O'Donovan Rossa (1831–1915) (the last name added because of his birthplace), with some other young men, founded the Phoenix National and Literary Society, which soon began to grow into an island-wide political organization. About the same time in the United States, two refugees from the 1848 uprising, James Stephens (1825–1901) and John O'Mahony (1819–1877), formed the Fenian Brotherhood in 1858, and the latter presided over a national convention in Chicago in 1863. Simultaneously with the foundation of the Fenian organization in America, a Fenian organization was founded in Dublin, calling itself the Irish Republican (or Revolutionary) Brotherhood, which almost immediately won the support of the spreading chapters of the Phoenix National and Literary Society. The Fenians took their name from the Fianna, the heroes who had fought for Fionn MacCumhaill. The Fenians were committed to forceful revolution. The constitutionalism of O'Connell was discarded; the irenic spirit of Davis abandoned; the militancy of Mitchel adopted.

By one of those curious twists of fate in which Clio, the muse of history, delights, the famine that depopulated the Irish countryside gave strength to the Fenian movement. The reason for this was that the impoverished, starving Irish who fled to America, Australia, England, and elsewhere were able to work, thrive, prosper, plot, plan, and, above all, finance revolution. Money from overseas, chiefly American dollars, kept the Fenian movement churning in Ireland. The manpower for revolution came in good part from the ranks of the Irish veterans of the American Civil War, veterans of both the Union and the Confederate armies. Some of these were to mount three unsuccessful invasions of Canada from the United States. Many returned to Ireland ready for action. The English anticipated them. The American Civil War ended in 1865; the next year, the British suspended the right of habeas corpus in Dublin. James Stephens (not to be confused with the poet) had returned to Dublin and was editing a paper called *The Irish People*, chief writer of which was purblind Charles Kickham (1828–1882), whose novels would win him fame and the enthusiasm of the Irish people. The British, moving defensively, arrested John Devoy (1842–1929) and John O'Leary (1830–1907), two of the prime figures in the movement, and many of their Fenian supporters.

Devoy was transported, later became an Irish leader in New York City, and wrote *The Land of Eire, The Irish Land League,* and *Recollections of an Irish Rebel*. He was the only Fenian leader who would live until the 1920s to visit the Dail Eireann parliament of a free Ireland.

O'Leary was converted by Davis to the cause of political journalism and became editor of *The Irish People*. He too was sentenced for revolutionary activity, exiled, and not allowed to return to Ireland until 1885. His works include *Young Ireland, What Irishmen Should Read*, and *Recollections of Fenians and Fenianism*. It was he who was to influence, inspire, and even inflame William Butler Yeats.

The preventive arrests of such men as O'Leary and Devoy weakened the revolt the Fenians had planned for 1867, and the revolt failed. A man who believed piously in studied interventions of Providence, as distinguished from its sustaining power, could readily convince himself that God had no desire for any Irish revolution to succeed because chance and the natural elements conspired against it time and again, chance and the elements, to say nothing of the venality of some of the participants. Informers hurt the rebellion of 1867, and such villainy was not new in Ireland. The day of revolt was set for February 11, 1867, and postponed, after having been previously postponed.

As a result, a raid on Chester Castle in England was untimely mounted, and so was an uprising in Kerry, and both were quietly put down. March 5, 1867, was set as the day of revolution but the weather thwarted the Fenians. There was aimless fighting in half a dozen spots, and then the whole scheme collapsed. There were no heroes, yet the Fenians needed one badly. That September, they got three; if not heroes, martyrs. Three men were hanged in England for killing a constable while they were attempting the delivery of two Fenian prisoners. The three were hanged and have been known since as the Manchester Martyrs. The uproar over their deaths revitalized Fenian sentiment and, more particularly, kept it alive in the United States and England.

Throughout all this time, literature in Dublin was in thrall to politics. Men who might have been poets became political balladeers; men who might have been novelists became rabble-rousers; men who might have been essayists became conspirators. Kickham alone among revolutionaries extricated himself from the ruck and published his popular novels: *Rory of the Hill* in 1857, *Sally Cavanagh* in 1869, and *Knocknagow* in 1879. Yet, in a country as small as Ireland and a city as intramurally intense as Dublin, it is almost impossible to separate literature from politics, since failure to participate could be the same as to take sides.

Certain writers pursued their careers quite apart from politics. Some, like George Darley (1795–1846), a poet, educated at Trinity College, whose first book, *The Errors of Ecstasie and Other Pieces*, brought him to public attention, sought a career in London, but his pronounced stammer made him all but a recluse. He won little regard from his contemporaries, but, curiously, his poem *Nepenthe*, which he was forced to publish at his own expense, has won him a twentieth-century following.

In Dublin, William S. Trench (1808–1872) in 1868 published his *Realities of Irish Life*, which was to win republication a century later. Richard Whately (1787–1863), archbishop of Dublin for the Church of Ireland and an Englishman, wrote *Christian Evidences* while in Dublin and won himself the soubriquet "The White Bear," because of his huge white hat and huge white dog. He is perhaps best remembered today for an excellent study of rhetoric. His successor, Archbishop Richard C. Trench (1807–1886), was hailed in his day as an outstanding English poet, but is known widely today for neither his poems nor his theological works, but for *The Study of Words*, which, while philologically outdated, makes entertaining reading. John Francis Waller (1809–1894) succeeded Charles Lever as editor of the *Dublin University Magazine*, established a reputation as a poet under the pseudonym Jonathan Freke Slingsby, at the same time pursuing his legal and scholarly work. He supervised the publication of the *Imperial Dictionary of Universal Biography* and published an edition of the works of Oliver Goldsmith. Sir Martin Archer Shee (1769–1850), a distinguished portrait painter, published poetry and novels and *Outlines of a Plan for the Natural Encouragement of Historical Painting in the United Kingdom*. He was a native of Dublin, a scholar of the Dublin Royal Society, and later a member of the Royal Academy in London. George Croly (1780–1860), a clergyman turned journalist, wrote voluminously, tales, tragedies, poetry, until he dropped dead in the streets of London. The Reverend William Butler (1814–1848) was a scientist and poet and a brilliant contributor to the *Dublin University Magazine*, who died of fever near the end of the famine.

Dr. James Henthron Todd (1805–1869) was Regius Professor of Hebrew at Trinity College, and his work stands with that of O'Donovan and O'Curry in the resurrection of Irish manuscripts, as well as in numerous historical works. He was buried in the churchyard of Swift's old cathedral, an appropriate resting place for a man who had written a life of Saint Patrick. Among others working in the same vein was the Reverend Dr. John Lanigan (1758–1828), a formidable scholar, who was driven by the intransigence of the Catholic hierarchy from a seminary post to the Royal Dublin Society and the Gaelic Society of Dublin, in the formation of which he shared. His chief work was an *Ecclesiastical History of Ireland*. The Gaelic Society engaged in work similar to Petrie's at the Ordnance Survey Office and drew a group of luminaries to its projects. Among these were Edward O'Reilly (1770–1829), who compiled an Irish-English dictionary with the encouragement and assistance of Dr. Todd, and the first dictionary of Irish writers; the Halliday brothers, William (1788–1812) and Charles (1789–1866), historians; the Reverend Paul O'Brien, first professor of Irish at Maynooth, the Catholic seminary; and James Hardiman (1782–1855), associated with Dr. Lanigan in the Gaelic Society.

As a result of the discovery of Irish manuscripts on the continent, German scholars took the lead in the study of the Irish language and Kuno Meyer (1858–1919), a German who had taught in England, was to be the preeminent scholar and translator. However, the work of the Irish scholars was monumental, not least among whom was Whitley Stokes (1830–1909), whose father, a physician and also an antiquarian, wrote a life of Petrie and did significant work in Dublin in collaboration with John Strachan, a Scot.

After 1850 it took nearly forty years for the inchoate, amorphous situation in Irish letters to jell, to gather force, and initiate the Gaelic revival, which, while not truly a revival, since Irish letters were far from moribund, testifies by its title to the lack of focus on literature in Dublin because of the whiplash of political upheaval.

Kickham, as we have seen, struck out creatively after his prison days; Ferguson was publishing his staid but significant translations; and, more important, as evidence of creative vitality, Dion Boucicault, who was born in Dublin in 1820 or 1822 (there is confusion about the date and some evidence of illegitimacy), was in full swing as an inexhaustible playwright. His full name was Dionysius Lardner Boucicault, originally Boursiquot. His father may have been Dr. Dionysius Lardner (1793–1859), a native of Dublin who took several degrees from Trinity College. He is famous for his 134-volume reference work, *The Cabinet Cyclopedia*, although Charles Dickens thought him a "humbug." On the other hand, Boucicault's father may have been his mother's husband, Samuel Smith Boursiquot, who separated from her and went to his death leaping out a window in Athlone. Some say he was a suicide; others say he was impetuously fleeing from an irate husband who had found him in bed with the wrong woman.

In any event, Dionysius went on to become a phenomenon in the theater. He was educated in London but at eighteen (or sixteen) went away to join the theater and in 1841 saw his first successful play produced under the pen name Leo Moreton. The play was *London Assurance*, a five-act comedy of manners centered in a love triangle with the heroine promised to an old rake whose son wins her heart. It ran for sixty-nine nights, which, at the time, was accounted highly satisfactory. Boucicault's unabating career lasted until 1890, when he died in New York City. He married twice and probably three times, the last some months before his second wife had gotten her divorce. He wrote more than one hundred plays, acted, directed, produced, and was at once eminently successful and always in financial straits. In 1860 *The Colleen Bawn*, a play adapted from Gerald Griffin's novel *The Collegians*, ran for 278 performances in London, a record run at the time. The novel deals with the murder of an Irish beauty by the willing tool of her husband at the latter's ambivalent direction, but surveys the sweep of Irish society in the eighteenth century. It was successful as a novel, as a play, and much less so as an opera.

Boucicault adapted other novels for the stage and plundered

French dramatic literature for ideas, at the same time fighting for copyright laws to protect his own plays. His weakness was his obvious desire to please the groundlings, which led his play-writing into an exaggerated theatricality. Comedy was his strength, and many of his scenes, even today, are most amusing and often tender and touching. He has been accused of invent-ing the "stage Irishman" but that factitious individual was already achieved in Lover's *Handy Andy* and the novels of Lever and others. Boucicault moderated him sufficiently in order to portray him and not outrage Irish audiences. Boucicault is credited by scholars with having influenced Shaw, Synge, O'Casey, and some playwrights in the United States. His por-trayals, it could be, influenced Yeats and his circle in reverse, for they may well have stirred in them a determination to put in their dramas Irish people who had dignity.

A far more important influence in the latter half of the nine-teenth century on the shape of the great things to come was Standish James O'Grady (1846–1928), who has been called the father of the Irish revival. He was a journalist, novelist, and historian, schooled at Trinity, of a prominent Protestant family, a relative of Standish Hayes O'Grady (1832–1915). The latter was a civil engineer who, nevertheless, worked with O'Curry and O'Donovan in the library of Trinity College and published two volumes of translations from Irish texts under the title *Silva Gaedelic*.

The younger and more eminent O'Grady's influence came not so much from his scholarship but the afflatus of his prose, beginning with his *History of Ireland: Heroic Period*, published in 1878, which offers a picture of the Celtic period through the "biography" of Cuchulain. To sample his florid style, see how he recounts the death of Fardia (or Ferdia) in combat with his friend Cuchulain, whom he has been forced to fight.

But Cuchulain plucked out the spear and stood above him, panting, as a hound pants returning from the chase, and the war-demons passed out of him, and he looked upon Fardia, and a great sorrow overwhelmed him, and he lamented and moaned over Fardia, joining his voice to the howl of the people of Fardia, the great-hearted children of Mac Erc, and he took off the cathbarr from the head of Fardia, and unwound his yellow hair, tress after bright tress, most beautiful, shedding many tears, and he opened the battle-dress and took out the queen's brooch—that for which his friend had come to slay him—and he cursed the lifeless metal, and cast it from him into the air, southwards over the host, and men saw it no more.

Here was magic and mystery, and music that sifted into the bones of the coming generation. If it was the ambition of Ferguson to raise Irish history and myth to a dignified level, O'Grady elevated it above that to the near-mystical. The next step would be taken by Lady Gregory, Synge, Yeats, and the other revivalists.

Politically, this was the period in which Fenianism, having failed in its military aspiration, gave way to the moderation of Isaac Butt (1813–1879), a distinguished Dublin lawyer, who had been a Unionist at first, opposing O'Connell, but had come to alter his views. When William Smith O'Brien was captured in the abortive Young Ireland insurrection, Butt defended him, and later he defended Fenian rebels.

Butt had studied at Trinity College and helped found the *Dublin University Magazine*. Before being called to the bar, he served as professor of political economy at Trinity. The famine and its unrelieved tragedy turned him from a Unionist to an advocate of home rule, a phrase he is credited with coining. Home rule would have given Ireland independence on its own soil and left its foreign policy to Westminster. Butt sensed that Westminster had neither the intention nor the ability to deal properly and fairly with Ireland. His moderation in politics and his immoderation in high living weakened his effectiveness as a political leader and he had to give way to Charles Stewart Parnell (1846–1891), a reserved, taciturn landowner, the son of an American mother, who was one of the most charismatic figures ever to appear in Irish politics, and one of the most tragic. Besides the convictions about independence which he drew from his mother, his grandfather had bequeathed to him a legacy of liberalism. His grandfather, William Parnell, had opposed the Union and had written *An Enquiry into the Causes of Popular Discontent in Ireland* and *An Historical Apology for the Irish Catholics.*

In Charles Stewart Parnell, Ireland had, for the first time, a Protestant aristocrat leader with the Catholic people behind him. John O'Leary had said quite rightly that the Fenian revolution had been one of the masses not the classes. In 1872 the secret ballot came to Ireland and in 1873 Butt founded the Home Rule League. Two years later Parnell decided to enter politics and in the following June rose in the House of Commons to electrify the members with his brief defense of the Manchester Martyrs. His leadership would collapse in 1890 when his love affair with Kitty O'Shea was brought to public attention by a divorce suit. She was divorced and became Mrs. Parnell, but in the fall of 1891, having lost his party's leadership, he was dead. With Michael Devitt he had solved the land problems which had plagued Ireland since the plantations, but he had not achieved home rule. More than any other political leader he was the uncrowned king of Ireland.

Such was the background against which appeared in 1888 an anthology of poetry, a trivial event in such swirling political turmoil but the first unfolding of what was to be a prodigious efflorescence. The book was *Poems and Ballads of Young Ireland,* and the three men responsible for it were the old Fenian John O'Leary; William Butler Yeats, whose father had long before made his reputation as a painter; and Thomas William Rolleston (1857–1920), a graduate of Trinity College and the first secretary of the Irish Literary Society of London, himself a poet. Its dedication to O'Leary gave it the popular appeal it deserved, but its significance was its seminal relationship with William Butler Yeats.

What these men now looked back to, discovered, as it were, and began to exhume and explore was one of the most astounding literatures in all Europe, the oldest literature in Northern Europe. It was also one of the largest and most refined, although marred by the facts of its history, primarily, the absence of a written language until the monks came. Incredibly, a prodigious mass of manuscripts had survived the rapine of the Vikings, internecine quarrels, the Draconian impositions of the English crown, spoliation of the monasteries and the persecutions that had followed the Reformation. Gaelic had been spoken in Ireland since 350 B.C. It had been written in Ireland since the fifth or sixth century A.D. and was still being written when Thomas Moore made some of its rhythms and some of its sentiments familiar to every drawing room in Europe and America. In brief, they were uncovering a literature of two thousand years' standing, the oldest manuscript of which did not go back beyond the twelfth century although some recorded material had been composed six hundred years earlier or more than that and transmitted by the living voice.

Irish, with Scottish Gaelic and Manx, forms the Gaelic branch of the Celtic language. An allied branch is the Brythonic, which consists of Welsh, Breton, and Cornish. Gaelic is called Q-Celtic and Welsh P-Celtic so that what would be Penmawr in Welsh would be Kenmore in Irish. Their likenesses are basic, and to students of comparative philology, both are fascinating. Today Irish is written in both Gaelic and Roman letters. The former uses eighteen characters of an antique Roman style and achieves additional effects by aspirations indicated by dots placed above the aspirated letters. When modern Roman types are used, to achieve the aspirations, instead of a dot over the letter to be aspirated, an *h* is placed after it. The result to American eyes is strange and appears extremely awkward. The phonetics of the system are quite foreign to English practice, which makes many of the Irish words for any literate man, however well educated, if unacquainted with the system, quite impossible to pronounce correctly.

Today there are three if not four dialects of Irish (which, by the way, should never be called Erse) spoken in Ireland

—the Ulster, the Munster, and the Connacht—and besides differing in the pronunciation of certain vowels and aspirated consonants, they vary in stress-accents. (When we consider that Laoghaire is pronounced Leary, we can appreciate somewhat the difficulties involved.) The language is made additionally difficult by being highly inflected like Latin and Greek and by its practice of "eclipsing" initial consonants. Thus *bo* is "cow" and pronounced as an American would pronounce it, while *a mbo* is "their cow" and pronounced *ah moh*. Moreover, all consonants have two sounds, one broad and one slender, and vowel sounds are varied by a covey of diphthongs. There are nine parts of speech, two genders (there used to be a neuter as well), and three numbers, singular, plural, and, as in ancient Greek, a dual, used of two of anything. There are five cases: nominative, genitive, accusative, dative, and vocative, each with its own ending. There is no indefinite article, but the definite article is quite complicated, sometimes aspirating the initial consonant of the word it precedes, and at other times prefixing to it an *n*, a *t*, or an *h*. Nouns have five declensions and the adjectives four, all with their own endings, and adjectives can, like nouns, be eclipsed or aspirated by the article. The pronouns are far more complicated than in English and combine with prepositions in a bewildering set of associations which leaves the Italian practice of combining articles and prepositions simple by comparison. There are only two conjugations for verbs, but there are irregular verbs, and, as in Spanish, two verbs "to be." Proper pronunciation can be learned only from use, and often, it seems, has no relation to the antic agglutinations of consonants which appear on paper.

That much said we can add that Irish is a language of grace and vigor, expressive in the extreme, lively and melodious, soft as the Irish brogue which takes its softness from it, and admirably suited to poetry and song. An old saying has it that Irish is the language in which a man should make love. Another avers that anyone under indictment should plead his cause in Irish.

As a literary language, it is highly polished and shows the

effects of having been the language of aristocrats, of courtliness, of warriors, of feudal life, and never the language of an urban society or the countinghouse, and hence, a language of the tongue rather than the pen (although it remains the oldest written language north of the Alps) and of the heart rather than the head. The ancient Irish not only loved poetry, they gave it magical significance and held poetry-storming sessions as American businesses today hold brain-storming sessions. They gathered for public poetry contests, valuing impromptu composing, a practice still maintained in the Feis, an open-air competition in all the arts.

A civilization that depends for its continuity, as did that of the Celts of Ireland, not on documents, but on memorization, must, of necessity, eschew the convolutions of ratiocination, the delights of analysis, and the complications of philosophy. Hence, it is no surprise that when the monks arrived with their pens and their lettering, they found a literature composed mostly of entertainment and history, strong on genealogy, with some law and medicine thrown in. The entertainment included the great sagas of Ireland, written in prose, and lyric poetry, much of it dealing with love or laments.

What must be remembered here as well is that Irish literature gave courtly love to the world. The Tristan and Isolde legend takes its roots in Ireland, and the grand passion, love at first sight, love for one woman leading to happiness but more often to tragedy and death, came out of the Celtic mists and is strong in Irish folklore. Isolde was an Irish princess. Irish mythology is a mythology untouched by the Greek and Roman mythologies, which got themselves mixed up with other mythologies in Europe. The Irish mythology remained pure of such admixture, and throughout it we can see a magnificent polarity of man and woman, and it becomes quite clear as one reads the subsequent history of the island why Ireland is always symbolized as a woman, the Dark Rosaleen or Cathleen ni Houlihan or Kathleen Mavourneen, and never any figure like John Bull or Uncle Sam, or the Bear That Walks Like a Man. Nor is the woman a swooning damosel, but a queen like Maeve of Connacht; or Grania, the pirate, who defied Queen Elizabeth; or the older Grainne, who pursued Diarmuit; or a femme fatale like Deidre, the central figure of a thousand stories; or a matriarch that runs the family while the husband fights in the hills.

The literature ran back two thousand years, or better. The monks transcribed all they could and saved all they could. The late-nineteenth-century scholarship under the leadership of Kuno Meyer, a German, divided the material into periods. One scholar puts them thus: Old Irish, A.D. 700 to 950; Middle Irish, A.D. 950 to 1350; Early Modern, A.D. 1350 to 1650; and Late Modern from 1650 to the men and women who are writing Irish literature in Ireland this minute. Old Irish is the province of specialists; it is extremely difficult; and there isn't too much of it. Of the rest there is a great deal which includes in it innumerable references which let us know that still more was lost.

Down to 1800 the great majority of the people of Ireland were Irish-speaking, and had not read, and perhaps had not heard of, Jonathan Swift and his English-speaking contemporaries. The great mass lived outside the Pale in humble and humiliating circumstances. Some possessed manuscripts they could not read but happily cherished. In turn, Swift knew no Irish and little of the Irish people, and his colleagues at Trinity College possessed a number of manuscripts they could not or would not read. By Swift's day the communication gap was broad indeed. Dublin, founded by the Vikings, long occupied by them and the British, while not unused to the sound of Irish being spoken, was never an Irish-speaking city, Irish though it became and Irish though it remains. It was in the nineteenth century that the Irish language began to die out rapidly. Not only had the terrible penal laws had their effect by denying schooling to the great majority of the people, but two major benevolent forces impelled the Irish people along the courses that led them to become English-speaking. One of these forces

was the Catholic church, which, while it was vital to the preservation of Irishness, and to the determination on independence,
nevertheless, since it conducted its services in Latin, failed, unlike the Protestant church in Wales, to preserve the vernacular
of the people. Another major force was Daniel O'Connell, who,
while able to speak Irish himself, insisted on English, sensing
that only through a mastery of English would the people be
able to further the constitutional struggle that would bring them
their freedom. With all these forces working against its reten-
tion, the Irish language died. When the Irish people came to
their senses and sought to preserve it, fewer than fifty thousand
persons remained in Ireland who spoke only Irish, and, of
course, the number is less today, although the number able to
speak Irish and read it and write it is far greater than it was
at the end of the nineteenth century.

Thus when Ferguson and others turned to the mass of Irish
manuscripts that abounded, it was as if they had discovered
a new world. To be sure, there had been a Celtic Revival (with
capital letters) as early as 1750, which had taken its impetus
from some Welsh translations and reached a climactic point in
the famous duplicity of James Macpherson (1736–1796), a
Scot, after he published his *Fragments of Ancient Poetry, Collected in the Highlands of Scotland and Translated from the
Gaelic or Erse Language.* This, and subsequent books, contained his controversial poems of Ossian, which became extremely popular, but were finally denounced as forgeries and
shown to be Macpherson's own poems offered as translations
from third-century manuscripts. The controversy, which brought
about Dr. Samuel Johnson's famous letter rebuking Macpherson's threats to him helped turn popular attention to the extensive remnants of Celtic literature. Twenty-nine years after
Macpherson perpetrated his fraud, Miss Charlotte Brooke
(1740–1793) published in Dublin her *Reliques of Irish Poetry.*
The work is a landmark in the revival of Irish, for while she
watered the vigorous Irish with the poetical clichés of her generation, she nevertheless worked with taste and scholarship. She

had learned Irish in her father's library, where she, one of twenty-two children in the family, would read while the others slept. Her father, Henry Brooke (1703–1783), was also a writer, author of *The Fool of Quality*, a novel that first appeared in 1766, and of innumerable other works, a man prolific in his works and in his children, only two of whom, however, outlived him. One was Charlotte, who published a posthumous collection of his poems. Like Dean Swift, who adapted a poem from a translation of the Irish provided him and took his cue for *Gulliver's Travels* from an Irish tale, Miss Brooke had no conception of the amount of literature in Irish that lay around Ireland and Europe.

The first age of written Irish literature ran from the arrival of the monks with their Latin and their alphabet to the establishment of the Viking kings. We must remind ourselves again that during those centuries Irish was a language superior to what was being spoken in England, and the rival of Latin in its refinements. Down to Elizabeth's day it remained a superior language, or at least was so considered by the Irish feudal nobility, and was preferred by the Anglo-Norman settlers. When the Normans brought French to England, the evolving mixture of the two languages sounded coarse to the cultivated Celt. In Elizabeth's court *The O'Neill* refused to speak English and referred to it as a "barbarous jargon." Elizabeth, on the other hand, thought Irish sounded like the "bark of a dog." However, the language of Shakespeare had not yet made its immortal impact on the world.

The Irish manuscripts that were now being examined contained language of a highly developed nature, a language with a long history, that had a dictionary before A.D. 900, eight hundred years before Dr. Johnson published his famous dictionary. What remained in manuscript, of course, was slight in comparison to what had been destroyed. Armagh, where thousands of students attended classes, was sacked or burned a dozen times between A.D. 800 and Brian Boru's victory at Contarf in A.D. 1014. Other centers of learning suffered as well.

The greatest literary treasure of pagan Ireland, *The Cuilmenn*, was lost, along with innumerable other treasures, with the destruction of the monasteries following the Act of Supremacy that made Henry VIII the head of the church.

What remained, however, was enormous. Matthew Arnold, who misunderstood the Celtic temperament but had insight and knowledge, referred to the remains as "truly vast." In the Royal Irish Academy and Trinity College's magnificent library, for example, more than sixty thousand quarto pages of ancient Irish manuscripts repose. Others are to be found in the Bodleian Library at Oxford University in England and in the British Museum. Many more, and they the oldest, are held on the continent, taken there by monks who fled before invasion and persecution. There are more manuscripts, scholars aver, than have been preserved of ancient Latin or Greek. In these remains are grammars and glossaries, prose, poetry, histories, genealogies, mythological and other tales, vivid sagas, satires, lives of the saints, explications of the Brehon laws—the ancient law of Ireland—sciences, particularly medicine, miscellaneous works, and translations from other languages into Irish.

The great volumes have fascinating names: *The Book of the Dun Cow*, the *Book of Ballymote* (where the key to Ogham script was found), the *Book of Lecan*, the *Book of Leinster*, the *Book of Armagh*, the *Speckled Book*, and the *Yellow Book of Lecan*. Most of them, if not all, were compiled by monks of the type whose artistic hands were responsible for the *Book of Kells*, which adorns Trinity College and is proclaimed the most beautiful book in the world.

Besides these there are the various annals, of which the most important is the *Annals of the Four Masters*, an outstanding compilation of history and pseudo-history. Others are the *Annals of Tighernach*, the *Annals of Ulster*, the *Chronicum Scotorum*, the *Annals of Innisfallen*, the *Annals of Loch Ce*, the *Annals of Connact*, the *Annals of Clonmacnois* (which begins with the Creation and ends with the year 1408), and the *Annals of Boyle*.

The *Annals of the Four Masters*, which is correctly called
the *Annals of the Kingdom of Ireland*, was compiled by Michael
O'Cleary (1575–1643), who was the most voluminous compiler
the country ever had. He was known as Teigue of the Mountain
until he became a Franciscan and took the name Michael. His
elder brother, Bernardin, was superior of their monastery in
Donegal. The book is misnamed since there were at least six
masters. Other masters who worked with him were Conary
O'Cleary, Peregrine O'Clery, and Ferfeasa O'Mulchrony. Their
patron was a Protestant Gaelic chieftain. Their history was
finished in 1636, part of it done in Ireland and part of it in
Louvain. In 1848 John O'Donovan, working in Petrie's Ordnance Survey project, published his translation in seven large
quarto volumes. His colleague O'Curry said at the time, "We
regard the *Annals of the Four Masters* as the largest collection
of national, civil, military and family history brought together
in this or perhaps any other country." To gauge it in perspective, an American might match the accomplishment, all done
by men under legal sanctions, against the somewhat meager
accomplishment of the Puritan and Pilgrim settlers in the New
World about the same time.

Among the other annals and histories that awaited the explo-
ration of the scholars were *The Wars of the Norse* by Dr.
Geoffrey Keating (1570–1644?), and the *Chronicle Book of
Genealogies of the Irish* by Dugald MacFirbis (1580–1660), the
first a stylist and poet as well as a historian; the second a first-
rate scholar.

The scholars of the day were dedicated men who worked
under great hardships. MacFirbis received no recompense for
his work and died in his eighties when, walking from the west
to Dublin, he was set upon by a Cromwellian and beaten to
death. Dr. Keating, who had studied on the continent, began
his history while living in a cave where he had fled from the
authorities because of his preaching. The cave, called Poll
Granda, is seven miles west of Cahir and still pointed out to
travelers. Despite the law that kept him on the run, or forced

him into hiding, Protestants as well as his own Catholics honored his scholarship by sequestering him. He completed his work in 1834, a monument of Irish literature, sometimes too full-blown in its style, a passionate apologia for the Irish, but a philological treasure house because of its extensive vocabulary. By some scholars it is deemed the beginning of modern Irish literature.

The annals and the histories entranced the scholars, but it was the pagan sagas and the lyric poetry preserved by the monks that played a salient role in the Irish literary revival that turned the end of the century into a torch that lighted the world. The poetry and the mythology were rich in the extreme and are still challenging the abilities of translators or inspiring Irish writers to further flights of imagination and drawing them to rarefied creative heights.

V I I

The sagas of Ireland deal with the most ancient traditions of the island. Writes Edmund Curtis in his *History of Ireland*,

> The traditions of the Irish people are the oldest of any race in Europe north and west of the Alps, and they themselves are the longest settled on their own soil. When they learned to write, they recorded the tradition that they originally came from northern Spain. The ancient *Leabar Gabala* (the Book of Invasions) tells how the three sons of Mileadh of Spain, namely Hermon, Heber and Ir, came to Erin about the time of Alexander the Great and conquered the land from the Tuatha De Danann. Of the races that were in possession before them the Tuatha De Danann were a superior race, semi-divine in their arts of magic and wizardry. The Firbolgs were a race dark, short and plebeian, the Fomorians were gloomy giants of the sea. From the three sons of Mileadh descended all the royal clans of later Ireland. To this day wherever Irish is spoken, the story of "Meela Spaunya," is remembered, and to be of the old Milesian race is an honorable distinction.

Modern Irish scholars set the facts somewhat apart from the traditions and, with Curtis, place the arrival of the Celts about 350 B.C. They may have come from Spain as well as France, where the Gauls and Gaels were the same breed.

The sagas which clothe much of this history and the stories of these peoples in fantasy and fable are grouped in four preeminent cycles. The first is the mythological cycle of Tuatha

De Danann, that semi-divine people (the Tribes of the Goddess Danann) and their conquests of their predecessors, the Ne-medians (ancestors of the Tuatha De Danann), the Fomorians, and the Firbolgs. In one legend the Fomorians were people with only one leg and one arm and three sets of teeth, but in other stories they do battle with the customary assortment of limbs and dentition. In one major romance, *The Battle of Moytura*, the Tuatha De Danann, having routed the Firbolgs, find their King Nuada has lost an arm. Their great physician—the Tuatha De Danann were the technicians of their day—whose name is Diancecht, makes him one of silver, which is pretty good but not good enough. Two young physicians turn up, Omiach and Miach, actually the sons of Diancecht, who dig up the king's lost arm and put it back in place. They also put a cat's eye in the socket of Nuada's steward, who had lost one eye fighting the Firbolgs, but it continues to behave like a cat's eye, much to his irritation, forever awake and looking for mice when he wants to sleep, and forever closing when he wants it open. So much for the first surgical transplants!

Such charming if macabre incidents dot the sagas, and in the mythological cycle magic runs high. The paladin of the Tuatha De Danann is Lugh, semi-divine for all practical pur-poses, and evidently a god clothed in golden armor and quite indestructible. His father, not quite so durable, is murdered by the three sons of Tuireann, who, for punishment, are ordered on forfeit (called an *eric* in Irish) to perform seven tasks that would embarrass Herakles. They are to bring back from the Hesperides apples the pulp of which will cure a dying man; from Greece, a pigskin that will also heal; from Persia, an indomitable spear with a flaming tip that must be stored in a cauldron of water; from Sicily, two legendary indestructible horses, and so on.

The three sons of Tuireann (the tale is known as *The Fate of the Children of Tuireann*) set off to fulfill the terms of the eric, using a magic boat that whips them over the seas in an eye's twinkling. Well, they bring it all off, but die afterwards, the godlike Lugh refusing to intervene, when he might have, and so save their lives. Violence, fantasy, and magic mingle with tragedy in the saga as they do in a similar one, *The Tragedy of the Children of Lir*, another Celtic classic.

One of Lugh's feats on the field of battle must be recounted. The Fomorians had a champion, Balor (some put him down as a Firbolg), who was fierce indeed. He it was slew Nuada of the Silver Hand. His dread power lay in his single eye, which opened only in warfare and required four men to raise the lid. Whomever Balor scanned with that evil eye was rendered unable to resist his enemies. Lest that awful eye fall on Lugh, who ached to do combat with Balor, the Tuatha De Danann surrounded him with nine guards to hold him in reserve to give counsel. But Lugh broke away. Four men raised the awful eyelid, but Lugh, sling at the ready, sent a rock whistling against the eye. The shot passed through Balor's head, carrying the eye with it from front to back so that it then looked on the Fomorian and Firbolg host, who were as a result soon put to flight.

Lugh was also known as Il-Dana (meaning "of the many arts") and was a half-breed, son of a king of the Tuatha De Danann and a Firbolg queen, and indeed, some say, Balor was his grandfather. He moved in battle with a nimbus about him, was a man of prodigious knowledge as well as a warrior (hence valued for his counsel), and rode a god's horse over land and sea. His armor, like the horse, came from the god Mananaan, an even earlier Celtic deity and somehow set apart from the pantheon in which Lugh moved. In that distinguished company was Daga, which means "good god" and his son, Oengus. The mother of Oengus, the legends record, was Boann, who was the river Boyne or the goddess for whom it was named. Later we shall see that these gods all became mixed up with the fairies, or Daoine Sidhe, for when the Milesians came to the island, the Tuatha De Danann retreated into the fairy mounds which to this day are pointed out in Ireland.

Love as well as violence dominates the sagas. In them are

the roots of the Arthurian cycle as well as of Tristan and Isolde. One of the loveliest of the stories is The Wooing of Etain. Without recounting the entire story, which has, unlike many of the sagas, a happy ending, let us remark that Etain was the wife of a fairy king, Midhir, but because of the jealousy of his second wife is turned by druidic magic into a dragonfly, only to fall in a chalice of wine being drunk by a woman who gives birth to a child named Etain. Meanwhile, a thousand years have passed. Etain marries Eoai, a king, only to have his brother, Ailill, fall tragically in love with her. He begins to pine away from desire for her and is near death. An understanding druid suggests that Etain be kind to Ailill and she nurses him back to health but not to a complete cure. He points out that the complete cure awaits her final favor, and when can he have it? She agrees because her husband has told her to do her utmost for his brother, but declines to sleep with him in her husband's house. She suggests a nearby wood. There she repairs each day and meets a man she thinks is Ailill. Well, the poseur turns out to be Midhir, her divine husband, some reincarnations back, who has cast a spell over Ailill, which is raised, so the stricken is cured much to the delight of Eoai, who returns from a trip to find him so. Midhir then appears to Eoai in the form of a warrior and suggests a chess match with, finally, a kiss from Etain as the prize. Midhir wins the kiss and claims it at a great dinner. When Etain and Midhir kiss, they shoot straight up through the roof, and fly off as a pair of swans. A happy ending though not for Eoai the hospitable!

To separate the mass of myth and legend into suitable divisions is not easy. Some of the characters move back and forth, it seems, from one cycle to another; and certainly the themes do. Just as Etain's mother became pregnant from drinking an insect that had once been an earlier Etain, so with Cuchulain's mother, who somehow swallowed the god Lugh from a chalice. Cuchulain (or Cu Chulainn) is the preeminent Irish hero, the central figure in the second cycle, the Ulster cycle, taking its name from the Ulaid, who peopled the north of Ireland. The name Cuchulain means the "hound of Culann," and the superman was so called because, having accidentally killed Culann's hound, he had to serve in the role himself. He is the hero of Ireland's greatest epic, the *Tain Bo Cuailnge*, which means *The Cattle Raid of Cooley* or, as sometimes written, *The Cattle Spoil of Cooley*, "spoil" in the sixteenth century having a substantive meaning now rarely used.

The story, which stands to Irish literature as the Iliad to Greek (but is quite inferior to that masterpiece), tells of the invasion of Ulster by Queen Maeve of Connacht (which probably never had a queen) for the purpose of stealing the famous bull of Cooley whose youthful lord is Cuchulain. Maeve has a large army, and the army of King Conchobar (sometimes incredibly pronounced cru-hoor), who rules Ulster, is stricken with a mysterious illness, a sleeping sickness, so that Cuchulain must stand off the invasion by himself. He does so until the Ulster army awakes, although it involves slaying in single combat his boyhood chum Ferdia. Awakened at last, the men of Ulster rout Maeve's army. The epic ends with a mortal combat between the great Brown Bull of Cooley and Maeve's great bull. The brown bull wins and comes home with remnants of his enemy on his horns, but dies from his wounds in the exhilaration of triumph.

The *Tain* is the greatest of the Irish sagas and has inspired any number of preliminary and epilogic tales, none rivaling the original but, nevertheless, dramatic, poignant, and vital.

In one of them Cuchulain, in combat, kills his own son, not recognizing him until after he is slain. Here too is a recurring theme and indeed there is an old Irish word for the slaying of a kinsman. In another saga, highly regarded, called *Scel Mucce Mic Da Tho* or *The Story of Mac Da Tho's Pig*, heroes fight in mortal combat to determine who shall have the right to the first cut of the roast in the king's hall, a custom, barbaric and brutal, but evidently not uncommon in the halls of the Gaulish chiefs of the continent as well as in Ireland.

In the Ulster cycle also we have the great legend of Deirdre, Synge's *Deirdre of the Sorrows*, whose tragic fate has so appealed to scholars and poets since she was brought over into English prose. Of Deirdre when she was born, it was predicted that she would bring ruin to Ireland. King Conchobar, or Conor, has her consequently reared in isolation, planning to marry her because of her beauty, but she falls in love with Naoise, the eldest of the three sons of Usnach, or Usna, and sometimes the story bears their name, *The Fate of the Children of Usnach*.

Naoise and Deirdre run off to Alba (Scotland) together, his brothers attending them. The four live there for seven years until the Scottish king falls in love with Deirdre and they have to flee again. They at length return to Ulster, where King Conchobar has promised them no harm, but he double-crosses them. He kills Naoise and takes Deirdre, who refuses him and finally kills herself. The tale has been retold in a thousand versions and each version a thousand times. Without question, it is one of the world's great stories, and beautifully told in Irish, fast-moving, dramatic, heart-rending.

If the Red Branch cycle, as the Ulster cycle is sometimes called, is the more profound, the Fenian cycle, our third, became the more popular. It was in a way the south's response to the poets of Ulster. The Ulster cycle indeed excels the others in heroic grandeur, for the semi-divine must always exceed man in heroism. The Fenian cycle is the one that burrowed into the hearts of the people and even today Finn MacCumhaill (pronounced McCool) is more familiar to the people of Ireland than is Cuchulain, just as Deirdre is more often mentioned than Maeve or Etain.

One reason for Finn's popularity lies in the presentation of him in rhymed verse (which by the twelfth century, when he was first written down, had become commonplace, the Irish having led the way in this) whereas the older mythological stories were done in prose, although interspersed with verse.

Fionn or Find or Finn Mac Umaill or MacCumhaill or Mac-

Cuhal—but always pronounced Finn McCool—is to the Fenian cycle what Cuchulain is to the Ulster, and scholars trace his mythological origins back to Lugh. Sometimes Finn is a giant, a mixture of Paul Bunyan and Horatius at the Gate, but with a gift of clairvoyance and a magic thumb and a magic tooth. Hero though he is he is a tragic figure in the love story of Grainne and Diarmuit (Grania and Dermott), for Grainne spurns his suit and runs off with Diarmuit and to this day the Irish countryman will point out a massive dolmen as the bed of Grainne and Diarmuit.

Finn was the leader of the Fianna, the crack troops of King Cormac Mac Airt, and the two, because of a literary accident, became the subjects of a proliferating ballad literature. Cormac Airt was the grandson of Conn of the Hundred Battles, another hero, and Finn, besides being Cormac's paladin, was the father of Oisin, the poet who met with Saint Patrick. Cormac is himself a great folk figure and is quoted at length.

"O Cormac, grandson of Conn," said Carbery, "what is the worst thing you have seen?"

"Not hard to tell," said Cormac, "faces of foes in the rout of battle."

"O Cormac, grandson of Conn," said Carbery, "what is the sweetest thing you have heard?"

"Not hard to tell," said Cormac.

"The shout of victory,

"Praise after wages,

"A lady's invitation to her pillow."

Cormac's opinion of women was somewhat low, and his remarks on the subject are amusingly translated by Micheál MacLiammóir:

Although he distinguished women, he saw no distinction amongst them. "Women are crabbed as constant companions and have tell-tale faces. They are quarrelsome in company, steadfast in hate, and forgetful in love, never to be trusted with a secret; boisterous in their jealousy, sorrowful in an ale house,

tearful or talkative during music, lustful in bed, late in keeping
appointments, furies when themselves kept waiting, sulky on a
journey, most troublesome bedfellows, craving for delicacies
whenever they wake, dumb on useful matters, eloquent on
trifles, looking on one another with utter loathing. Happy the
man who does not yield to women. They should be dreaded like
fire and feared like wild beasts for they are moths for tenacity,
serpents for cunning, bad among the good and worse among the
bad."

King Cormac, like King Conor, however, is a secondary character. What the ancient sagas gave to the emerging nation was
not merely an autochthonous literature excelling that of England, the ancient enemy, and so inspiriting a people, but also
heroes of classical dimensions, particularly Cuchulain, the hero
without flaw, a man of preeminent virtue, and Finn McCumhaill,
no Achilles like Cuchulain, but a paladin nevertheless with just
a touch of the rogue. The exploits of both, as recounted in the
ancient manuscripts or extrapolated in folk creation, rivaled
those of Greek, Roman, and Teutonic mythology, involving
as they did fantastic physical feats, the accomplishment of Her-
culean chores, the whole touched with the preternatural and the
supernatural, the magical and the divine. What uniquely marks
them is their particularly Celtic touch: exquisite dialogue.

What more could be asked for the making of a new literature, or the making of a new nation, than these incomparable
heroes and the sagas' equally incomparable love stories: Tristan
and Isolde, Grainne and Diarmuit, Naoise and Deirdre, Etain
and Midhir. The temptation is always present to recount more
of the tales, but they have been retold by masters and in those
texts should they be read.

From those early ancient myths the fairies came into Irish
folklore. The Tuatha De Danann were deemed to have been a
fairy people who, defeated by the Milesians, retreated into *sid*,
or mounds, to an underworld of magic, and the fairy people
in Ireland to this day are called the *sidhe*. Few countries have

kept alive the happy belief in fairies as well as Ireland. The truth of the matter is, of course, that the belief of the Irish in the fairies is not as strong as the belief outside Ireland that the Irish believe in the fairies. But the fairies are real enough in Irish folklore and in Irish literature and in Irish night tales. They are not the neuropterous elves familiar in children's books, but rather a variety of beings not pure spirits nor yet human, halfway between men and angels, beings without souls who live for ages and ages but die, at last, into nothingness. They have a sinister side to them and interfere commonly in the lives of people. They are best avoided.

The Irish fairies were not only the most numerous but sometimes the most snobbish. The Daoine Sidhe were the most regal of all, having kings and queens and clans, and having little to do with humankind.

The Irish fairy tales are among the oldest in the world, and, of all the fairies, the leprechaun, which is the most familiar, is perhaps the least of them. Irish folklore has a diversification of fairies that must be unmatched in the world. There are the *sidehogs*, or land fairies, and there are the *merrows*, or sea fairies, not merely mermaids, but mermen. In Irish the word is *moruadh* and means a sea maid. The *sidehogs*, or *sheoques*, can entice you into their world or steal a child and leave a shriveled fairy in its place. From this legend came "Up the Airy Mountain," the most popular poem by William Allingham (1824–1889), friend of Thomas Carlyle, Leigh Hunt, and Dante Gabriel Rossetti, no Irish chauvinist yet infected by the new spirit.

> Up the airy mountain
> Down the rushy glen
> We daren't go a-hunting
> For fear of little men
> Wee folk, good folk
> Trooping all together
> Green jacket, red cap
> And white owl's feather.

But they are *sheoques* and they steal away "little Bridget/ For seven long years/ When she came down again/ Her friends were all gone." That theme is returned to again and again in Irish literature—the traveler to a distant land returning to find what were merely days or years in the far land, Hy Brasil or Breasil they called it, or Tir-na-nOg, were centuries in Ireland. The man is away a week and finds it has been centuries. "The Stolen Child" by Yeats is the finest poem on the theme of a child taken by fairies.

The *merrows* came out of the sea frequently, sometimes as cows without horns, or more often in their own shape—that of men and women, the men with fishes' tails, green hair, and red noses; and the women, beautiful, who often take Irish fishermen as lovers. The leprechaun is a shoemaker, a little man who sits under hedges working away. Catch him and he'll give you a pot of gold. He usually wears a red coat and can stand on his head and then spin like a top. If the sun is shining during a rainstorm, the pookha appears, usually in the shape of a horse, or goat, or donkey or eagle, and is happiest if he can get a drunken rider on his back and speed away across the countryside, breakneck. The banshee is a woman fairy who can be heard keening, or wailing, when someone dies. These are not all. There are the *sowlth*, the *far gorta*, the *leanhaun shee*, the *thivishes*, the *dullahan* (that carries its head under its arm), the *far darrig*, the *gonconer*, and the *cluricaun*, and even that does not exhaust the list.

Many of the songs, stories, fairy legends, and tales of the peasantry were diligently gathered by T. Croften Croker (1798–1854), a Cork-born writer who was a secretary at the Admiralty in London but found his career in literature and research. He supplied many airs to a grateful Tom Moore while compiling *Fairy Legends and Traditions of the South West of Ireland*. That the Grimm brothers translated them into German is not without interest. Croker did for the fairy tales what Ferguson and Mangan did for the poetry, Moore for the songs, O'Donovan, O'Curry, Petrie, and others for the manuscripts, and Mrs.

S. C. Hall (1800–1881) for common stories in her *Popular Tales and Stories of the Irish Peasantry*. Like Moore and Croker, she was widely read in England.

The belief in fairies was common throughout Europe, and authorities do not agree on the origin of that belief. Some think them an outgrowth of the ancient gods who faded before the illumination of Christianity. They stood somewhere between men and angels, supernormal or preternatural beings, lacking souls and hence immortality, but having superhuman longevity and magical powers. They were far more Ariel than Tinkerbell, and the prettification of them is a debasement that robs them of their idiosyncratic charm. This is the true aspect of them that was retained in Ireland beyond its time and gives Irish stories a unique overtone. What was quite certain always was that the fairies—every type of them—were better left alone and we had best leave them here.

They have never done as much for Irish literature as Cuchulain and Finn McCumhaill but they must not be ignored. They don't like that.

VIII

An aspect of Dublin life that it shares with European capitals—
in the smaller countries particularly—and which America lacks
is the integral and vital role of journalism and its ancillaries:
the street ballad and gossip. All three differ in their relationship to Dublin's literary heritage from their counterparts' relationship in the United States to its literary history, and to grasp
the nature of Dublin's literary tradition, one must understand
the differences.

The multiplex of intellectual exchange in Dublin that we
have called the Dublin Dimension gives journalism there a role
it has not held in the United States since the days of the Fed-
eralist papers. One result is that, on the average, Dublin's literary figures are to those in any American city as chessmen are
to checkers. If the leading American writers lived in Washington, D.C., if the New York theater centered there, if the city
was the seat of Harvard University and the Massachusetts Institute of Technology as well as Georgetown University, and if
the leading figures in government, as well as writers and educators, were frequent contributors to the daily newspapers, and
there were a half dozen of those, we would have a situation
analogous to that which exists in Dublin. We can thus assess
the salient place that journalism holds in Dublin and how it
differs from its role in the United States.

The place of journalism in the career of the Dublin writer
has been heightened by history. To repeat, the man who has
another's will imposed on him by arms and is without arms

himself must argue his case where he can. Thus journalism has been central to the career of the literary man in Dublin, or his acquaintance with it has enabled him to find a career in it abroad when exile, voluntary or involuntary, becomes his lot.

Journalism in Dublin began, as it began elsewhere, with the broadside and the anonymous pamphlet or letter. Dean Swift wrote his letters of outrage anonymously or under a pseudonym. The first newspaper in Dublin appeared in 1659, thirty-one years before the first newspaper in the American colonies was published in Boston and promptly suppressed. The papers shared somewhat similar names. The Boston paper was called *Publick Occurrences Both Forreign and Domestick*; the Dublin paper *An Account of the Chief Occurrences of Ireland*. It was followed by the *Dublin Newsletter* (1685) and the *Dublin Intelligencer* (1690–1693). From that day to the present the city has enjoyed a multiplicity of newspapers, many of them short-lived and most of them linked more or less to one political faction or another. No American city has as many newspapers as Dublin.

From the earliest days in Dublin's history under British rule there was a prodigious flow of Irish journalists to England and parts of the British empire and to the United States. One of the first newspaper publishers and book publishers in the United States was Mathew Carey (1760–1839), Dublin-born, who, fleeing British oppression, landed in Paris, where he worked for Benjamin Franklin; with a loan from the Marquis de Lafayette, he began his newspaper publishing career in Philadelphia. The first daily newspaper in London was the *Daily Courant*, founded in 1702, which had for its second editor Samuel Buckley. In 1709, the genial Richard Steele, tired of editing the *London Gazette*, founded *The Tatler* and later *The Spectator* to win appreciative London audiences. Steele's ambition was to "publish a Paper which should observe upon the Manners of the Pleasurable, as well as the Busie Part of Mankind." He was thirty-seven years old at the time, and already had a reputation as a dramatist. With Swift he shared the pseudonym Isaac Bickerstaff, taken from an earlier Dublin writer and a rather disreputable one. Perhaps the name was an in joke between Swift and Steele. In 1710, when Tory leaders founded *The Examiner*, its chief contributor was Swift, who can claim a place in the history of journalism as "the father of the leader" or, to give it its American name, the editorial. Swift was the *The Examiner*'s main thrust until he left in 1711 to take his post as dean of St. Patrick's. His contribution to English journalism was as important as his contribution to Irish journalism.

The Public Advertiser, London's outstanding daily paper of the eighteenth century, had as its most distinguished contributor Philip Francis (1740–1818), who was at the center of the impeachment of Warren Hastings, who had wounded him in a duel in India. Francis was most probably the author of the famous *Letters of Junius* which attacked the government of George III and his ministers with a unique gift of vituperation and a prose style to rival Macaulay's. He set a fashion in journalistic invective that was influential for a hundred years. The letters gained in popularity because of the mystery attendant on their authorship, and because the publisher of them was brought to trial (as was Swift's publisher) and acquitted of seditious libel. The trial was as significant in the British Isles as the trial of Peter Zenger in the United States, a landmark, in brief, in the long struggle for a free and untrammeled press. Junius had written in one letter, "The liberty of the press is our only resource: it will command an audience when every honest man in the kingdom is excluded," and again, "They who conceive that our newspapers are no restraint upon bad men, or impediment to the execution of bad measures, know nothing of this country." His words were tocsins of liberty.

Even if Francis is challenged as the author of the celebrated, tempestuous letters, Dublin is not to be denied the honor of their composition because the next most likely candidate for authorship is Hugh Macaulay Boyd (1746–1794), another Dublin man, whose life was devoted to journalism and to the British foreign service.

To estimate the number of Irish journalists who went through —and still go through—Dublin to London or America would be an impossibility. For better or worse, Dublin gave London Alfred Harmsworth, the celebrated Lord Northcliffe, and his family troupe. Northcliffe has been called the English Hearst and was the genius who launched the age of mass media in England. Justin McCarthy (1830–1912), author of *The History of Our Times* and numerous novels and biographies, is an example of a whole breed of Irish journalists working in England in the generation preceding the first world war; Michael MacDonagh (1860–1946), who was chairman of the press gallery in the House of Commons, whose career spanned two world wars, is a paradigm of his generation; while Alan Bestic, author of *The Importance of Being Irish*, is a present-day example. Along with them there have been thousands.

For the Irish in England, journalism was a door to political advancement. T. P. O'Connor (1848–1929) was an Irish journalist elected to the House of Commons first from Ireland and in 1885 from Liverpool and returned regularly for the rest of his life. He founded *The Star* and, later, *T.P.'s Weekly* (pronounced, of course, Tay Pay's weekly), and broadened English concepts of editorship. His *Memoirs of an Old Parliamentarian* gathered strength from his length of service, which made him near the end of his life the oldest member of the House of Commons in years of service.

With his flair for journalism and his itch to travel, we should expect the Irishman to make a good foreign correspondent. He does. Sir William Howard Russell (1820–1907), a graduate of Trinity, has the distinction of being history's first foreign correspondent. Jacob Fugger and other renaissance bankers had correspondents writing privately to them from distant parts, but in the modern journalistic sense, Russell is the prototype. He began as a parliamentary reporter for the London *Times*, and then was sent to report on O'Connell's mammoth rallies, and then to cover the Crimean War, from which he sent back brilliant dispatches—one on the famous Charge of the Light Brigade which inspired the poem by Lord Alfred Tennyson.

Russell's disclosures exposed the incredible incompetence of the British military at that time. From the Crimea he went on to cover other wars, including the Indian mutiny in 1847, the American Civil War, in which he so displeased both sides by his factual reporting that he was banished, and then the Franco-Prussian war. The talent continues among Dubliners today, one of the most recent being Cornelius Ryan (1920–   ), a correspondent during World War II, and author of the best-seller *The Longest Day*, which is the story of the invasion of Normandy by the Allies. Between the nineteenth-century Russell and the twentieth-century Ryan, Dublin has produced hundreds of peripatetic, far-ranging journalists. The name Ryan is a solid one in Dublin journalism. W. P. Ryan (1867–1942) was, like George Moore, an Irishman who returned to Dublin from a career in London to edit rousing political journals in the years before World War I, returning to London on the eve of it. His son, Desmond Ryan (1893–1964), who was educated at Padraic Pearse's St. Enda's school, and fought in the 1916 Rising, also found his career in journalism.

Within Dublin itself the procession of newspapers and journals resulted in an extraordinarily high incidence of periodicals per person. This has been true from the days of Dean Swift and Dr. Thomas Sheridan, who together for a short while published a journal, until today. Although the longest-lived paper in Ireland is in Belfast, Dublin's *Freeman's Journal* ran from 1763 until 1924, a publication, which, while its views varied over the years, traditionally maintained a moderate tone. It supported Grattan and it supported O'Connell. The Great Liberator, however, had his own paper, *The Pilot*, which published from 1828 to 1849. Parnell helped launch *United Ireland*, which had for its editor William O'Brien (1852–1890), who, like many another, wrote verse and novels.

Of all the political papers, Thomas Davis's *The Nation* still stands, in relation to the Irish renaissance, preeminent, a paper suffused by an indomitable spirit that imprisonment, banishment, exile, and death could not quench. Dublin boasts a statue honoring Davis, a remarkable piece of work in bronze, with an angel at each of its four corners blowing the trumpets of Ireland's resurrection. The irascible John Mitchel, who broke with *The Nation* and founded *The United Irishman*, was transported in one of the hideous British prison ships, escaped, and became a journalist in New York. Directly after his transportation, his colleague, John Finton Lalor, founded a successor to *The United Irishman* and named it *The Irish Felon* in semantic defiance of the legalisms of England. The Unionists had their publications also, of course, among them the *Dublin Evening Mail*, which lasted from 1821 to 1962.

Before the *Dublin Evening Mail* closed its doors, *The Irish Times* was begun, an Anglo-Irish paper, Unionist in principle, royalist, and pro-England which, managed by astute journalists, however, survived the Rising, and the Troubles, and the Irish civil war, and flourishes today a respected, literate, responsible, fairly liberal paper, no longer a toady to English policy. The more determinedly nationalist papers, however, have the larger circulation.

The Irish Republican Brotherhood at the beginning of the twentieth century published *Irish Freedom*, pledged to seek "the independence of Ireland by every practicable means, including the use of physical force." To list the publications that came and went in the cause of Irish freedom would make a tedious litany. Most were closed by British oppression, some stilled by the church's indirect censorship (such as Ryan's *The Irish Peasant*, so that he went on to write a protest novel about it, *The Plough and the Cross*). Other papers served less revolutionary purposes, prospered and died, among them *The Irish Homestead* edited by AE. *The Irish People* was revolutionary in tone and purpose and spoke for the Fenians, and it was in its office that John O'Leary and O'Donovan Rossa were arrested to be exiled. The Irish editor's life was not a placid one.

The Irish Protestant was a different sort of brief excursion into print, a paper not merely violently anti-Catholic, as was Caesar Otway's publication that first brought Carleton to light, but determinedly anti-High Church. Both passed away for lack of support.

Poet Plunkett's violent revolutionary language ended *The Irish Review* in 1910. When one of Griffith's papers ended in bankruptcy, he started another, living like a medieval ascetic, fed by his patriotism. Socialist James Connolly, one of the most original of Dublin's political theorists, published *The Worker's Republic* to argue the case that "private property [is the] fundamental basis of all oppression national, political and social." Like many another Irish political leader, he was a two-fisted journalist as well who wouldn't think of leaving his speeches or editorials to a ghost-writer.

The Gaelic League had its own publication, *An Claidhmeamh Soluis*, with Michael Joseph O'Rahilly, who boasted the honorific The O'Rahilly, as managing director. In its pages, Eoin Mac-Neill (1867–1944), scholar, historian, revolutionary, and minister of state, in brilliant articles sought to resolve the widening split between the south and most of Ulster. A profusion of papers took sides in the turbulent days of the first two decades of the century. *An tOglach*, edited by Piaras Beaslai, denounced conscription of Irish troops and protested Irish service in the British armed forces, as did another of Connolly's publications, *The Harp*. At the height of the Anglo-Irish war, *An Poblacht* was edited by Erskine Childers and Frank Gallagher on behalf of the Republican cause. Short-lived and short-tempered, dozens of such papers came and went. Journalism in Dublin is likely to be everyone's business.

No political movement of size was truly established in Dublin until its newspaper spoke. In order to come to power, and because all the newspapers were opposed to the Fianna Fail, De Valera's party, he founded *The Irish Press* in 1931. The first editor was Frank Gallagher, who had worked with Childers. M. J. MacManus, known to readers as EmmJay, was its first literary editor and set the pace for the city. Today it has the most lively literary pages in Ireland, edited by David Marcus (1926–   ), one of the founders of the periodicals *Envoy* and *Irish Writing*, both of which in their brief existences did much to bring young Irish writers into print and Irish writers to the attention of American readers.

The quality of some of the men who abandoned Dublin to make their careers in journalism is by today's standards formidably high. Preeminent nineteenth-century examples are Francis Sylvester O'Mahony (1805–1866) and William Maginn (1794–1842). Maginn was a child prodigy who was graduated from Trinity College with distinction at the age of seventeen. He began teaching school in Cork while contributing to *Blackwood's* magazine, the leading literary publication of the day. He finally became a regular contributor and is credited by some scholars as having been the originator of the famous Noctes Ambrosianae that appeared in *Blackwood's*, written chiefly by Christopher North (John Wilson). Maginn in any event was a major contributor. He was unfortunately an alcoholic, and this played a part in his wandering from one publication to another. He wrote brilliantly for a number of English magazines including *The Representative, The Standard*, and *The Literary Souvenir*. He helped found *Fraser's* magazine, which rivaled *Blackwood's*. He was a master linguist, a writer of style and wit. When Daniel Donnelly, the heavyweight boxing champion, died, Maginn in one of his magazines set out to honor his countryman. He wrote poems in half a dozen languages eulogizing the pugilist and pretended the tributes had come from around the world. He also rhymed as readily in Greek and Latin as he did in English.

This gift was even more marked in the puckish Francis Sylvester O'Mahony, who sometimes dropped the *O* but was best known under his pen name, Father Prout. He was, like Maginn, a native of Cork, and would in turn be a stellar contributor to *Fraser's* magazine.

He was educated for the priesthood and studied in Rome. For a short while he taught at Clongowes, the Jesuit college, but left the Society of Jesus and became a professional journalist. He it was introduced Maginn to William M. Thackeray and the three collaborated on one magazine. Daniel Maclise (1806–1870), Irish painter of historical scenes, did a group portrait of the writers for *Fraser's* magazine, showing Maginn, O'Mahony, and Crofton Croker seated with such giants as Thackeray, Robert Southey, Samuel T. Coleridge, and others. He soon established himself as a journalist in Dublin and London, and, in 1846, at the suggestion of Charles Dickens, became a foreign correspondent. He sent a brilliant series of dispatches from Rome under the signature Don Jeremy Savonarola. He knew Rome well, having been a student there, and it was in that city that he wrote his extremely popular poem "The Bells of Shandon."

Like Maginn, he was a formidable linguist. An earlier Cork poet, Richard Alfred Millikin (1767–1815), had written a humorous poem called "The Groves of Blarney." Father Prout rewrote it in French, Italian, Latin, and Greek. That sort of composition was something he enjoyed immensely, much to the despair of Thomas Moore, for Father Prout made the distinguished Irish poet the goat of a scholarly jape. He translated several poems of Moore into foreign languages and pretended that the translations were the originals and that Moore had plagiarized them! The literary and linguist virtuosity is magnificent, and there are those critics who believe that his Latin rendition of Moore's *To a Beautiful Milkmaid* is a better poem than Moore's, particularly since the archaisms of the early-nineteenth-century English are avoided in the Latin.

Without question, O'Mahony and Maginn were a pair of journalistic geniuses, but they perhaps had their match in Brian O'Nolan (1911–1966), who wrote a column in *The Irish Times* for more than a quarter of a century, using Irish, English, and Latin with equal facility. Without the scholarship, but with wit and facility, Seamus Kelly today, under the pen name Quidnunc, writes a sparking column for *The Irish Times*.

The myriad literary magazines that have come and gone or publish in Dublin today would make a chapter in itself. Of them all *The Bell* was the most famous. The *Dublin University Magazine* emblazoned the nineteenth century, and Seumus O'Sullivan's *Dublin Magazine* did the same for the twentieth. Another magazine of the same name flourishes today. Some others from the past were *The All Ireland Review*, which Stanish O'Grady edited for five years (1900–1905); and the *Shan Van Vocht* (1896–1899), edited by Ethna Carbery and Alice Milligan, in Belfast, which won a wide Dublin audience. *The Irish Monthly* was edited by the Reverend Matthew Russell from 1873 to 1912. This is to mention only a handful. Richard Robert Madden (1798–1886) wrote *The History of Irish Periodical Literature from the End of the 17th to the Middle of the 19th Century.* Someone should do the same for the century that followed. Richard J. Hayes, LL.D., director of the National Library of Ireland, has edited "Sources for the History of Irish Civilization: Articles in Irish Periodicals," in thirteen massive volumes, culling an index of articles, poems, essays, etc., from more than 150 periodicals, some still flourishing, others gone with the soft Irish wind. It makes our mention of half a dozen presumptuous. Dr. Hayes's massive index has been published by the G. K. Hall Co. of Boston, which has been described as "the next Irish city to Galway going West."

In Dublin, the same hands that write for the daily newspapers are, more often than not, the ones that contribute to the scholarly monthlies, quarterlies, and annuals. For the Dublin Dimension is seen here in full force. One cannot compartmentalize Irish writers, and we can see the link between journalism and literature later in our discussion of present-day Irish novelists.

To understand further the Dublin Dimension, one must understand another means of human communication and the exchange of ideas and information: gossip. You can look through a thousand books on political science, or a thousand books on Ireland and the indexes will carry no mention of gossip. Indeed, encyclopedias as well fail to mention it, and dictionaries are little help, for they list only the very commonplace widespread meaning of the word, "to tattle," or "to exchange light talk." The serious nature of gossip is not mentioned by the dictionaries, yet its role in the formation of a public mood, in the formal estimation of public characters, in the final turn that makes or breaks a reputation, a business, or a nation is always present and can be decisive. The intensity of its significance lessens in some sort of proportion to the extension of a nation, so that in the United States gossip of the sort rampant in Dublin (or even London or Paris) is almost totally absent. For just as there are words that are known to everyone but cannot be used in public, *a fortiori* there are facts that can be told in private that cannot, because of propriety, libel, or human decency, be told in public. The absence of gossip can be detrimental to a country, and no better example need be sought than the 1972 uproar over the selection of Senator Thomas Eagleton of Missouri as Democratic vice-presidential candidate and then his dismissal because it was disclosed that he had had electric shock treatments for mental depression and had not informed Senator George McGovern, the Democratic candidate for President, who had selected him as his running mate. The gossip about Senator Eagleton's previous ill health had been all over Missouri but had not reached the United States Senate chamber nor the headquarters of the Democratic National Committee. In Dublin gossip would have prevented the choice of an Eagleton, the subsequent embarrassment to him and to McGovern, and the disastrous consequences to the nation which could follow on such a contretemps, and some think, did.

Just as there are intimacies in a family circle, known to all and never mentioned, except one-to-one, so there are intimacies among persons in a literary circle, a club, a profession, a trade, a union, a legislative assembly, or a nation itself. The etymology of the word helps our understanding, for a gossip was originally a godparent, a person who was sponsor at another's baptism, in brief, a god sibling, hence an intimate. New York is filled with literary and publishing gossip (that author A is sleeping with the wife of actor B and so must not be invited to gathering C), and Washington is filled with political gossip (that the woman who committed suicide last Thursday was the mistress of Congressman E). In Dublin the intensity of gossip, dealing as it does with the electric, synergetic interchange of all the professions, has an intensity that the United States does not know. To make up for such a lack (for there is something in the human heart that lusts for such intimacies, the desire to be on the inside, to be in the know, which really means up on the gossip) Walter Winchell invented the gossip column, which, of course, was a synthetic thing, since the point about gossip is that for one reason or another, good or bad, it cannot be printed.

The real thing is very European. The sidewalk cafés of those countries fortunate enough to have them are, of course, gossip shops. In Ireland, the role of the pub is the same. Mile upon mile of prose has been written about the Irish pub without emphasizing this aspect of it. Dublin is one of the truly democratic nations of the world, and the pub helps keep it so. In no other capital of the Western world are legislators, cabinet members, or a prime minister himself likely to be found chatting at the same bar as laborers, brokers, doctors, journalists, or other ordinary or extraordinary citizens. To be sure, there are pubs that the nation's rulers would not frequent unless they were seeking election, and there are pubs where a longshoreman might not find the companionship he desires, but none of them is too expensive for the ordinary man, and none will exclude a toper because of his dress. Nor will a literary editor shun some popular pub lest he be approached by favor-seekers, for the Irish have a natural courtesy and reticence in that regard that differs from American practice, which makes public men more ready to sequester themselves.

This is a long digression to explain a much-observed but little-understood feature of Irish life. The pubs are indeed gathering places where a casual visitor can hear good conversation, for they are much more like clubs than are American bars. Often there is a general conversation going that anyone can join, as well as tête-à-têtes which are not to be intruded on. If the visitor is fortunate some of Ireland's best minds may be participating in the general conversation. Here again we see a facet of the oral culture of the Celt.

I X

What we have said about journalism and gossip gives a background against which subsequent Irish history, particularly the Irish literary revival, must be seen. But before we approach it, we must deal with the Irish street ballad, which we have subsumed under the head of gossip. It might just as well have gone under the heading of song or poetry, but essentially it is most closely allied with journalism and gossip. It was a way of making a protest or a point. At its best it could merge into poetry, even as it grew out of poetry. Once again the Celtic mnemonic gift played a part. Many of the ballad writers (and singers) are nameless, but many are known, remembered, and honored. Strange descendants of the old bards, heirs of the harpists, they sang their songs and won their applause, and took their payment in food or a drink and died anonymously, revered perhaps by a circle of friends, sometimes nationally known, often submerged by the endemic popularity of their work.

Alfred Percival Graves (1846–1940), a Dublin native and father of the poet Robert Graves, published several collections of Irish songs and ballads, many of them his own. His most famous composition is the song "Father O'Flynn," and he himself told of being asked by a woman why it was that men of his day did not write wonderful songs like "Father O'Flynn." She did not know he was the author of the composition, so popular had it become, so traditional did it seem, so much was it part and parcel of the country's folklore within his own day. The Graves family is as literary as the Sheridans. Graves's father, bishop of Limerick, was a writer, as was his uncle, as are his two sons, Robert and Charles.

In this century James Stephens and Padraic Colum also lived to see poems of their composing sung as street ballads, although offered anonymously to the public, who perhaps had never heard their names, or knowing them, failed to associate them with the passing song. One street balladeer, James Hiney, possessed of the Dublin wit, told an amusing story on himself. His mother-in-law on meeting him for the first time, and surveying his diminutive size, said to her daughter, "Well, if you get nothing else from him you'll always get a laugh." Brendan Behan's brother Dominick (himself a playwright), a few years back, dashed off a street ballad (they need not follow the traditional form) when zealots blew up the famous Nelson Column, honoring the indomitable English admiral, in O'Connell Street, Dublin. To be sure, the council had talked often of taking it down, but the $70,000 it had cost to erect would have been near double that to raze. Leaving it was the softer course. Dynamite brought it down; and Behan's ballad swept the country.

The street ballads blend three distinct aspects of Dublin's literary life: journalism, wit, and song. They are matters of wit because they were often done extemporaneously or struck off topically, occasional verses some of which bristle with satire; matters of journalism because they brought news (and propaganda) to the illiterate; and they were sung as well as printed, sung in the streets, sung at political gatherings, sung in homes and sung in the hearts of tens of thousands, who, unable to read, exercised their memories.

In this last aspect, they linked the balladeer with the bards of Ireland, who in turn were the heirs of the Celtic *filidh*. The Last of the Bards is a title given to Turlough O'Carolan (in Irish, Toirdhealbhach O Cearbhallain) (1670–1783), blind from his youth as a result of smallpox, who was trained at the expense of patrons in English, Irish, and music, and became the foremost harpist in Ireland. Scholars rebel at calling him a bard, seeing him more as the descendant of the *ollavs*, the

highest rank of the Celtic poets. He was preeminently a musician, and a better composer than a harpist, nine-tenths of
whose works have been lost, whose harp was burned by the
loutish servants of his patron after his death, whose son lacked
his musical genius. While we do not know what words he set
to his religious music, those verses we have from him are of
the more ephemeral nature of the ballads. His lines are often
in praise of the masters and mistresses of the houses that had
him as guest, and his convivial nature made him welcome wherever he went. Indeed, several of his verses celebrate conviviality itself or the whisky that excites it. He was probably
much more welcome in homes than another poet, also blinded
by smallpox, Anthony Raftery, who, honored among the hills
and islands, could, nevertheless, outwear the welcome Celtic
tradition demanded for the poet. By that tradition, a poet, guest
in a house, could never be asked to leave. One story tells of a
woman recruiting Blind Raftery to help her twist a hay-rope.
As it lengthened, she maneuvered him beyond the threshold
and, when he was well beyond, slammed the door against him.
She had rid herself of him without asking him to leave. Raftery
was illiterate and his poetry would all have been lost except
for a chance meeting between Douglas Hyde and a Dublin
beggar who directed him to the house in Galway where the
wandering poet had died. Raftery's famous poem, given here
in Hyde's translation, tells with heartbreak the story of the
nomadic Irish poets, as they wandered with their dying Gaelic
speech through the shrinking Gaeltacht. Fiddling at a wedding
one day, Raftery overheard a man ask, "Who is the old fellow
over there?" Raftery replied:

> I am Raftery the Poet
> Full of hope and love
> With eyes that have no light,
> With gentleness that has no misery.
> Going west upon my pilgrimage
> By the light of my heart
> Feeble and tired
> To the end of my road.

Behold me now,
And my face to the wall
A-playing music
Unto empty pockets.

The poem could be spoken for them all, O'Carolan, as well as Raftery. A surprising number of the harpists were blind, or perhaps it is not surprising. The blind must cultivate their hearing, and they cannot run with the seeing, but must sit by themselves. Raftery's poem loses in translation; for example, Irish has more than one verb for "to be" and the one that Raftery uses means "to be forever." In brief he proclaimed his own immortality of genius over against the transience of his surroundings. In Irish it gives the poem the sting of wit.

The balladeers of the nineteenth and twentieth centuries are the descendants of these men, the harp gone, the concertina in its place, the Irish gone, the English that O'Connell wanted for political reasons now serving all purposes. Indeed, balladeering became so popular that John Mitchel's newspaper felt revolutionary energy was being wasted on them, and O'Donovan Rossa wanted fewer songs and more action. Others, like Gavan Duffy, felt them very important, and not only gave them prominence in his newspaper but collected them in an anthology. In their history, we can see, once again, how Thomas Davis and *The Nation* were a turning point, a climacteric.

Few of these ballads mounted the rungs of poetry, but hundreds of them have survived as songs and are still sung in Dublin drawing rooms. They have the naïve charm of primitive art, and in several instances rare dignity—"The Croppy Boy" and "Michael Boyland," to take two examples—while "The Night Before Larry Was Stretched" stands out as one of the best poems ever written in the argot of criminals. It could have been done by an Irish Villon, but has been attributed sometimes to that genius John Philpot Curran. By way of digression, we might quote here a poem he did write, which is a minor Dublin masterpiece.

If sadly thinking with spirits sinking
    Could more than drinking my cares compose,

> A cure for sorrow from sighs I'd borrow
>   And hope tomorrow would end my woes.
> But since in wailing there's no availing
>   And death unfailing will strike a blow,
> Then for that reason and for a season
>   Let us be merry before we go.

In addition to their charm, the ballads such as "The Wearing of the Green," which is perhaps the best-known of all, serve to illuminate history, revealing as they do the concerns, the manners, and mores of their periods. They do this not only for Dublin but for New York and Boston, where they were brought by the immigrants.

Take this excerpt from an Irish street ballad sung in the Old World and the New but composed in America.

> I'm a decent boy just landed from the town of Ballyfad
> I want a situation, yes, I want it mighty bad.
> I seen employment advertised. "Tis just the thing," says I.
> But the dirty spalpeen ended with: "No Irish need apply."

Like the popular songs of America, ballads were meant to be sung and so they lose strength in the silence of type. Such lyrics need their melodies. Few Irish ballads dealt with satire, although many dealt in irony. The law had little chance of dealing with them, although singers were arrested. The sting of satire could, on occasion, cause libel actions, however, but it was a railroad company that sued William Percy French (1854–1922) for one of his popular songs that ridiculed it. French was one of those extraordinary Trinity College graduates, a man who took his degree in civil engineering and ended up editor of a comic magazine, songwriter, librettist for operas, and a performer himself. His most famous composition never earned him a penny, but is still sung wherever English is spoken. The song was "Abdullah Bulbul Ameer," which he published anonymously only to have it stolen and copyrighted by an English firm. No other balladeer is more often quoted in the obscure semantic parodying of Joyce.

James Joyce

Parodies, of which Joyce was the master, mounting parody on parody, were, and are, in Dublin a great weapon of satire, as well as keen instruments for insight into and beyond the masks men wear, the personae they either manage or are. In his famous novel *At Swim-Two-Birds* Flann O'Brien (Brian Nolan) wields parody with the adroitness of a master fiddler sawing his bow. To parody is to mimic, and the Irish shanachie is also the master of accent and intonation, mocking the variations of sound one county in Ireland mounts against another. Ireland is the land of song and the land of satire, and her native sons have carried it over the world wherever they have sought their expatriation or suffered their exiles.

Who today will scoff at the power of a song? Shelley's aphorism that he didn't care who made a nation's laws may be rodomontade, for we have seen that the lawmakers of the totalitarian state can smother song entirely, but there is no question that song can still be deadly. The English still fear the power of the Irish songmaker and satirist and in 1971 banned from the air a song of Paul McCartney, the Liverpool Irishman, the wit of the Beatles quartet. The song, "Give Ireland Back to the Irish," was more than the British conscience could stand as the pathetic remnant of its imperial army sought to pacify by the machine gun the six counties of the north of Ireland. Who can fail to see the direct line between McCartney and the Irish minstrel starving in Dublin and threatening the Viking warlords with his words.

There are some excellent collections of Irish ballads, many well-known. Everyone is familiar with the lilting "The Girl I Left Behind Me," sung by the Irish youth going off to fight in England's war, but a few know the ballad "Johnny, I Hardly Knew Ye," which tells of his return.

Johnny, I Hardly Knew Ye

> While going the road to sweet Athy,
> Hurroo! hurroo!
> While going the road to sweet Athy,

Hurroo! hurroo!
While going the road to sweet Athy,
A stick in my hand and a drop in my eye,
A doleful damsel I heard cry:
    "Och, Johnny, I hardly knew ye!
    With drums and guns, and guns and drums
    The enemy nearly slew ye;
    My darling dear, you look so queer,
    Och, Johnny, I hardly knew ye!

"Where are your eyes that looked so mild?
    Hurroo! hurroo!
Where are your eyes that looked so mild?
    Hurroo! hurroo!
Where are your eyes that looked so mild
When my poor heart you first beguiled?
Why did you run from me and the child?
    Och, Johnny, I hardly knew ye!
      With drums, etc.

"Where are the legs with which you run?
    Hurroo! hurroo!
Where are the legs with which you run
When you went to carry a gun?
Indeed, your dancing days are done!
    Och, Johnny, I hardly knew ye!
      With drums, etc.

"It grieved my heart to see you sail,
    Hurroo! hurroo!
It grieved my heart to see you sail,
Though from my heart you took leg-bail;
Like a cod you're doubled up head and tail!
    Och, Johnny, I hardly knew ye!
      With drums, etc.

"You haven't an arm and you haven't a leg,
    Hurroo! hurroo!
You haven't an arm and you haven't a leg,
You're an eyeless, noseless, chickenless egg;
You'll have to be put wid a bowl to beg:

Och, Johnny, I hardly knew ye!
   With drums, etc.

"I'm happy for to see you home,
   Hurroo! hurroo!
I'm happy for to see you home,
   Hurroo! hurroo!
All from the island of Sulliloon,
So low in flesh, so high in bone;
   Och, Johnny, I hardly knew ye!
      With drums, etc.

"But sad as it is to see you so,
   Hurroo! hurroo!
But sad as it is to see you so,

   Hurroo! hurroo!
But sad as it is to see you so,
And to think of you now as an object of woe,
Your Peggy'll still keep ye on as her beau;
   Och, Johnny, I hardly knew ye;
      With drums and guns, etc.

Written in Dublin slang of the late eighteenth century, "The Night Before Larry Was Stretched" has enchanted all students of Irish street ballads, and among them all it stands surely immortal. If it was Curran's creation, and no doubt he knew the argot of criminals as well as any cultivated man could, he was the genius popular tradition claims.

The Night Before Larry Was Stretched

The night before Larry was stretched
   The boys they all paid him a visit;
A bait in their sacks, too, they fetched;
   They sweated their duds till they riz it:
For Larry was ever the lad,
   When a boy was condemned to the squeezer,
Would fence all the duds that he had
   To help a poor friend to a sneezer
     And warm his gob 'fore he died.

The boys they came crowding in fast,
  They drew all their stools round about him,
Six glims round his trap-case were placed,
  He couldn't be well waked without 'em.
When one of us asked could he die
  Without having duly repented,
Says Larry, "That's all in my eye;
  And first by the clargy invented,
    To get a fat bit for themselves."

"I'm sorry, dear Larry," says I,
  "To see you in this situation;
And blister my limbs if I lie,
  I'd as lieve it had been my own station."
"Ochone! It's all over," says he,
  "For the neckcloth I'll be forced to put on
And by this time tomorrow you'll see
  Your poor Larry as dead as a mutton."
    Because, why, his courage was good.

"And I'll be cut up like a pie,
  And my nob from my body be parted."
"You're in the wrong box, then," says I,
  "For blast me if they're so hard-hearted:
A chalk on the back of your neck
  Is all that Jack Ketch dares to give you;
Then mind not such trifles a feck,
  For why should the likes of them grieve you?
    And now, boys, come tip us the deck."

The cards being called for, they played
  Till Larry found one of them cheated;
A dart at his napper he made
  (The boy being easily heated:)
"Oh, by the hokey, you thief,
  I'll scuttle your nob with my daddle!
You cheat me because I'm in grief,
  But soon I'll demolish your noddle,
    And leave you your claret to drink."

Then the clergy came in with his book,
   He spoke him so smooth and so civil;
Larry tipped him a Kilmainham look,
   And pitched his big wig to the devil;
Then sighing, he threw back his head
   To get a sweet drop of the bottle,
And pitiful sighing, he said:
     "Oh, the hemp will be soon round my throttle
     And choke my poor windpipe to death.

"Though sure it's the best way to die,
   Oh, the devil a betther a-livin'!
For, sure, when the gallows is high
   Your journey is shorter to Heaven;
But what harasses Larry the most,
   And makes his poor soul melancholy,
Is to think of the time when his ghost
     Will come in a sheet to sweet Molly—
     Oh, sure it will kill her alive!"

So moving these last words he spoke,
   We all vented our tears in a shower;
For my part, I thought my heart broke,
   To see him cut down like a flower,
On his travels we watched him next day;
   Oh, the throttler! I thought I could kill him;
But Larry not one word did say,
     Nor changed till he come to 'King William'—
     Then, musha! his color grew white.

When he came to the nubbling chit,
   He was tucked up so neat and so pretty,
The rumbler jogged off from his feet,
   And he died with his face to the city;
He kicked, too—but that was all pride,
   For soon you might see 't was all over;
Soon after the noose was untied,
     And at darky we waked him in clover
     And sent him to take a ground sweat.

The Celtic Renaissance

X

William Butler Yeats (1865–1939), the genius behind the Celtic renaissance at the turn of the century, was born in Sandymount in Dublin. His father, John Butler Yeats, was a distinguished painter and poet of the pre-Raphaelite movement, and his mother was Susan Pollexfen of Sligo. They had married in Sligo in 1863 and William was their first child. He had two younger brothers, Robert, who died as a child, and Jack B. Yeats, who became the most distinguished Irish painter of his age. Yeats's lineage was Anglo-Irish Protestant, but the father, trained first for the law, and before that intended for the Church of Ireland, turned artist and agnostic. His interest was in the physical world, the world an artist could see and paint, and he had the conviction that exaggerated ideals could dehumanize a man. He had seen them do so on both sides of Ireland's political quarrels. Mrs. Susan Yeats was no intellectual, to use that dreadful current term; she read little and was so indifferent to her husband's work she is said never to have visited his studio. She had, however, an imaginative gift that sometimes sparkled in her letters but more frequently in loquacious story-telling to her children. Besides three boys, she bore two daughters called by the nicknames Lily and Lolly.

Three years after William was born, John Yeats took his wife and the child to London, where he studied art and pursued his talent unprofitably. William was to go to school in England but his summers were spent in Sligo at the home of his grandfather, William Pollexfen, and it was Sligo that acquainted him with folklore and fairies and it was Sligo that entered his marrow as, indeed, it did that of his brother Jack (1871–1957), several of whose excellent paintings today adorn the walls of a pathetic little museum there. If all the scholars of the world who have made their reputations and their fortunes writing and lecturing about the poet and his work were to pay tithes for the upkeep of the museum it would rival the national museum in Dublin. At the age of nine, Willie, as he was called, was sent to the Godolphin School at Hammersmith, a school which shared the usual brutal and vicious aspects of the English public school. Yeats endured it quite well but hated London and longed for Sligo. When he was fifteen his family took him back to Ireland, to the opposite side of the island from Sligo, and acquired a thatched cottage in Howth, just outside Dublin, overlooking the sea, and Willie was sent off to Erasmus High School in Dublin, commuting daily by train in the company of his father, whose studio was in the city.

In 1883, the family moved from Howth to Rothgar, a Dublin suburb, and Willie again changed schools. His father, to supplement his income, had been teaching at the Metropolitan Library of Art on Kildare Street in the heart of Dublin and it was there Willie was enrolled. One of his schoolmates was George Russell, poet and painter, who would become famous under a pseudonym that was the result of a printing error: AE. The two students shared a curious interest in the occult, the mystical and the unseen, and later, in the pagan myths of Ireland, and would work together in the theater. Yeats had been writing verse for several years by now, but it was 1885 that became a fateful year for him, for it was that year that he published his first poems and in that year he met John O'Leary, the old, bearded Fenian leader, just returned to Ireland after nine years of exile. O'Leary was a literate giant and a political hero to the people of Dublin. His sister, Ellen O'Leary (1831–1889), was a respected poet who was among the many who contributed to *The United Irishman* and other journals.

"We of the younger generation owe a great deal to Mr. John

O'Leary and his sister," Yeats would write later. "What nationality is in the present literary movement in Ireland is largely owing to their influence—an influence all feel who come across them." On another occasion he would say more passionately, "From O'Leary's conversations and from the Irish books he lent or gave me has come all I have set my head to since." O'Leary it was who first brought Ferguson and Davis to Yeats's attention, as well as the work of other Irish writers in the swelling body of translations from the Irish.

O'Leary turned the young poet from a career in painting to the literary life, but above all it was O'Leary who enunciated the majestic principle that would be for Yeats forever the *lettre de cachet* to keep his dedication above all to art.

"There are some things," O'Leary said, "that a man must not do to save a nation." This insight, this vision, was the key to all that had gone wrong before. While our concern here is only with the literary aspect of Ireland's nineteenth-century failure, the vision of O'Leary can put all Irish history in a new light: Yeats applied it effectively to art.

England had done things to Ireland, intended to save England, which a man must not do to save a nation (permitting the famine, for one), and is paying for it today. The Catholic church had done things to save Ireland which a man must not do to save a nation by giving a frigid face and an iron heart to Catholicism, which is alien to its essence. More pertinent to our study, the poets had done things that a man must not do to save a nation. They had violated the autonomy of art and put it at the service of politics, and so had vitiated their genius. Poetry had created Cathleen ni Houlihan and Dark Rosaleen but instead of remaining her lover it had become her slave, poetry soured to propaganda, and for most of the decades of the century the worth of a poem was calculated by the hyperbole of its political bias. Hysteria and a martial cadence were mistaken for passion and inspired rhythm. This sad syndrome proved a spiraling descent from the aspirations to the actualities. Davis himself could offend.

This downward spiral was broken by Yeats, who rightfully chose as his saints the apolitical Ferguson and the inspired Mangan. These two had not abandoned the autonomy of art to the exigencies of politics; they had sought, with varying success, the perfection of the poem, the integrity of the work. Yet, the influence of Davis played its part by intensity of national feeling.

In 1887 the elder Yeats took his enlarged family back to London, and Willie, now a young man, launched himself on a literary career. Behind him in Dublin, Yeats had left a friendly circle which included not only the O'Learys, but Katharine Tynan (1861–1931), a poet and critic, deemed a major poet in her day, and author of more than one hundred volumes of prose and verses; T. W. Rolleston (1857–1920), poet and translator; Douglas Hyde (1860–1944), a poet who wrote in Irish, a language which he acquired in the west, who would be the first president of Ireland; and John F. Taylor (1850–1902), a writer with extraordinary oratorical gifts—all of whom made a deep impression on the young Yeats.

Although Yeats had had a somewhat disturbing experience at a Dublin séance, he was no sooner in England than he joined various occult groups, including the Theosophical Society headed by the remarkable Madame Blavatsky. He met his fellow Irishmen Oscar Wilde (1854–1900) and George Bernard Shaw (1856–1950), who, seemingly of two generations, were born in almost the same year. Up to this time Yeats's poems had sought themes from the Orient, Hungary, or never-never land, but O'Leary's influence now took hold, for O'Leary's other great principle that impressed itself on Yeats was that there is no literature without nationality and no nationality without literature. Yeats not only adopted that aphorism but would repeat it in varied phrases. O'Leary was a liberation for him, and if a further liberation followed it would not have been possible without the first.

In 1888, the O'Learys, with help from their literary circle, including Yeats, published an anthology of poetry with the

W. B. Yeats

ambivalent title *Poems and Ballads of Young Ireland*. This title not only turned the minds of readers back to the cultural surge of the 1840s and *The Nation* but, of course, stood for the new young Ireland the compilers saw waiting in the wings. The book was a literary success despite the weakness of some of its content, and the emphasis had been turned from politics. Perceptive critics sensed the change.

Besides Yeats, with his new Irish themes, other contributors were T. W. Rolleston, John O'Leary, Douglas Hyde, Rose Kavanaugh (sickly and soon dead), Katharine Tynan, John Todhunter, and George Noble Plunkett, who became a Papal count and was father of Joseph Mary Plunkett (1887–1916), like his father a poet (and a better one) and one of the hero-martyrs of the 1916 Easter Rising. Most of the other contributors faded into obscurity. Nevertheless, the overall quality was far superior to the mass of balladeering of the 1840s, which, as one sardonic latter-day critic remarked, had been a "great age for the feeble-minded." The 1880s were something else.

The significance of the anthology lay in its new emphasis, a poetry that had extricated itself from the cloying aspects of Victorian or Augustan diction, poetry with most of the encrusted rhetoric scraped away, poetry that looked to art rather than argument.

The next year was even more memorable for Yeats. He brought out *The Wanderings of Oisin and Other Poems*, completed in Sligo in 1888, and published through the good offices of John O'Leary. The book was a mixture of traditional weary nineteenth-century romanticism plus some contrasting exuberant poems with Irish themes. The work was well received in Dublin as well as London, and Yeats was compared flatteringly to Tennyson. However, what was clear at this time was that the man's voice was his own.

He had returned to London and it was there that another gesture on the part of his friend O'Leary changed his life. Miss Maud Gonne, one of the most beautiful women in Ireland and certainly the most beautiful revolutionary, who was to become a legendary figure, stepped from her carriage in Bedford Square with a letter of introduction from O'Leary to Yeats père. She was already a determined rebel and neither romance nor art was going to distract her from her ambition to see Ireland free. Yeats fell madly in love with her but her heart lay elsewhere and her favors were withheld. Later he would propose to her daughter and be again rejected. Maud welcomed Yeats as a friend but refused, despite his imploring, to become either mistress or wife. She would have been pleased if he devoted his genius to writing political ballads and raucous propaganda. To woo her he drove himself deeper into politics than he cared and marched in at least one anti-British demonstration. She was to inspire his most nationalistic play, *Cathleen ni Houlihan*, and, indeed, to inspire him for many years afterwards.

In 1890 Yeats published *The Lake Isle of Innisfree*, which was like a gonfalon hoisted on a lance. He became busy in London with the Rhymer's Club, a literary circle he had helped form, met with the circle surrounding *The Yellow Book*, and clubbed with occult groups. In that year Charles Stewart Parnell lost his leadership of the Irish Parliamentary party as a result of his marriage to the divorced Kitty O'Shea, who had already borne his child. Despite the intensity of party politics, Yeats founded first the Literary Society of London and in 1892 the Irish National Literary Society of Dublin, and it was before that group on November 25 that Douglas Hyde delivered a famous lecture, "The Necessity for the De-Anglicising of the Irish Nation."

Here was a clarion call that was too clamorous even for Yeats but it was in the right direction, and Yeats was to agree with it in principle. The man who took up the opposing view was a friend of the Yeats family, Edward Dowden (1843–1913), professor of English literature at loyalist-royalist Trinity College, author of *Shakespeare: A Critical Study of His Mind and Art*—which owed much to German higher criticism—who accused the new movement of running around "plastered with shamrocks and raving of Brian Boru." Dowden was a brilliant man, prejudiced against Irish literature and a

devoted advocate of cosmopolitanism, but when he insisted that
Irish writers need not adopt Irish subjects he became a foe
of Yeats.

Before the time of Thomas Moore, most of what had been
written by Irishmen was indistinguishable in style and subject
matter from English literature. What Yeats and O'Leary and
others were grasping for was a distinctive Irishness, a style that
would be unique, deliberate, and forceful. Hyde and some
others insisted that true Irishness had to be found in Gaelic,
and in his *History of Irish Literature*, which was to be published in 1899, Hyde included no Irishmen who wrote in
English. Yeats was somewhat handicapped in the ongoing
debate and in the attempt to transform the autochthonous
Irish past into a new national literature because he knew no
Gaelic, nor did he attempt seriously to master the language.
He had his supporters, of course, who maintained with him
that a true Irish literature could be written in English, and
indeed that an Anglo-Irish language was a possibility.

Before this discussion bubbled in Dublin, two very distinguished Irish poets had been writing not only in English but
after the traditional English manner. They were William Allingham (1824–1889), whose death came in the year Yeats's *The
Wanderings of Oisin* appeared, and Aubrey De Vere (1814–
1902), who, on the death of Tennyson in 1892, became the
dean of English verse.

Allingham was born in Ballyshannon in Donegal on the banks
of the Erne river, and received his education there, and also
what proved to be his best inspiration. He had a long literary
career in England, where he edited *Fraser's* magazine. In 1887,
he published *Irish Songs and Poems*. Yeats praised it highly
but found that Allingham's lack of sympathy "with the national
life and history had limited his principles and driven away from
his poetry much beauty and power—thinned his blood." Tennyson said of him, "The man has a true spirit of song in him, I
have no doubt of it." But in *The Age of Tennyson*, published
in the decade after Allingham's death, the critic Hugh Walker
wrote, "His inspiration is strangely fitful and uncertain, and

after his removal to London, in consequence of the success of his earlier verses, it seemed almost wholly to desert him." It is interesting to speculate on what might have been Allingham's place in Irish letters if his life's itinerary had taken him from Donegal to Dublin rather than to London.

Like Ferguson, Allingham eschewed political themes and stood apart from the Young Ireland movement. "Learn your trade," Yeats was to cry out to the Irish poets and praised Allingham for having chosen the best English models for style while clinging to Irish subjects. He put Allingham with Ferguson, Mangan, and De Vere in the front rank. He mourned that Allingham was not "national" enough and had in his later years fallen into cosmopolitanism. Insularity was the fault of the Young Ireland poets and cosmopolitanism was the error that stood in polarity.

De Vere was born at Adare in County Limerick and educated at Trinity College, and, while he became a Catholic in 1851, he abhorred the violence or "jacobinism" of the Fenians. More than Allingham he was to turn deliberately to Irish themes, not the ancient myths which so interested Ferguson, but Irish national history. It was a mild nationalism; and his ideal in poetry was a Wordsworthian one. His most Irish book was *Inishfail*. In his *Recollections*, he would write, "No other poem of mine was written more intensely, I may say more painfully, from my heart than, *Inishfail*."

The national passion that was on Ireland at the time left Allingham and De Vere neglected; it was not enough to be national, one had to be nationalistic. Yeats urged their true claim. As Austin Clarke was to point out later, Ferguson, Mangan, De Vere, and Allingham never were at home in the English canon. They were Irish and Yeats knew it was important for Ireland to see them so. Allingham had made a significant point in one of his poems:

> We're one at heart, if you be Ireland's friend,
> Though leagues asunder our opinions tend.
> There are but two great parties in the end.

Certainly the English were never going to warm to De Vere's *Inishfail*. His intention had been to present climacterics of Irish history in poetry.

> Contemporary historic poems [he wrote] touch us with a magical hand but they often pass by the most important events and linger beside the most trivial. Looking back upon history, as from a vantage ground, its general proportions become palpable; and the themes to which poetry attaches herself are either those of critical junctures upon which the fortunes of a nation turn, or such accidents of a lighter sort as illustrate the character of a race. A historic series of poems thus becomes possible, in interest of which is continuous, and the course of which reveals an increasing significance.

His prose works attracted attention, and his *English Misrule and Irish Misdeeds* was a defense of the Irish against the calumny of English critics.

Allingham's most aspiring effort was a novel in verse entitled *Laurence Bloomfield in Ireland*, but later criticism did not deem it successful. Yeats found it lacking in national sympathy, and cried out:

> What a sad business this non-nationalism has been! It gave to Lever and Lover their shallowness, and still gives to a section of Dublin society its cynicism. Lever and Lover and Allingham alike, it has deprived of their true audience. Many much less endowed writers than they have more influence in Ireland. Political doctrine was not demanded of them, merely nationalism. They would not take the people seriously—these writers of the Ascendency—and had to go to England for their audience. To Lever and Lover Ireland became merely a property shop, and to Allingham a half serious memory.
>
> To the great poets everything they see has its relation to the national life, and through that to the universal and divine life; nothing is an isolated artistic moment; there is a unity everywhere; everything fulfills a purpose that is not its own; the hailstone is a journeyman of God; the grass blade carries the universe upon its point. But to this universalism, this seeing the unity everywhere, you can only attain through what is near you, your

nation, or, if you be not travelled, your village and the cobwebs on your walls. You can no more have the greater poetry without a nation than religion without symbols. One can only reach out to the universe with a gloved hand—that glove is one's nation, the only thing one knows even a little of.

Yeats echoes the voice of O'Leary.

No better statement of the case could be made by Yeats. He had forecast his own career. Regretfully Allingham missed his chance when he walked the streets of Ballyshannon and listened to the songs of the girls of the district, completing them if they were incomplete and "refining" them, Arthur Hughes tells us, "where they were improper." It was once again the English prurience emasculating Irish literature, but, in any event, the livelier songs were lost.

While Allingham and De Vere moved between two worlds, their eyes pointed toward London and their hearts rooted in Ireland, another graduate of Trinity College was to overwhelm London with his wit. This was Oscar Fingal O'Flahertie Wills Wilde (1854–1900), literary son of literary parents. After excelling in classics at Trinity College, Oscar went to Oxford and won the Newdigate poetry prize with his poem "Ravenna," and came under the influence of John Ruskin and Walter Pater. From that influence, a highly intellectualized devotion to "art for art's sake" should come as no surprise, and Wilde was soon the superaesthete of his day. Although W. S. Gilbert in satirizing the aesthetic movement in *Patience* in 1881 had Dante Gabriel Rossetti in mind when he created the character of Bunthorne, and Lily Langtry insisted James McNeill Whistler was intended, the general public thought of Wilde.

In that year, Wilde published *Poems*, which, slight though it was, enjoyed five editions. Wilde had the same gift his fellow Dubliner George Bernard Shaw would display without disaster —self-promotion. Wilde's book, despite his mother's early patriotism, showed little Irish influence. He was an Irishman in the tradition of Goldsmith, Darley, and Canning. His Dublin heritage showed in his wit and his conversation, for he was, admittedly, the greatest conversationalist of his day, and his wit, though scintillating, was rarely bitter. In 1882, Wilde set off for the United States and a lecture tour to tell his audiences that "art is not something you can take or leave. It is a necessity of human life," and that "bad art is worse than no art at all." He returned to England to marry Constance Lloyd, who had more money than he, and to become editor of *Woman's World*. For his two sons, Cyril and Vyvyan, he wrote *The Happy Prince, and Other Tales*, delightful fairy stories, and *A House of Pomegranates*. Besides his souped-up personal style, his essays were winning him attention, and in 1890 his only novel, *The Picture of Dorian Gray*, was published, first in serial and then in book form, to be promptly attacked as immoral. Even before his lecture tour in America, his first play, *Vera*, had opened and failed. A second play, *The Duchess of Padua*, was also no success, but in 1892 his genius shone forth in *Lady Windermere's Fan*. At this time, George Bernard Shaw (1856–1950) was a relatively obscure journalist, writing novels that were either not published or little read when they were, but slowly building fame as a socialist lecturer and perceptive music critic.

Wilde followed the success of *Lady Windermere's Fan* with three other comedies. These were *A Woman of No Importance* (1893), *An Ideal Husband* (1895), and his most popular and classic comedy, *The Importance of Being Earnest* (1895). Before these had won him fame, his play *Salomé*, written in French, had won him notoriety. Sarah Bernhardt was to appear in it when the English censor barred it from the stage because it dealt with Biblical characters.

The English translation of *Salomé* was done by Lord Alfred Douglas, a young aristocrat with whom Wilde took up in 1891 and who was to bring about his downfall. Before this, Wilde had been indulging his homosexuality with street louts and stable boys, likening it to "feasting with panthers," because the danger heightened the excitement. The Marquis of Queensberry, Lord Alfred Douglas's father, tried to break up the attachment between Wilde and his overbearing, egotistical son. His harassment drove Wilde to sue him for libel and when the suit failed, Wilde found himself open to arrest and criminal prosecution. A hung jury ended the first trial but a second jury found Wilde guilty of homosexual practices. He was sentenced to two years' imprisonment at hard labor. Found bankrupt while in jail, he emerged impoverished in 1897. While in jail he wrote *De Profundis*, a long recriminatory letter to Lord Alfred Douglas, and while in exile on the continent, living first in Italy and Paris under the name of Sebastian Melmoth, he wrote "The Ballad of Reading Gaol," his most famous poem. The name Sebastian Melmoth, there is good reason to believe, was chosen by him with deliberation. Sebastian was the Christian martyr who was tied to a pillar and then used as a target by bowmen trying not to hit a vital part in order to prolong the torture. In Reading Gaol the prison garb was gray cloth printed with black arrows. Melmoth came from *Melmoth the Wanderer*, the most celebrated novel by the Dublin clergyman-eccentric Charles Maturin, whom Wilde claimed as his grand-uncle. The arrows of outrageous fortune had driven Wilde to wander the continent. His letters from this time show that his literary powers had not diminished and that his wit was intact, but he composed nothing.

"I am dying beyond my means," he told his friends. To this day the scandal and social aspects of his life have delayed first-rate scholars in critical appraisal of his literary work. He told André Gide that he had put his genius into his life and his talent into his writings. His conversation was the conversation of genius, the peculiarly Celtic thing about him, and Walter Pater was to say of his writings that they had always "the quality of the good talker." What he had done was to go to the opposite pole from the Young Irelanders and to carry Yeats's dictum to extremes: "If one loves Art at all," Wilde said, "one must love it beyond all other things in that world, and against such love, the reason, if one listened to it, would cry out. There is nothing sane about the worship of beauty. It is too splendid to be sane. Those of whose lives it forms the dominant note will always seem to the world to be pure visionaries." O'Leary would have said to him that there are not only things a man must not do to save a nation there are things he must not do in the name of art. By 1900 Wilde was dead, but we cannot say the English-oriented Anglo-Irish tradition died with him.

In the great Anglo-Irish tradition, even then withering, stands William Edward Hartpole Lecky (1838–1903), a historian of first rank, whose major works are a *History of England in the Eighteenth Century* (1878–1890) and a *History of the Rise and Influence of the Spirit of Rationalism in Europe* (1865).

Lecky was born in Newtown near Dublin and educated at Trinity College. His father had been an Anglo-Irish landowner and throughout his academic career and his years in parliament, where he represented the university, he was pro-Irish but anti-home rule. He was trained for the Irish church but turned to literature. His first work was *The Religious Tendencies of the Age*, which was published anonymously in 1860. His second effort, *The Leaders of Public Opinion in Ireland*, appeared in 1861, also anonymously. Two years later he published an essay entitled *The Declining Sense of the Miraculous*, which won him a good deal of attention and set the tone for his famous history of the influence of rationalism. Four years after that came his *History of European Morals from Augustus to Charlemagne*. All attempt a naturalistic explanation of the religious beliefs and practices of the centuries and seek to demonstrate the natural evolution of Western ethics and morals.

Outraged by the bias of James Anthony Froude, an English historian (whom the Irish-Americans in Boston were to stone), Lecky produced his most celebrated work, *A History of England in the Eighteenth Century*, which in its final form contained seven volumes on England and five on Ireland. The work is, where Ireland is concerned, remarkably objective for one who might be expected to have a Unionist bias, but Lecky has been deemed a fair and impartial historian, concerned with his Irish heritage, seeking to regard the evolution of political and other institutions from social and economic viewpoints. His work is said to have made a home-ruler of Gladstone if it did not do it for himself.

Lecky traveled on the continent, married Elizabeth van Dedem, who was a lady-in-waiting to the Queen of the Netherlands, served in the House of Commons, and died in London full of honors.

In the old Ascendancy manner, the remarkable writing team of Edith Anna Oenone Somerville (1858–1949) and Martin Ross, a pen name for her second cousin, Violet Florence Martin (1862–1915), heirs to the tradition of Lover and Lever, contributed much to the Irish novel. They drew cruelly accurate pictures of Irish society in their day. Because of their pejorative characterizations, the collaborators were very popular in England but disliked in Ireland, particularly by the Irish nationalists. They knew the Irish people, however, and portrayed them skillfully, and they knew Dublin well, where Miss Martin had been educated. Their first work, *An Irish Cousin*, appeared in 1889, written by Miss Martin and illustrated by Miss Somerville, who, however, was to be the dominant member of the writing team, and who, after the death of her cousin, would continue to sign both names to her creations, claiming she was in touch with her partner through the Ouija board. Among their fourteen books the most popular are *The Real Charlotte* (1894) and *Some Experiences of an Irish R.M.* (1899) and its sequels. Miss Somerville was a horsewoman, a master of foxhounds, and she published a hunting anthology, *Notes of the Horn*. Miss Martin also rode to the hounds and was invalided after a fall from her horse.

More in the swelling current of the new nationalism, yet apart from it, were the novels of the Reverend Patrick A. Sheehan (1852–1913), which were extremely popular in Catholic circles. The three best known are *My New Curate, The Blindness of Dr. Gray*, and *Luke Delmege*. Closer to the resurgence stirring the land was *The Graves at Kilmorna*, which deals with the Fenians and sees them, as indeed many of them were, martyrs to a dream of national independence which they knew their deaths could not make palpable but would keep alive.

X I

The last decade of the nineteenth century was one of preparation for George Bernard Shaw (1856–1950), who was born in Dublin, attended a Methodist school, and went to work at the age of sixteen as a clerk. He was not yet twenty and pretty much self-educated when he determined on a career as a writer. His mother, who was a musician, more or less supported him by teaching music and took him to London with her in 1876 when she went there to be near her music teacher. Shaw remained with her until he married in 1895. He wrote five novels, either unpublished or unsuccessful, including *Cashel Byron's Profession* (1886), which would be turned into a play, and *The Unsocial Socialist*, which was his first novel, published in 1887 as a book. In 1885 he caught on as a book reviewer for the *Pall Mall Gazette* and then as art critic on the *World* (1886–1888), and then as a music critic, first on the *Star* (1888–1890), and then on the *World* (1890–94), but would not make a splash until as drama critic on *The Saturday Review*, under the editorship of Frank Harris, another Irishman, beginning in 1895, his excoriation of the current theater won him a reputation. In 1892, his own play *Widowers' Houses*, an attack on slum landlordism, foundered in two nights, and his great days as playwright would not come until after the turn of the century. His talent was annealing in London while the Irish revival churned at home.

At the heart of the strength of that revival as much as anything else was the Gaelic League, which was founded in 1893. By the 1880s the Irish language was fast dying out in Ireland. The ancient, indigenous tongue was not taught in the schools, and in Dublin a person could spend half a lifetime and never hear a word of Gaelic. The famine had hit hardest the Gaeltacht, the name given to the Irish-speaking sections of the country, and all who faced emigration or dreamed of it felt compelled to learn English if only to read the help-wanted advertisements when they went abroad. The situation was so bad that the Irish tongue as a spoken language was in danger of disappearing altogether, as, indeed, Cornish has.

Against this background and stimulated by the tonics distilled by Davis on the one hand and Ferguson on the other, three scholars joined to form the league. They were Douglas Hyde (1860–1949), Eoin MacNeill (1867–1945), later professor of early Irish history at University College, Dublin, who first suggested the idea, and the Reverend Eoghen O'Growney (1863–1899), who taught the Irish language at Maynooth, the Catholic seminary, and wrote the outstanding textbooks for its study. He would later edit the league's publication, the *Gaelic Journal*, which, significantly, had to be written in English as well as Irish. There existed also a Society for the Preservation of the Irish Language, but it had become inanimate as a result of minor disputes. Thus it was the intention of the founders of the Gaelic League that it should not become politicized, that it should not become a party instrument, as had the Gaelic Athletic Association, formed some years earlier. For twenty years they were able to keep it pure, and during that time it would attract, stimulate, and inspire a large number of writers.

The movement became first fashionable and then extremely popular, and it had the ecumenical thrust that Davis had so hungered for. In the same year the league was formed Yeats wrote *The Celtic Twilight*, giving a name to a mystic mood that he would tire of. *The Celtic Dawn* would have been a more appropriate title. In that same year Douglas Hyde published his *The Love Songs of Connacht*, a pioneer work of translation and a literary landmark. By this time the dimensions of the ferment were forming in sufficient focus for W. P. Ryan (1867–1942), journalist and critic, to write *The Irish Literary Revival*, and so give it a name, and the *New Ireland Review* was founded. Dublin's electric air acquired an unprecedented amperage.

The aims of the Gaelic League were already being achieved in part even as it was formed. Its purpose was the preservation of Irish as the national language, and consequently the broadening of its use as a spoken everyday speech, and the publication of Irish texts old and new, that is, the creation of a modern Irish literature. One major boost to the first and last aims was given by the Reverend Peter Leary (1839–1918), a native of Cork, whose *Seadna*, a novel (for want of a better word) written in Irish, appeared in serial form in the *Gaelic Journal*. With this and other of his writings he helped give Gaelic a modern idiom. Besides his fiction, Father Leary translated the Gospels and published an Irish rendition of *The Imitation of Christ*, which became one of the most popular books of devotion in Irish, its Augustinian strictures at that moment nicely suiting the history-induced gloom of the Irish nature. Leary's own writings are marked occasionally by moralizing, and his translations by unconscionable bowdlerizing. His contribution to the popularization of Irish, however, was enormous and gives him a preeminent position in the movement.

Almost equal in influence to Douglas Hyde and, indeed, a forerunner of him was Dr. George Sigerson (1836–1925), like Wilde's father a physician as well as a man of letters, whose home was a literary salon after the manner of Lady Morgan's. As early as 1860 his translations had appeared, and his *The Bards of the Gael and the Gall* (1897) had wide popularity. He was chosen to give the inaugural lecture to the Irish National Literary Society in 1892, and while neither his scholarship nor his poetic gift was as strong as those in Douglas Hyde, he, nevertheless, also played a major role in reviving interest, popular interest, in Irish poetry.

While some were insisting that any Irish literature had to be written in Irish, Yeats, as we have seen, was insisting that a genuinely and uniquely Irish literature could be written in English. The two major collaborators who would join him to prove him right were Lady Augusta Gregory (1852–1932) and John Millington Synge (1871–1909), and, as many critics have said of them, it is impossible to discuss them separately.

Isabella Augusta Persse was born in Galway and grew up there a typical daughter of the Protestant Ascendancy with numerous brothers devoted to riding raucously to the hounds and shooting snipe and woodcock throughout the countryside. Her little pony Shamrock would become more famous than any of their mounts, but her literary career would not begin until after she had been widowed. Her husband was William Gregory, a landowner and member of parliament, whom she married in 1880, and it is as Lady Gregory that she is famous. His work as governor of Ceylon took her there and to India and other distant parts of the world, but in 1892 he died leaving her with a son, whom she sent off to Harrow. But the son returned, evidently with homesickness in his heart, and with some sense of the Irish revival in his soul. With his mother, he set out to learn the Irish language. Lady Gregory had been brought up with a household of Irish servants and was familiar with their gift of storytelling and vaguely with the continent of mythology and culture that lay behind their humble creativity. To learn Irish, she borrowed books from a neighbor and friend, Edward Martyn (1849–1923), an extraordinary figure, an aristocrat and a contemporary of hers, like her a wealthy landowner, but a Catholic, and a musician, who, with her, would become famous as a playwright. On reading *Love Songs of Connacht*, which brought to book some of the oral tradition of the Irish which was all around her, and *The Celtic Twilight*, a collection of Irish folklore which gathered "the simplest and most unforgettable thoughts of the generation," Lady Gregory invited the authors, Hyde and Yeats, to Coole Park, her Galway estate. There in the summer of 1896 Yeats first met Lady Gregory and, as he later wrote, "when I went to Coole the curtain had fallen on the first act of my drama." Until this time, the Irish revival dealt almost solely in poetry and the prose recounting of myths. Drama was on Yeats's mind. When the literary movement was launched, the general Irish public were not habitual readers. They had been denied books too long. Yeats dreamed now to put something on the stage because he felt the orators and priests had at least made the Irish people intelligent listeners. Lady Gregory brought him to Martyn, whom he had not met before, and the three of them in 1898 planned and initiated the Irish national theater.

Lady Gregory's contribution to that theater would be immense, and some would say she *was* the Abbey. She wrote or translated more than forty plays, offered management, direction, encouragement, guidance, patronage, and criticism. She most graciously lent Yeats money he did not need to pay back (but did) and she aided the impoverished Sean O'Casey, who treated her badly in return. Her plays won the ironic criticism of some Dubliners, and the language in them, which she adapted after the peasant speech of the west, is still referred to (sometimes sarcastically) as Kiltartanese, taking a name from a village on the great estate at Coole, but as stagecraft it worked and still works. It was she also who insisted, when Yeats would have turned to London, that the place for a national Irish theater was Ireland, and that Dublin must be the site.

It was Yeats who first broached to Lady Gregory the subject of forming an Irish theater. Edward Martyn soon became the third collaborator. He had had already two plays published, *Maeve* and *The Heather Field*, and the latter was about to be produced in Germany. Instead, it was decided to open the Irish theater with it. For a companion piece, the three elected Yeats's *The Countess Cathleen*. A fourth figure was destined to play an important part in the formation and launching of this theater group. He was the novelist George Moore (1852–1933), a native of Mayo, who, having failed as a painter in Paris, was supporting himself by his writings in London. He was a friend of Martyn's, the two, as Yeats was to say, bound together by mutual contempt. Martyn was somewhat stuffy and clerical-minded, a Catholic filled with Protestant scruples; while Moore, born a Catholic and a renegade, had neither manners nor morals. He wrote such bitter things about Martyn in his celebrated memoir *Hail and Farewell* that their friendship finally foundered. At this moment he was intent on helping. To get professional actors one had to go to London and rehearsals on both plays began there. Moore, Lady Gregory recorded (she didn't like him), was very helpful in getting actors. Moore claims he saved the whole project from disaster, worked his head off in a number of ways, and got the company off to Dublin, notoriety, success, and prosperity.

Before the plays got off the ground, before the curtain rose, protests alleging that *The Countess Cathleen* (she sells her soul to the devil for the sake of her starving tenants) was blasphemous were voiced in Dublin. A pamphlet by Frank Hugh O'Donnell, a Dublin writer and would-be playwright, attacked it, and Cardinal Logue, having read only the extracts in the pamphlet, pronounced that only a Catholic deficient in religion and patriotism could tolerate the play. Martyn, devout as ever, wanted to resign, but Yeats was determined that his play, which had the Countess Cathleen apotheosized for selling her soul to ransom those of the peasants, would be staged and not be made the occasion for political demonstrations. He found two priests who approved it as a work of art and then called in the constabulary to prevent any outbursts. *The Countess Cathleen* with May Whitty (later Dame May Whitty) in the title role was performed in the Antient Concert Rooms in what is now Pearse Street and the Irish Literary Theatre was launched on May 8, 1899. Dublin was polarized, it seems, between the pros and the cons. The audience which saw the play on opening night rose to its feet at the curtain, the vast majority applauding or shouting praise, a minority hissing protest. Yeats responded to a curtain call and shook hands with May Whitty and Florence Farr, and was able to telegraph George Moore that the evening had been a success.

The next night, Martyn's play, *The Heather Field*, a drama of a mismarriage that ends with the mental collapse of the idealistically minded husband, was presented and met with popular approval and critical kudos because of its basic spirituality. *The Irish Times*, which was wrong about *The Countess Cathleen*, was also wrong about *The Heather Field*, faulting, as it did, both. Sometime later Martyn's second play, *Maeve*, met with even greater success, for the nationalistically-minded found comfort in it, much to the surprise of Martyn and Yeats. The play deals with a young woman half deranged by love of Ireland's heroic past and the prospect of a marriage of convenience to an Englishman she doesn't love. That she was unhappy at marrying an Englishman to save her father's already diminished fortunes was not what caught the crowd's ear as much as what amounted to a throw-away line by an oracular old crone—"You think I am only an old woman, but I tell you that Eire can never be subdued." That won loud applause. At the first opportunity the audience rose and sang patriotic songs, including "The Wearing of the Green," and some in Irish.

But Martyn and Yeats were at cross-purposes. Yeats wanted a poetic folk theater while Martyn was taking his inspiration from the middle class and Henrik Ibsen, whose realism was fashionable at the time, in great part due to the enthusiasm of George Bernard Shaw. Yeats was the one who was experimental and disturbing, and while Martyn departed, Yeats's dream would not triumph but was altered by the genius of others.

Moore and Martyn collaborated on a play, as did Moore and Yeats. The first was *The Bending of the Bough*, dealing with Irish tax problems, and the second, *Diarmuid and Grania*, dealing with an old pagan romance. The latter was produced in 1901, the year Moore decided to return to Ireland from London. His move was most significant, a tribute to the strength and vitality and lure of the revival, and although Moore returned to England in 1911, what he found in Ireland provided the material for his most memorable work, *Hail and Farewell* (1911–1914), an autobiographical trilogy recounting, in vivid detail and with a spendid lack of accuracy, his experiences in Dublin at this time. His years in Ireland resulted in two other books, *The Untilled Field* (1903), a collection of short stories, and *The Lake* (1905), a poetic novella. All his Irish work was in contrast with the writing he had done in London and the equal of it, although his novels, *Esther Waters* and *A Mummer's Wife*, had won him a reputation as a realist and a groundbreaker in English literature. He was also the first distinguished Irish writer since Swift to make a name for himself in London and then return to Ireland to find his true genius and greatness.

The literary activity of the decade beginning in 1899 with the founding of Yeats's Irish Literary Theatre is so complex, comprehensive, and exciting that it is impossible to limn it all. Any outline would be a confusing tabulation of titles and authors. The intellectual excitement was intense, not in Dublin alone, but throughout Ireland, and in England and the English-speaking world. Max Beerbohm, the celebrated English critic, came over from England at the very beginning to comment favorably. John Quinn, the New York attorney famous as a patron and collector of the literary memorabilia of T. S. Eliot, James Joyce, and others, came to Dublin to observe, and of course, all the players would travel to England and to the United States. Later on, Quinn would defend the players in a Philadelphia court and win acquittal for them from an absurd charge of conducting an immoral performance.

In 1900, the theater movement presented its second series of plays, including *The Bending of the Bough*, which, though presented as a middle-class comedy in five acts by George Moore, was Moore's rewrite of Martyn's original play entitled *The Tale of a Town*. Two nights later, on February 22, 1900, two plays were presented, Martyn's *Maeve*, with the attendant jingoist demonstration, and Alice Milligan's *The Last Feast of the Fianna*. Miss Milligan (1866–1953) was a remarkable literary figure, a poet, novelist, playwright, and journalist. She was born in County Tyrone and educated at the Methodist College in Belfast, and in London, but was an Irish nationalist all the way. Under the pseudonym Iris Olkryn, she contributed to a number of Dublin journals, including Griffith's *Sinn Fein*, and then founded her own, the *Shan Van Vocht*. Many of her ballads were set to music by her sister. Her novel, *A Royal Democrat*, appeared in 1892, and her biography of Wolfe Tone in 1898. She collaborated with her scholar father, S. F. Milligan, an antiquarian, on *Glimpses of Erin*. Another play of hers, *The Daughter of Donagh*, was presented some years later. Her play *The Last Feast of the Fianna* was the first in the Irish Literary Theatre to take Irish history and legend for its subject, but the newspapers reported the audience as "wretchedly small." Although she hoped the play would be translated into Irish and performed in that language, the first play in Irish ever to be performed publicly was Douglas Hyde's *The Twisting of the Rope*, in which he himself acted a leading role with exuberant flair. The year was 1901, and the Gaiety Theatre was rented for the occasion. The same evening, October 21, the Yeats-Moore collaboration *Diarmuid and Grania* was performed with Frank R. Benson as Diarmuid and his wife as Grania. The play was not a hit, and Hyde's Gaelic play received the plaudits, effusively given by those Dublin papers that ascribed to the revival of Irish. They praised the play, the actors, the way the language was used, and the language as a dramatic instrument.

Besides the activity of the Irish Literary Theatre, there was, of course, in Dublin other literary excitement. In the year 1901, Stopford A. Brook and T. W. Rolleston (to whom Moore had dedicated *Esther Waters*) published *A Treasury of Irish Poetry*, and a young man named James Joyce made his first impact on the Dublin scene with his reading of a paper, *Drama and Life*, at the Literary and Historical Society. The rising political figure of the hour was Arthur Griffith (1872–1922), who that year took over the editorial leadership of *The United Irishman*, which had been founded two years before. Griffith despaired of winning Irish independence either by constitutional means at Westminster or by armed insurrection against British military forces. He urged a policy of massive resistance plus boycott of English goods (shades of Swift) and withdrawal of association with all things English. He railed against British recruitment of Irish soldiers and when Queen Victoria, nearing her end, visited Ireland he spoke of her coming "in her dotage . . . to seek recruits for her battered army." Yeats and AE, as well as Alice Milligan and other major literary figures, contributed to his paper, and did so without payment, for Griffith was without funds and lived in impoverished asceticism. He became the first president of the Irish Free State, the government that preceded the present Irish Republic. He proved a better statesman than drama critic, but it is the peculiar mark of Dublin that its statesmen are sufficiently au courant with literary activity to make such public judgments at all.

The 1901 drama series was presented by Yeats and Lady Gregory. Martyn had withdrawn because of Yeats's insistence on "peasant plays," while Martyn's concerns were more with the middle class. His withdrawal this time was final, although his plays would be presented by other groups in Ireland. James Joyce (1882–1941) had praised the Irish Literary Theatre at first for exposing and opposing the "sterility and falsehood" of the theater of London, but that fall he denounced it for catering to "the rabblement," by its insularity, a criticism not too far removed from that of Martyn, and one the philistines applauded in order to beat the Irish Literary Theatre with as many sticks as possible. Joyce was still a student at the university at this time and did not meet Yeats and AE until the following year when his essay on Mangan won him increased attention and respect.

In December of 1901, a sort of preview of AE's play *Deirdre* was performed by a group headed by the Fay brothers, William G. and Frank, who for ten years had been connected with the world of the Dublin theater, drama schools, and semi-professional and professional productions. The two Fays, natives of

Dublin, taught elocution and stagecraft, performed themselves, and managed about ten productions a year in halls and clubs throughout Dublin and the countryside. In 1898, they formed the Ormonde Dramatic Society and performed a number of worthless comedies until in December, 1901, at the Coffee Palace theater they undertook AE's *Deirdre*. Evidently it was through AE that the Fays met Lady Gregory and Yeats, who later connived against them. Never was there a happier marriage of genius, short-lived though it was.

AE, George William Russell (1867–1935), who had been at the Metropolitan School of Art with Yeats, was born in Lurgan in County Armagh, began his career as a clerk in a draper's shop, but at the age of thirty began to organize agricultural cooperatives. Like Yeats, he made his reputation as a writer rather than a painter but he continued to paint pictures of a theosophically mystical sort, landscapes with fairies dancing like Grecian figures. He was, like Yeats, a firm believer in the spirit world and its palpability, and his poetry and prose as well as his paintings reflect this bent. In 1899 he joined the Irish Agricultural Organization Society and in 1904 became editor of its journal, *The Homestead*, which was concerned chiefly with Ireland's ongoing question of land reform. As early as 1894, his first book of poetry appeared, *Homeward: Songs by the Way*, and more would follow. Two of his political works are *Cooperatives and Nationality* (1912) and *The National Being* (1916). Russell was a saintly man in many ways (and a bit of a bigot) who made his home a salon for writers. As an influence on the young, he rivaled Yeats. Like Moore, Joyce, and others he left Ireland but not wholly because of intransigent politics, clericalism, and attendant intolerance, but because of the loss of his wife and his declining influence. Russell was brought into the agricultural work by Sir Horace Plunkett (1854–1932), a Unionist M.P. from Dublin, who spent many years in Wyoming because of his health. He was an author as well as a politician and reformer and two of his books are *Ireland in the New Century* (1904) and *The Rural Life Problems of the United*

States (1910). One of his last works was *The Interpreters* a fascinating reflection on government.

AE's *Deirdre* was his only work for the theater. After the December preview, it was given a full-scale production in April, 1902, along with Yeats's *Cathleen ni Houlihan*, in which Maud Gonne took the title role. The two plays were produced by the Fay company, called the Irish National Dramatic Company, in St. Teresa's Hall on Clarendon Street. Maud Gonne was sensational in the leading role of Yeats's most nationalistic play, and the two performances were determinative in the Fays' deciding to form a permanent repertory group producing only Irish plays. Yeats was asked to be president and the next year, the Irish National Theatre Society was formed, a combination of the Irish Literary Theatre and the Fays. Frederick Ryan was secretary, a playwright who would die too soon; AE was a vicepresident, along with Maud Gonne and Douglas Hyde; W. G. Fay was stage manager. They hired a hall on Lower Camden Street, behind a warehouse, ill-lighted and drafty, with no room backstage. Several plays were staged in the fall of 1902, and in the following year, the Irish National Theatre Society performed in Molesworth Street. There, they had a stage twelve feet deep instead of six, and two dressing rooms, whereas at Camden Street they dressed in the wings. They opened their season in March with *The Hour-Glass* by Yeats and a play by Lady Gregory, *Twenty-Five*, and in between plays, Yeats, as requested by the Fays, lectured. In September of the same year they produced Yeats's play *The King's Threshold*. In this play Yeats turned to the great sagas, as Miss Milligan had already done. So, too, Lady Gregory, who published in 1902 her *Cuchulain of Muirthemne*, a narrative of the majestic pagan hero written in her peasant prose.

In October, 1903, the trend of the Irish theater was to be immortally altered, for that month saw the first Synge play. The centrality of Yeats to the Irish revival is seen again in the career of John Millington Synge (1871–1909). As Yeats had started out to study painting, so Synge began with music. He

J. M. Synge

was born at 2 Newtown Villas, Rathfarnham, near Dublin, and began the study of the violin in the city before entering Trinity College. He furthered his music studies at the Royal Academy of Music and became proficient enough to play in its orchestra and win a scholarship. His continued interest took him to the continent in his early twenties, but the itch to write was in his skin. He took off for Paris to try his hand at writing but not with the intent of abandoning his Irish heritage because he also pursued his study of Gaelic.

In 1896, he met Yeats in Paris and soon was told by the poet to go back to Ireland and find his subjects there, to go to the Aran Islands and to listen and to observe. Synge, who had twice been rejected by a woman he loved, and was already ill with Hodgkin's disease, but innocent of its inevitable consequences, did as Yeats bade him. In retrospect, Yeats recorded his advice in these words: "Give up Paris. You will never create anything by reading Racine, and Arthur Symons will always be a better critic of French literature. Go to the Aran Islands. Live there as if you were one of the people themselves; express a life that has never found expression."

Synge's first visit to the islands was made in May, 1898, and he was to return for varying periods in the next four years, having made five trips in all, filling his notebooks, observing, and listening to the gulls with as much attention as he gave the inhabitants, and charming the natives with his tunes on the penny whistle. Synge is now acknowledged by many as the second genius of the Irish revival, next to Yeats, and the equal of O'Casey, and its greatest lyrical dramatic genius; and he had the stuff of romance and tragedy woven into his life. (The name, incidentally, is pronounced Sing and was thrust on one of his Millington ancestors by King Henry VIII, who had liked the forebear's voice.)

In 1901, Synge, or "the man who is staying at Patrick Mc-Donagh's," as he was known to the islanders, finished his book, *The Aran Islands*, only to have it rejected by Grant Richards, the publisher. In the same year, Lady Gregory spurned his play

When the Moon Has Set. Synge, however, was in a swirl of creativity, writing not only numerous plays, but critical articles for a variety of journals, and his first stage production was not far off. In Dublin, at that time particularly, controversy lay in wait for every genius. When his play *In the Shadow of the Glen* was produced the same night as Yeats's *The King's Threshold*, a storm broke about his head, a storm minor to what would come later. A discerning minority, however, sensed that the Irish National Theatre Society had found another genius.

The play was denounced as an affront to Irish womanhood, a travesty on the mores of the good people of Ireland, an insult to the race. In it, an old man pretends death in order to test the fidelity of his young wife, who, in the end, runs off with a tramp. Arthur Griffith in *The United Irishman* condemned the play as "a lie" and declared with the literal-mindedness that is ever the foe of art, and which Cardinal Logue had displayed earlier, that "all of us know that Irish women are the most virtuous in the world" and "in no country are women so faithful to their marriage bonds as in Ireland." The young Irish theater came under fire for being at once "too national" and "not national enough," for being insular and too cosmopolitan, too simple and too sophisticated. Lecky, the historian, who was a member of the board, withdrew because of the exaggerated nationalism of Yeats and Lady Gregory.

In 1904 (the same year that James Joyce left Ireland) the society's problem over suitable quarters was solved when Miss Annie Elizabeth Fredericka Horniman (1860–1937), an English heiress to a tea fortune, who had been secretary to Yeats for a while, in response to a public appeal by him for a donation, responded simply, "I will give you a theater." In 1903, the Dublin company had taken five plays to London, one of them *The Laying of the Foundations* by Fred Ryan (1870–1912), who was secretary to the society. Their performances incited the interest of Miss Horniman, who was a leading force in England at the time in the advancement of repertory theaters.

She was no stranger to the troupe, of course, for besides her friendship with Yeats, she had sat backstage at the Camden Street quarters stitching costumes. True to her pledge, she bought for the company and renovated the Mechanics Institute Theatre in Abbey Street and the adjoining City Morgue (which had been a bank) in Marlborough Street. Thus, the Abbey was born.

On December 27, 1904, the first productions in the theater were staged under the direction of the Fay brothers. The plays were Lady Gregory's peasant comedy *Spreading the News* and Yeats's tragedy *On Baile's Strand*, which deals with one version of the death of Cuchulain. When it was published he dedicated it to Frank Fay because "of the beautiful fantasy of his playing in the character of the Fool." The theater had found native actors and actresses worthy of its dramas. Among them that opening night was Sara Allgood, who won international fame, and whose sister Molly (Maire O'Neill) became the fiancée of Synge. She had a walk-on part the next year (1905) when his *The Well of the Saints* was performed and later starred in *Playboy* and *Deirdre*.

Another major figure had now appeared on the Dublin scene, Padraic Colum (1881–1972), who had Gaelicized his English name, Patrick Colm. Whereas Synge was the youngest child of a family of eight, Colum was the oldest of a family of seven. His father was master of a workhouse and a stationmaster, and Padraic followed his father into the railway system. His work took him to Dublin, and he began, there, to write poetry and plays. As early as 1903 a play of his, *Broken Soil*, was mounted at Molesworth Hall.

In 1905, his play *The Land* was produced at the Abbey, along with *The Building Fund*, the work of another new playwright, William Boyle (1853–1922). By this time Colum had quit the civil service and was devoting himself full-time to his writing. He later became one of the most prolific writers of the revival.

When Miss Horniman bought the theater a thank-you note

was sent to her, signed by W. B. Yeats, F. J. Fay, William G. Fay, James S. Starkey, Frank Walker, Udolphus Wright, Miss Garoby, Vera Esposito, Dora L. Annesley, George Roberts, Douglas Hyde, Thomas E. Keohler, Harry F. Norman, Helen S. Laird, G. Russell, Miss Walker, J. M. Synge, Sara Allgood, Frederick Ryan, and Padraic Colum. Later they had more reason to be grateful to her, for she gave them eight hundred pounds a year to cover salaries. Her presence and presents however caused difficulties, and finally she withdrew in pique. Lady Gregory, who was fifty years old when she began her literary career, was now making major contributions to the repertory, and in 1905, when Synge's *The Well of the Saints* was produced, two of her plays, *Kincora* and *The White Cockade*, were performed, and the following year three more. Boyle, a civil servant and a political figure, friend to Parnell and his successor John Redmond, an authority on the writings of James Mangan, also had two more of his plays presented, *The Eloquent Dempsey* and *The Mineral Workers.*

It was on January 26, 1907, a Saturday night, when Synge's masterpiece, *The Playboy of the Western World*, was performed at the Abbey with William Fay as Christy Mahon; Maire O'Neill, Synge's fiancée, as Pegeen Mike; and Sara Allgood, her sister, as the Widow Quin. That first performance passed off without too much trouble until the third act, when, as Lady Gregory wired Yeats, the "Audience broke up in disorder at the word 'shift.' " There was no performance on Sunday, but Monday night the philistines had mobilized. Forty men, more or less, made a block in the audience, bent on disruption, and although Synge summoned the police, the uproar was such that the players could not be heard from start to finish. The men had tin horns to supplement their hooting, hissing, and catcalling. The next night was little better. Yeats came from Scotland, where he had been lecturing, and he and Lady Gregory persisted, realizing they were in a death struggle with "mob censorship." They were not the only Irish company to be so challenged. Popeyed Irish Nationalists, salivating in rage elsewhere in the country, had either barred performances of various plays or prevented audiences from attending. The Abbey won the fight. The *Playboy* was not barred from the stage and at week's end won applause. Four years later, on an American tour, it received worse treatment in New York City from Irish-American audiences, whose romantic view of the "Ould Counthry" could not tolerate the hilarious, poetic realism of Synge. Potatoes and even watches were hurled at the players in New York and police threw demonstrators into the streets. In Philadelphia narrow-minded clerics combined with an out-raged liquor dealer to bring the Abbey players into court. The courtroom scene had some of the comic qualities of the plays the protestors were denouncing. Attorney John Quinn managed to get one priest-witness to admit that even in Ireland the word "God" was sometimes used as a profane expletive and not confined to prayers and blessings. The episode was merely another instance of a blind nationalism seeking to subvert not merely art but truth to its service. Chicago's city council might have sought to ban the performance of The *Playboy* if it had not been for William Dillon, the brother of the Fenian patriot, whose calmer judgment prevailed. Two years later, Lady Gregory recounted the story in her memoir, *Our Irish Theatre*, a pleasant, personal book, and quite reliable although she be-lieved "Newhaven" and Yale University were in Massachusetts.

The year of Synge's triumph was the year of his physical decline. He had earlier been operated on for swollen glands in his neck. Now he was operated on again, but also became aware of a swelling in his side, the tumor that told him his hope of life was fading. In 1908 he was again under the knife and it was determined that the new tumor was inoperable. The next year he was dead.

His *The Aran Islands* had appeared and a book of his poetry had been accepted for publication by the Cuala Press, which was run by Yeats's sisters, Lolly and Lily. Synge also had lived to hear of the success of his plays before audiences in London and Oxford and even on the continent. Left unfinished at the time of his death was his *Deirdre of the Sorrows*. It was produced by Maire O'Neill at the Abbey the next year.

What the passage of the years has shown is the essential Irishness of Synge, the man and his work, for, if he disappointed Yeats by dissipating the mists of the Celtic twilight, he proved, above all others, including Yeats, that there is an English-language literature that is quintessentially Irish. To the discerning, it was no surprise that the hundredth anniversary of his birth, April 16, 1971, found the Irish nation rising in tribute to him and scholars from around the world traveling to Dublin to honor his memory and his work. In that year Harvard University Press in Cambridge, Massachusetts, published his *Letters to Molly: John Millington Synge to Maire O'Neill*, edited by Ann Saddlemyer, which reviewer Thomas McDonnell, literary editor of the Boston *Pilot*, founded by Irish exile John Boyle O'Reilly, proclaimed one of the most tender books of the century. The genius of the revival was still alive.

In the year that Synge died, the Abbey Theatre was involved in another conflict with attendant controversy. Lady Gregory undertook to present George Bernard Shaw's play *The Shewing-Up of Blanco Posnet*, which English censors had barred from performance in London. Shaw's spectacular career in the theater did not begin until after the death of Oscar Wilde in 1900. To be sure, he was, before that, a public figure, a popular platform lecturer, a friend of Sidney and Beatrice Webb and, like them, a leader of the Fabian socialist movement. Indeed, it was at the Webbs that he met his wife, Charlotte Payne-Townshend, an Irishwoman of fortune and liberal political views. They were married in 1898 and not until that year did Shaw leave his mother's home. He was then forty-two. He had reached the point also where he had abandoned his ambition to be a novelist and had turned playwright. His first novel to appear was *The Unsocial Socialist*, which ran as a serial in 1884. His most celebrated novel, *Cashel Byron's Profession*, also ran as a serial in the socialist monthly *Today*, in 1885–1886, and appeared in book form in the latter year. Two others were *The Irrational Knot* and *Love Among the Artists*. From 1886 on, for more than a decade, he worked as a critic (books, art, drama, music) for several publications. He was, in the main, self-educated and his music and theatrical experience began in the home. His mother sang in a number of operas and Shaw learned the scores listening to her rehearse. When she and her music teacher parted ways, Shaw would accompany her on the piano. His own acting experiences began in Dublin with a falsetto performance as Othello that turned high tragedy to comedy, but in England he appeared in a play, *Alone*, staged by the Fabians. In Dublin he had attended the variety of productions that came to the Gaiety, the Theatre Royal, and the Queen's Theatre and decades later could recall them vividly.

His first theatrical success as a playwright came in 1894, the year after *Widowers' Houses* closed. *Arms and the Man* was a theatrical delight and from then on the theater became his chief medium of expression and of social criticism. While the Abbey Theatre was rising in eminence and bringing playwright after playwright out of the Irish soil, Shaw was carrying on the tradition of Southerne, Sheridan, Goldsmith, Farquhar, Congreve, and Wilde by dominating the London stage. From 1904 to 1907 he was "house playwright" at the Court Theatre. But it was *Candida*, with Harley Granville-Barker starring, which began the brilliant runs at the Court which made him world famous.

From the beginning Shaw was as popular in America as in London, perhaps more so. *The Devil's Disciple* was performed in New York City, successfully, as early as 1897, aided no doubt by its American Revolutionary War setting. In 1906 his first great play, *Caesar and Cleopatra*, was put on at the Court, the year after, *Man and Superman*. His coruscating wit had by this time captivated England.

Shaw always thought of the Irish theater as "our theater," and London as "the English theater," and his play *John Bull's Other Island* was written specifically for the Abbey, although not produced there until long afterwards. But it was at the

Abbey that *The Shewing-Up of Blanco Posnet* was performed after being barred from the London stage. The incident was another milestone in the history of the Abbey and reflects nothing but credit on the courage of Lady Gregory and Yeats. Although Miss Horniman had been the financial backer of the Abbey Theatre, the patent for the theater could not be issued to her because she was English. From the beginning it was issued in the name of Lady Gregory. Now Dublin Castle, angered at the word that the Abbey Theatre was about to present a play in Dublin that had been barred as blasphemous in London, threatened her with retracting the patent. Despite the threat, and sensing that martyrdom loomed (Shaw promised to burn brighter than any of Foxe's martyrs if Dublin Castle dared interpose), Lady Gregory and Yeats produced the play. The house was jammed. Scores of enthusiasts came from London hoping to see the opening only to be disappointed because of the limitations of seating. The production was a success. The sky did not fall. Dublin Castle did nothing, perhaps because the laws of Ireland differed considerably from those in England, and no powers of censorship were specifically granted anyone. The play ended with the audience cheering. In fact, crowds in the street, not quite sure of the issue, but informed that English authority had been defied, took up the cheer.

Changes were altering the complexion of the Abbey, and a dominant figure, Lennox Robinson, was in the wings. A succession of lesser playwrights was adding their productions to the repertory, some successful, some less so. Among them were names distinguished in other arenas besides the theater: Seumas MacManus (who had gone off to establish a brilliant reputation in the United States); James Cousins; Wilfrid Scawen Blunt (an Englishman who would be imprisoned in Kilmainham Jail for anti-British activities); George Fitzmaurice, civil servant; W. F. Casey, who went off to London to help edit the *Times*; Daniel L. Kelleher, a schoolteacher turned travel writer; Norreys Connell, whose offerings were booked almost as much as Synge's; Seumas O'Kelly, close friend of Arthur Griffith and a

George Bernard Shaw (after the Karsh photograph)

distinguished short-story writer; Samuel Waddell, brother of
Helen Waddell, the celebrated Latinist, who wrote under the
pseudonym Rutherford Mayne; R. J. Brophy, who used the
pen name R. J. Ray, and dropped dead too, too young in the
streets of Dublin; Joseph Campbell, poet who would die in
poverty in the Wicklow Hills; and that strangest of originals,
Lord Dunsany.

Three of the more significant, however, were T. C. Murray
(1873–1959), St. John G. Ervine (1883–1971), and Lennox
Robinson (1886–1958). Ervine managed the Abbey briefly
and contributed some excellent plays, but Robinson was connected with it in one way or another for close to half a century.
In 1907, he had gone to see the performances there and had
been captivated. In 1908, his first play, *The Clancy Name*, was
produced there, to win denunciation from a benighted Irish
newspaper. The next week, *When the Dawn Is Come* was produced, a passionately nationalistic play by Thomas MacDonagh
(1878–1916), a poet and teacher (who had been a co-founder
with Martyn and Joseph Plunkett of the Irish Theatre). Both
signed the famous proclamation of the Irish Republic. Both
Plunkett and MacDonagh died before British firing squads
following the Easter Rising. Their deaths ended two literary
careers full of spectacular promise.

Under Robinson's management, Miss Horniman withdrew
her support. She was outraged that the Abbey had not closed
its doors in mourning for the death of King Edward VII, as
she had requested. Actually, her message never reached Robinson but explanations were futile. She, who had done so much
for the theater and without whose support it might never have
flourished, departed. The Abbey, however, by then was able to
stand on its own and went on to its successful international
tours.

Some of the troupe had left the Irish National Dramatic
Society when Miss Horniman had come in, fearing that what
had been a spontaneous Irish movement was now becoming a
commercial enterprise restricted in its freedom because of Eng-

lish backing. Others would also leave. Among the dissidents were Martyn, Colum, and the Fays.

When World War I came others departed. Momentous events were impending for Ireland and the world. At this point in the Abbey's history, the eve of World War I, we may well pause to consider the political situation. We can simplify the matter by stressing three figures, Arthur Griffith (1872–1922), John Redmond (1856–1918), and Sir Edward Henry Carson (1854–1935). The last was Dublin-born and in the great tradition of courtroom lawyers, a barrister of first rank, who was admitted to the Irish bar in 1877 on his graduation from Trinity. As a trial lawyer and superb advocate he was in the tradition of Curran, Plunkett, and Butt. A Protestant, he came to distrust the Irish home rule movement and would be its foremost opponent as a member of the House of Commons, although he took no political office until after 1900. Before that time he was perhaps the outstanding barrister in England, and it is one of the ironies of history that it was his devastating cross-examination of Oscar Wilde that led to the latter's conviction and disgrace—two Trinity men in intellectual combat! Throughout the earlier part of the twentieth century, because of the political leadership of John Redmond and the need of the Liberal party for Irish M.P. votes, home rule was becoming more and more a reality for Ireland. Prime Minister H. H. Asquith had eliminated the veto of the intransigent House of Lords, and home rule seemed imminent. Carson fought it desperately, threatened armed rebellion, and demanded that Ulster be exempt and so remain part of the United Kingdom.

Redmond, a member of parliament and the son of a member of parliament, who had as a boy clerked in the House of Commons, had an uncommon respect for the constitutional process. Both he and Griffith were disciples of Parnell. When Parnell died in 1891, however, his party split. The two factions in time reunited and Redmond was named the head of the so-called Irish Nationalist party, bent on home rule by constitutional progression. Griffith, a printer by trade, was virtually unknown at this time but became the spokesman for the Sinn Fein, which would eventually replace the Nationalist party as the dominant force. The outbreak of World War I ended the wrangling of these parties and imposed something of a truce. The situation, was, however, explosive, because volunteers, with differing views, were drilling in the north and the south, and both were seeking German guns.

Griffith's paper, *The United Irishman*, in 1906 changed its name to *Sinn Fein* (Irish for "ourselves alone") and in the next year appeared as a daily paper, albeit short-lived. Although he had opposed armed resistance to England, when he learned that Carson's volunteers were mustering in the north with German arms, he helped organize the Irish Volunteers. When the Easter Rising came, although he took no part, he was interned, but would return to Ireland to see the subsequent victory of the Sinn Fein. Before that, came the assassination at Sarajevo and World War I.

XII

The outbreak of World War I was traumatic for the literary history of Dublin as well as for its political history. The years immediately preceding World War I were made literarily bright in Dublin by the publication of the first volume of George Moore's greatest work, *Ave atque Vale*, which he had written in England after leaving Ireland for good, and by the founding of the *Irish Review* by Joseph Mary Plunkett (1887–1916), poet and son of a poet, who had worked with Edward Martyn and Padraic Colum in promoting the Irish Theatre, and who was one of the patriots executed as a result of the Easter Rising. In 1911, the year he founded the *Irish Review*, he also published a book of his own poetry, *The Circle and the Sword*.

In the next year, one of the most lovable of Irish writers made a scintillating appearance on the Dublin literary scene, James Stephens (1882–1950), a clerk in a law office. His famous book *The Crock of Gold*, which would be distorted into the musical comedy *Finian's Rainbow*, won him an international reputation. From 1912 until his death he published a succession of poems, essays, stories, and fantasies. Although he never topped *The Crock of Gold*, many critics deem *The Charwoman's Daughter*, which had preceded it by a year, to be its equal.

Like Sean O'Casey, who would come after him, Stephens came out of the Irish working class and had little formal education. It was AE who discovered and encouraged him, and helped him bring forth his first book, *Insurrections*, a volume of poetry, which appeared in 1909. In the same year that he published *The Crock of Gold*, he published a second book of verse, *The Hill of Vision*. Stephens was a dolichocephalic, lustrous-eyed gnome of a man, gentle by nature, with a surpassing love of animals. He helped Plunkett found the *Irish Review*, joined the Sinn Fein party, and dove into the seas of Irish mythology along with Yeats and the rest, and came up with his own version of the Deirdre legend. It was *The Crock of Gold*, however, that enabled him to leave the drudgery of the law office and seek his living by his pen. For a while he was the registrar at the National Gallery.

George Moore's second volume of *Hail and Farewell* appeared in 1912 with attendant sensation because of its gossipy nature. There would be a third volume later, and all three later would be published in two volumes. Yeats, of course, was continually publishing and had brought out *The Green Helmet and Other Poems* and had met his future wife, Georgie Hyde-Lees. Lady Gregory published *Our Irish Theatre*, which told the story of the beginnings of the Abbey Theatre, and Katharine Tynan Hinkson (1861–1931), who had been in O'Leary's circle with Yeats in the early days of the revival, and was now residing in England, published her *Twenty-Five Years*, which recounts those times and portrays its leading performers. Her reputation as a poet was then high and her literary work extremely varied. In 1893 she had married another Dublin author, H. A. Hinkson (1865–1919), and had gone to England with him when he was admitted to the bar there. In 1916, they returned to Ireland, three years before his death. Her husband had combined a literary career with the law and had written several novels, the last, *The Considine Luck*, in 1912. The lure of Dublin during this brilliant period took other writers from London, even as it took George Moore. Among these was the poet Joseph Campbell (1881–1944), who was born and educated in Ulster, and who turned like others with a knowledge of Irish to collecting and translating ancient songs and poems. His literary career took him to London, where he was secretary to the Irish National Literary Society. He had published three volumes of poems and songs before he made his way to Dublin, where the Abbey produced his play *Judgment* in 1912.

The previous year had seen the death in childbirth of Anna Johnston MacManus (1866–1911), who had made a slight literary reputation under the pen name Ethna Carbery, and with Alice Milligan had founded and edited the revivalist magazine *Shan Van Vocht*. Miss Johnston was the wife of Seumas Mac-Manus (1861–1960), who had written for the Abbey but whose literary reputation was made during a long career in America.

The impending world crisis fostered unrest in Dublin. As early as 1886, Protestants in Ulster, fearing that "home rule would mean Rome rule," had begun secretly to arm themselves, intent on resisting laws that would sever them from England. In that year, Gladstone's first home rule bill was defeated in the House of Commons. The London *Times* sought to destroy Parnell with forged documents only to have a special commission acquit him and the House of Commons rise to cheer his return. But by 1891 he was dead.

The great national revival then ensued, from the formation of the Gaelic Athletic Association to the Sinn Fein. John Redmond and John Dillon still hoped to win home rule by constitutional means, but Griffith opposed them and history was moving with him. In 1907, the year of the *Playboy* uproar, Thomas J. Clarke, a Fenian, reorganized the I.R.B. (whose members were bound by a secret oath) and founded its newspaper, *Irish Freedom*. The appeal to force was growing stronger than the appeal of boycott. In 1910 James Connolly returned from the United States to organize labor and preach socialism, and aligned himself with James Larkin to fight the massive 1913 lockout.

While Connolly (who was born in Scotland) was organizing labor in Belfast and in Dublin, Edward Carson was organizing Protestant resistance to home rule. In 1912, he brought about the famous Solemn League and Covenant, by which the Orangemen pledged themselves to armed resistance. By 1913, there were one hundred thousand armed volunteers in the north and German weapons were pouring in. It was illegal but the British Liberal party was unable to stop it because the Conservative party was involved in it. British troops told their government that they would resign rather than enforce the law in the north. The House of Commons passed the home rule bill for the third time when an amendment was added exempting some northern counties. The affair was still being negotiated when World War I broke out, and the guns of August boomed.

Although the majority of citizens in Ireland probably supported John Redmond and the home rule bill, it was the radical minority who determined the future of the country. In 1914, an estimated 150,000 volunteers were drilling under Eoin Mac-Neill. On a much smaller scale, Connolly and Larkin had been organizing similar volunteers. Only a small minority saw England's difficulties as Ireland's opportunity. Tens of thousands went to France in the British army.

At this moment, the dramatic conflict between politics and art intensified in Ireland, and the autonomy that Yeats and Lady Gregory had won for art would be lost again. The spirit of the revival had lured Campbell to Dublin, as it had lured Moore. The politics generated by Ireland's ongoing struggle for independence however lured other Irish writers, including Anglo-Irishmen, into its vortex. Two of the most romantic were Rogert Casement (1864–1916) and Erskine Childers (1870–1922), both of whom lost their lives in the conflict. Casement, born in Dublin, at Sandycove, was hanged in London as a traitor, and Childers, born in England, was executed in Dublin by the Irish Free State in the bitter years of the civil war.

Childers and Casement had both served England with distinction. Childers was primarily a military man, a historian of warfare and a theoretician, although he is best remembered today for his brilliant espionage novel *The Riddle of the Sands*, which was published in 1910. The next year he published a most significant book, *German Influence on British Cavalry*, warning of the changes the machine gun would necessitate in warfare. This book was comparable to General Charles de Gaulle's World War II volume on tank warfare, and similarly ignored, at heavy cost to the Allies. Early in the century, Childers, whose family home was in Ireland, became interested in Irish politics and played a vital role.

Casement had been knighted for his services in the British consular service, particularly for exposing the dreadful treatment of the natives in the plantations of the Congo and in Peru. His Irish nationalism was inflamed by his vacation contacts in Ulster and by his friendship with a remarkable woman, Alice Stopford Green (1847–1929), the widow of the English historian John R. Green. After his death in 1883, she completed his *Conquest of England* and turned historian herself beginning with a life of Henry II, the first English monarch to land on Irish soil.

With Carson's volunteers armed with German weapons in the north while England looked the other way, the nationalists sought arms. Mrs. Green raised money in London to aid a plan that she, Casement, Childers, and others devised to bring guns into Dublin. The method was ingenious and simple. They would smuggle them in on private yachts. Childers was an expert yachtsman. The trick worked. With his wife, a Boston society girl, aboard, Childers brought a shipment into Howth in his yacht, the *Asgard*. Two other yachts were also employed, and the guns were landed before the British could stop them. After a futile effort of the English troops to seize the guns, they shot and killed three persons and wounded thirty-eight others in a crowd that had stoned them as they returned to their barracks. The month was July, 1914, and Germany was ready to march. Nine days after the landing at Howth, the war began. Home rule was shelved for the duration.

In Dublin the years from 1916 to 1923 were dominated by World War I, the Easter Rising, fanatic English repression, the Anglo-Irish war, the establishment of the Irish Free State, and Irish civil war. No writer's febrile imagination could conceive the intricacies of politics, the quixotic revolutionary commitments, and the subsequent savage bloody fratricidal conflict that ensued. During these years in which a dozen poets and writers died untimely deaths, in battle, in internecine warfare, or before brutish British firing squads, some of Dublin's greatest poetry and greatest prose was being written, much of it outside Dublin, but more redolent of its quintessence than anything written hitherto.

These were the years in which Yeats brought out *Responsibilities*, taking a turn toward a new profundity, and also the years of his breathtaking poem on the Easter Rising that had won such little support from the mass of Irishmen when it was in progress, but which was to transform the thinking of the nation as the British executioners shot down the leaders in a prolonged sequence which proved to be a political mistake. Yeats summed up the vision that caused that change in his line, "A terrible beauty is born."

During these years, literature was in exile. Poets were shouldering guns or smuggling them, novelists were writing propaganda if they had not fled the country, critics were proclaiming politics. The Irish theater struggled on with contributions from a score of minor playwrights.

We may take then as a symbol of the new Dublin that was tempering itself in these years, the Dublin that was distilling a new sense of nationalism, the Dublin that was becoming a new Dublin, the figure of James Joyce (1882–1941), one of the outstanding novelists of the twentieth century, and one of the major figures of English as well as Irish literature. Joyce was born in Dublin and educated there, at Conglowes Wood, Belvedere College, and the University College, all conducted by Jesuits. He was a brilliant student who pondered a priestly vocation for a while but became more enamored of art and language. Finally he fled the Catholic church and Ireland to remain an exile from both but indelibly tinctured by both in the depths of his soul. He first attracted attention with his essays on the drama, and then met Yeats, who found him unbearably arrogant, even as Joyce found Dublin unbearably confining. He left the city in 1904, taking with him auburn-haired Nora Barnacle, with whom he lived until his death but did not marry until 1931, and then only to insure the legal rights of their children, Giorgio and Lucia.

His first book, a volume of poetry entitled *Chamber Music* (it has a scatological connotation), was published in 1907. As early as 1904 he had written a book of short stories called *Dubliners*, which for censorious reasons was not published until 1914 and then in London. In 1904, he began an autobiographical novel, *Stephen Hero*, that was put aside and not published for two decades more and then in uncompleted form. In the same year that *Dubliners* was published, his first novel, *A Portrait of the Artist as a Young Man*, began to appear seriatim. Meanwhile, he had composed a drama, *Exiles*, which was produced but was not successful.

By 1914, Joyce's most celebrated book was four years under way. *Ulysses* was begun in 1910 and was published in 1922 in Paris. The next year, 1923, he began work on *Finnegans Wake*, which was not completed until 1938. He died in 1941 with the literary world still puzzling over the semantic magnificences of that last book. The critical reception accorded it was not philistine but dubious enough to leave him disappointed and brooding. To this day, *Finnegans Wake* baffles the average reader and is psychic food only for an elite.

From 1907 until World War I, Joyce and Nora lived in Trieste, where he taught English to support them. The spread of hostilities drove them to Zurich, where they sat out the war, returning to Trieste briefly afterward, but moving on to Paris, where Joyce died. Sylvia Beach, an American and the proprietor of Shakespeare & Co., a celebrated bookstore in Paris, undertook the publication of *Ulysses*. The book created an international uproar. Adapting various narrative techniques, including representation of William James's stream of consciousness, *Ulysses* depicts a day in the lives of numerous Dubliners, particularly Stephen Dedalus, Leopold Bloom, and his estranged wife, Molly. Bloom is a Dublin Jew and thus somewhat withdrawn from the Irish Catholics Joyce portrays with so much ingenuity, realism, and humor, albeit with cynicism. The book moves through eighteen episodes, the whole related to Homer's Odyssey as a matrix.

Although the *Encyclopaedia Britannica* describes Joyce as "one of the greatest stylists in English literature," T. S. Eliot said of him that he was a man of many voices but no style. Joyce himself said *Dubliners* was written "for the most part in a style of scrupulous meanness." That could not be said of *Ulysses*, the eighteen sections of which are written in a variety of styles, parodies piled on parodies. The book was to play a salient role in the history of American jurisprudence and American social mores because a famous federal court decision ruled it not obscene.

The American court decision was a triumph for Joyce, who suffered more than his share of tribulation after leaving Dublin. Besides the ostracism of which he was conscious, the enduring neglect and poverty, the result of his own arrogance as well as the nationalistic bigotry in Ireland and its attendant arrant philistinism, he was the victim of a painful, recurring eye ailment, which brought on a continuing diminution of vision. The picture of Joyce under medical treatment with leeches applied to his eyes to clear the excessive bleeding readily makes the reader suffer with him. More agonizing was the mental illness of his daughter, Lucia, whose name had become an irony, for she was a schizophrenic. This sorrow plagued the famliy throughout the last decade of Joyce's life. In 1930 his own ill health interrupted his work and the fear of death and consequent legal problems that would have engulfed the children led him and Nora to marry, an act their rebelliousness had hitherto excluded.

Bernard Shaw and Lady Gregory chatting together had mused on the curiosity that the "three most indecent writers" of their day were Irishmen—Frank Harris, who would write his Casanovan memoirs; George Moore, father of the realistic novel and a man pursued by his own sensuality; and James Joyce, whose mastery of the interior monologue had brought into public print what had never before been there. G.B.S. and the Lady put it down to revolt against Catholic training, but, if it was, it was specifically Irish Catholic training, Catholicism stretched and strained by the nationalism that had soured Joyce.

This reaction by Joyce, who, refined in conversation as he was himself, at least in his mature years, would have been quite at home in the Catholicism of Chaucer and Dante, freed the novel of the sterile clichés of the nineteenth century and launched a new literature on the world. He was no more an innovator than Chaucer, or as much a one, say, for he adapted, with genius and encyclopedic knowledge (his Jesuit education aimed at a universal synthesis), leads taken from Dorothy Richardson, an English writer, and Édouard Dujardin, a French novelist, and brought the interior monologue to an apotheosis.

On December 6, 1933, Judge John M. Woolsey of the New York federal district court lifted a ban placed on *Ulysses* by customs agents and permitted it to come into the United States. The attorneys for the government had charged the book was obscene.

> . . . in *Ulysses* [the judge wrote] in spite of its unusual frankness, I do not detect anywhere the leer of the sensualist. I hold, therefore, that it is not pornographic.
>
> In writing *Ulysses* [he continued] Joyce sought to make a serious experiment in a new, if not wholly novel, literary genre. He takes persons of the lower middle class living in Dublin in 1904 and seeks not only to describe what they did on a certain day early in June of that year as they went about the city bent on their usual occupations, but also to tell what many of them thought about the while.
>
> Joyce has attempted—it seems to me, with astonishing success—to show how the screen of consciousness with its ever-shifting kaleidoscopic impressions carries, as it were on a plastic palimpsest, not only what is in the focus of each man's observation of the actual things about him, but also in a penumbral zone residual of past impressions, some recent and some drawn up

by association from the domain of the subconscious. He shows how each of these impressions affects the life and behavior of the character which he is describing.

The judge acknowledged the book contained words usually considered "dirty," but that he never found "dirt for dirt's sake."

By this time Joyce was a cult, the object of literary adulation on both sides of the Atlantic. In Dublin, where intensifying nationalism would further distort Catholicism, ultramontane Catholics marched through the streets to denounce dissenters. A ridiculous censorship was established which, curiously, never banned either *Ulysses* or *Finnegans Wake* while proscribing works much less, to use Bernard Shaw's word, "indecent." The reasons for Joyce's lack of popularity in Dublin at this time were numerous. No book in history has as much of Dublin in it as *Ulysses*, and Joyce himself said, if the city was destroyed, it could be rebuilt from his works. But many Dubliners saw Joyce as a man destroying the city as surely as British guns. He was sitting on the sidelines scoffing at his country in its hour of anguish and deliverance. An iron face of puritanism was turned against him. Many, like Shaw, found his work "indecent," and the Catholic clergy regarded him not as the heir to Rabelais, Chaucer, Boccaccio, and Dante, but as a lascivious renegade.

Not only was World War I engaging the attention of Dublin with its row over conscription of Irishmen into the British armed forces, but the Easter Rising had split Irish history in half, a rebellion spurred not, as the American Revolution, by money-minded merchants, but by poets and theorists. Three of the seven signers of the Proclamation of the Irish Republic, which Padraic Pearse (1879–1916) read out to uncomprehending foot traffic in Dublin on the day of the Rising, were poets and playwrights. Pearse himself, with his hunched shoulders, pink-and-white complexion, high forehead, and compelling blue eyes, was primarily a literary man and an educator whose gift for oratory reached its apogee in his funeral oration over the body of Jeremiah O'Donovan Rossa, an oration often quoted.

Life springs from death, and from the graves of patriot men and women spring living nations. The defenders of this realm have worked well in secret and in the open. They think they have pacified Ireland. They think they have purchased half of us and intimidated the other half. They think they have foreseen everything, provided against everything; but the fools, the fools, the fools!—they have left us our Fenian dead, and while Ireland holds these graves Ireland unfree shall never be at peace.

Pearse had been active in the Gaelic League and wrote his best work in Irish. To see that the Irish language was properly taught and available to the young he started a school, St. Enda's, where a young, curly-haired, talkative scholar joined the staff. He was Thomas MacDonagh (1878–1916), who also signed the proclamation, a poet whose study *Literature in Ireland* would be published after his death, a man who went from the lecture platform at the university to his death. The third poet to sign the proclamation was Joseph Mary Plunkett (1887–1916), the journalist who worked with MacDonagh and Edward Martyn in the Irish theater.

Pearse wrote in both Irish and English; MacDonagh wrote in English and did translations from the Irish; Plunkett wrote in English. MacDonagh argued in his *Literature in Ireland* that Irish poetry had to take its strength from its Gaelic beginnings. Pearse (in Irish: Padraic MacPiarais) was a barrister turned pedagogue, and was the leader of the Easter Rising which, like many an Irish rebellion, suffered from botched plans. The Rising itself was quickly put down by the British, but the rebels had been ready to lay down their lives and there is reason to believe that at least some of them desired martyrdom. One of Pearse's plays, *The Singer*, has the protagonist, MacDara, facing the English alone to die, saying, "One man can free a people, as one Man redeemed the world. I will take no pike, I will go into battle with bare hands. I will stand up before the Gall as Christ hung naked before men on the tree."

This strong religious identification in the struggle for freedom marked the three literary signatories, Plunkett, perhaps, most of all, for he was ennobled by a profound mysticism. It can be no surprise if such men and their admirers had little sympathy with an arrogant young novelist rusticating in Zurich, Trieste, and Paris during the Gethsemane and Good Friday of his native land, and then producing at last, however masterfully, a portrait of battle-scarred Dublin that seemed pejorative at best. The English critic Edmund Gosse expressed in 1924 the conservative view. *Ulysses*, he said, was an "anarchical production, infamous in taste [and] in style. . . . There are no English critics who consider Mr. Joyce an author of any importance." Mr. Gosse was often hard to take; but in this case his view was perhaps that of the majority at the time. Indeed, the irreverent Irish, always skeptical of foreign praise of their artists, regarded with ribald disdain the pilgrimages of Joycean cultists from around the world to the Dublin scenes that fill the pages of *Ulysses* and the more tortuously complicated pages of *Finnegans Wake*.

The deaths of the three poets (along with the other four signers and seven other patriots) were mourned in a poem by another Dublin poet who died the next year fighting along with thousands of Irishmen in the British forces in World War I. He was Francis Ledwidge (1891–1917), whose two volumes of verse, *Songs of the Field* (1916) and *Songs of the Peace* (1917), make him another example of that not unusual character, the Irish literary man of elementary education encouraged into a literary career by a sympathetic patron, in his case, Lord Dunsany. Ledwidge's elegy "The Blackbirds" honored Pearse, Plunkett, and MacDonagh. Like the careers of the men he saluted, his was truncated by war, and he remains more a poet of promise than full achievement. His lament for Thomas MacDonagh is one of his finest poems.

Lennox Robinson (1886–1958) had managed the Abbey Theatre in 1910 but resigned to write full-time and did not return until 1919. He stayed with the Abbey until two years before his death and no one did more to maintain the Irish theater than he. In his *Ireland's Abbey Theatre*, Robinson recorded:

> During those four years, 1914–1918, not very many great plays were being written. Perhaps the only ones to be noted are, in 1915, Lady Gregory's *Shanwalla*, a strange, moving play; St. John Ervine's masterpiece, *John Ferguson*; my *The Dreamers*. But in 1916, J. Augustus Keogh became the theater's producer. He knew Bernard Shaw's plays through and through, he had acted in them, he had produced them, and now, for the first time, since the production of *Blanco Posnet*, the Irish theater saw the plays of one of Ireland's greatest dramatists. They even saw the rejected *John Bull's Other Island*. From September, 1916 to March 1917 six great plays were presented. There were less important plays, pleasant comedies by Bernard Fluffy, and in December 1916, *The Whiteheaded Boy* by myself.
>
> In 1918 there came a fine one-act play by Lady Gregory *Hanrahan's Oath*; T. C. Murray's moving one-act tragedy *Spring*, and my pseudo-Parnellite play, *The Lost Leader*. But in spite of a few good plays the theater was in the doldrums.

Fate was on the side of the Abbey because each time it began to flounder new blood came in. In 1919 the Abbey produced *The Rebellion in Ballycullen* by John Weldon (1890–1963), who wrote under the pen name Brinsley MacNamara. He had joined the company as an actor but soon left to devote all his time to writing. The year before his play was produced his first novel, *The Valley of the Squinting Windows*, had caused a literary sensation (and was burned in his village). His second novel, *The Clanking of the Chains*, abjuring any romantic vision of the drive for national independence and emphasizing the disillusionment that could set in, received a like reception. He followed up his Abbey success with several other plays and produced also several collections of short stories.

In the literary host of these years in Dublin was the poet Frederick R. Higgins (1896–1941), a self-educated literary man, who began his apprenticeship in Dublin at fourteen years

of age, but was fired from his job as clerk because he founded
the Clerical Workers' Union. He worked on a number of unsuccessful or unprofitable journals in Dublin before establishing
his reputation as a poet. His books of poetry are *Salt Air,
Island Blood, The Dark Breed, Arable Holdings*, and *The Gap
of Brightness*. His finest poem for many is his elegy for Padraic
O'Conaire. His play *A Deuce of Jacks* was produced at the
Abbey and a few years before his death he became managing
director of the theater.

In 1918, the Dublin Drama League came into being for the
specific purpose of presenting first-rate plays regardless of their
national origin. For ten years it existed side by side with the
Abbey using Abbey actors and the Abbey quarters. It was during its decade that the Abbey was saved again, so to speak,
by two more discoveries, George Shiels (1886–1949), whom
Robinson called "the Thomas Moore of the Irish Theatre," and
Sean O'Casey (1884–1964), who was to prove the greatest
dramatist since Synge. Their day came after Dublin had gone
through incredible military trials, warfare of the bitterest kind,
the evil period of the Black and Tans, and the more tragic period
of the Irish civil war. Nor can it be forgotten that thousands of
Irishmen died fighting for the Allies in World War I, literary
men among them. Such trials, however, can anneal and temper
a man, and move him toward greatness.

XIII

The years from 1916 to 1922 are a major watershed in the literary history of Dublin, and the breach was to change much, but two constants of Irish life and literature remained, wit and exile—one an intrinsic manifestation of the Dublin Dimension and the other an external influence on that dimension and the literary history of the country. Let us deal with exile first, for the phenomenon itself and the conditions that brought it about, and still cause it, in themselves have prompted much of Dublin wit, for a good deal of Irish wit comes from Ireland's reflections on its tribulations.

The greatest Irish literary exile on the eve of World War I was James Joyce, and the most celebrated literary exile immediately following World War I was Sean O'Casey, and they can be used to make a point, for the first gained by the isolation of exile, and the second lost by it. Exile or expatriation, is, for all Irish writers, an emotional affair of frequently profound implications.

Islands much more than any other corners of a world are places where people come and go. The sea is always a barrier which makes return (or did so before the airplane) that much more difficult, and sometimes, because of fog or storms, impossible. Ireland has shared this attribute of islands to a greater degree than most (compare Iceland, for instance), and more than its neighboring island, Great Britain, which, thanks to the empire, has had more than its share of exiles. In Ireland, however, the phenomenon of exile has been intensified little by conquest or an international commerce, and more by ethnic, economic, political, and religious reasons. The result is that to this day exile is a phenomenon in the life of Ireland, although in the past decade emigration has dried to a trickle.

The song is quite correct in saying, "You'll find an Irishman no matter where you go." Men and women have left Ireland in extraordinary numbers although today it is mostly for economic reasons—Irish girls going to London to study nursing under the National Health plan, educated men and women coming to America for a variety of occupations, scholars seeking access to computers, scientists seeking use of equipment, trainees to find positions in some financial citadel, poets to read at the well-paying American universities, teachers to find departments at colleges eager for European erudition and insights.

The roots of Irish exile run deep. The Celts were driven by barbaric tribes to Ireland and possibly always carried within them a dream of return to a more beneficent land. Their mythology exalted the myth of a magical land, Hy Brassil or Tir-na-nOg, lands of eternal youth. Their explorers are personified in Brendan the Navigator probing the ends of the earth in restless searchings. Because they remained racially pure, relatively, in their Ultima Thule, the Celts and their gift for mnemonics kept their mythology from diminishing in force and intensified its own archetypes. This process was furthered by the attacks they suffered from more barbaric tribes—the Vikings or Danes, the Normans, the English—which made the dream of a land of peace and plenty even more alluring.

For centuries the call of Christian duty impelled hundreds of high-minded monks into exile so that Europe today is studded with monastic foundations which sprang from the industry and scholarship of these good men. No doubt they were eager not merely to preach the gospel of Jesus Christ and restore learning but to see something of the great world and to visit Rome.

The advent of the searoving Danes drove thousands more

of the Irish monks into exile, this time in involuntary flight. Others fled before the Normans. When the English came the rules and reasons altered. Stirrings of nationalism began to flutter the thinking of the Irish, but it was an uncertain nationalism; Christendom was still a dominant concept. Dubliners Nahum Tate and Ludovick Barry no doubt moved around London without too much sense of being alien. The pervasiveness of the Reformation modulated the game again, for as England became more and more Protestant (a religious conviction fortified by its compatibility with nationalism), Catholicism became more and more the mark of Irish ethnicity. English Protestantism, with its subjectivity and individualism, enabled a man in an expanding empire to make vigorous decisions in isolated places, and to have the forms of religion without compelling ritualistic and moral strictures. Irish Catholicism came more and more to emphasize the vale of suffering, the promise of heavenly reward for faith persisted in and worldly torment endured.

Adhering to the faith of Rome and adhering to nationalism became so intertwined for many that they were inseparable and the higher calling came more and more to be distorted through its interest in survival as well as in achieving the apotheosis of a nation—true independence—or opposing it as detrimental to the faith. For it must be remembered that Catholicism is of its essence universal, or to use the modern term, international, which applied to the church is inexact. Supranational would be the better term. In brief, the Catholic church and extreme nationalism (as distinguished from patriotism) are antipathetic, and must collide. In England, the conflict was resolved by jettisoning Papal authority and making the king (or the queen) the head of the church. All the marks of nationalism followed sooner or later: subservience of the Anglican church to the needs of imperialism, military conscription, anti-Catholicism (since Spain was the enemy and then France), education twisted to nationalistic indoctrination brooking no dissent, racism with its contempt for "the lesser breeds without the law."

Now in Ireland, the Irish were a conquered nation, threatened with extermination, absorption, or dispersion. The aim of England was to butcher them or to leave them in a state of irredeemable servitude that could be eluded by individuals only in their embracing the morals and manners, language and nationalistic ideals of the English, even as today, individual blacks can find full equality in Portuguese colonies. For these oppressed Catholics there were three choices: to renounce the Catholic faith, which was seen as treason to the Irish nation; to stand and suffer humiliation and hardship as inhuman as black slavery in America; or to emigrate to the continent or the United States. Throughout those two centuries, exile was a daily occurrence in any community or village; scarcely a family did not have someone overseas. Thousands went, of course, in prison ships to the Antipodes; or as slaves (under Cromwell's ministrations) to the West Indies.

In those two centuries following the Reformation and the utter subjection of the Irish, the Catholic church became the rallying post for nationalism and saw itself as such, a Catholic nation at war with a Protestant nation. Two things resulted. The church established an authoritarian priesthood. The priests alone had education, obtained often at the risk of their lives—sometimes from the heroic hedge masters who were laymen—and they most of all suffered at the hands of the invaders. The figure of Christ crucified was the identification Irishmen were offered to help them bear their torments during years when they were hunted for sport by English landlords. For women, chastity became the preeminent virtue, a very prudential insistence since the pathway out of starvation, rags, and squalor lay through dalliance with the local squire or his agents. In enforcing morals, the priest was the embodiment of the law. Perhaps the consequences were inevitable. Irish Catholicism took on the mask of Manichaeanism—the things of this world (denied to the Irish) were described as not worth having, wealth was an evil, and sex (for fear of assimilation or sellout) was a constant danger.

The frosty attitude of the Irish toward sex and the body itself has been shown in sociological studies of Aran Islanders and other Irish groups, by surveys of Irish art, by analysis of their speech, and by their curious official repugnance at the mildest erotic literature (unless written in Irish). For the Manichaean distrust of nature, reintroduced into Western civilization by Calvin, has remained in Irish life long after the reasons for its introduction were forgotten. It was dominant in Joyce's day and drove him from the precincts of the Catholic church if not from its penumbra.

The second thing the Catholic church in Ireland did which calcified the rigid morality necessary to survive the penal laws was to emulate the Protestant gentry. The servants copied the manners of their masters, and unfortunately, when, in the nineteenth century the Catholics were emerging from their deprived circumstances, the gentry they aped was the hypocritical bluenosed Victorian society. Shabby gentility was one of the outcomes, a ridiculous puritanism was another.

As early as the seventeenth century, this danger was seen. Even then we find an Irish writer, Dabhidh O Bruadair (1625–1698), in classic Irish verse denouncing the aping of the English conquerors. He shakes his head over the Irish mirroring their masters and adopting the English language. Even then the whole question of language was a major political issue. If at one time abandoning the Irish language was as treasonable as abandoning the Catholic faith, Daniel O'Connell and the Catholic church, more than any other influences, were to change that, and eliminate Irish from daily intercourse. The supervention of the famine played its part. This was not an antinational move on the part of the church. On the contrary it was a political move: the decision that independence could be achieved through constitutional means only if all the Catholics learned enough English to participate in the political process. Even today the overwhelming majority of masses in Ireland are said in English; the mass said in Irish is the exception, although to have them all in that tongue would not leave the average churchgoer any farther from the sacred mysteries than he was when they were offered in Latin.

By the end of the nineteenth century this combination of extreme nationalism and puritanism had bred a philistinism that became intolerable to artists. The political reasons for exile diminished. John Leary and the Fenians were welcomed home. The economic reasons for exile continued and took Bernard Shaw, George Moore, and hundreds of lesser lights to England. The growing philistinism (as the Catholic middle class spread and bettered itself financially) bolstered by the church, which, in proper balance, should be as contrary to philistinism as it is to nationalism, made new exiles, preeminently Joyce, but not him alone. George Moore returned to England. O'Casey in dudgeon took refuge there. Padraic Colum went to the United States. Colum was a new type of emigrant, the literary man seeking a living by his pen in the United States, which had received Irishmen before, but as political refugees, John Boyle O'Reilly, for example. Much of such exile is the inevitable fate of any small country that generates excessive talent.

No discussion of Irish exiles would have balance unless special reference were made to the hundreds of thousands of Christian missionaries—men and women—who have gone around the world, not merely as saintly and exemplary Catholic priests and nuns, but as dedicated educators.

The future of Irish life and Dublin's literary prospects are bound to the slow turning and unexpected revolutions of history's wheel. Ireland as an island will continue to have exiles but the reasons will more than likely in the future be chiefly economic, and the new tax laws introduced by Charles Haughey, which recognize the necessity of art to the life of a nation (or the soul of a man), will deter Ireland's writers from abandoning their homeland and, indeed, bring about a return of some of the prodigal sons.

The major movement in history today affecting Western civilization is the decline and death of Protestantism as a political force. The embracing by the Catholic church of the ecumenical movement is that church's latent acknowledgment that the Protestant heresy (as it regarded the theologies of the Reformation) is no longer a threat to the preservation of the purity of those Christian doctrines which Rome believes to be the essence of Christianity. From the sixteenth century, the Church of Rome believed itself locked in a death struggle with Protestantism and its derivative philosophies. To insure survival, it closed itself into an ironclad intellectual chamber. Theological discussion, which abounded during the Middle Ages and the early Renaissance, was denied even to scholars. Biblical studies became calcified. The liturgy insisted upon a Latin rigidity, and the daily practice of the conventions of the Catholic church became forbidding in their regularity. The Irish hierarchy accepted all this because they felt the Irish church was at the very heart of that struggle. It was difficult to see that in avoiding the heresies of Protestantism they were falling into the heresy of nationalism since the Italian popes seemed almost to have nationalized the church in Italy, with Italian pope succeeding Italian pope, Italians dominating the bureaucracy of the church, Italian saints canonized in excessive numbers, and the universality of the church scarcely visible in its administration. Such inbreeding, such a defensive posture, it can be argued, was necessary to save the besieged core of Christianity from what could be the fatally fragmenting influences of Protestantism, particularly when it was armed with the swords of England and the Germanies, and abetted by uncertain movements in the Catholic nations themselves.

Today that threat is past. There is no Protestant army left in the world (excepting perhaps South Africa) to conquer, colonize, or control. England, through the Common Market, is slipping back into Europe, from which, by courage and choice, it stood apart so long and so successfully. In the early 1970s, the British army which had ruled the world was reduced pitifully to chasing unemployed Catholic boys through the back alleys of Northern Ireland, dodging showers of rocks thrown by women and children, while the parliament at Westminster, despite all its experience, was unable to see that Polish corridors, German or English enclaves on foreign soil, cannot be maintained in a century which has repudiated colonialism as nothing but a milder form of slavery.

Vatican Council II was a theological recognition that Protestantism is no longer the enemy but an ally, and that the danger to the preservation of Revelation lies elsewhere. Since Ireland to this day is, of all countries, still most bitterly scarred by the Protestant-Catholic division and the Irish clergy in America as well as Ireland the most conservative in the church (more Catholic than Rome), because of the tragic political inheritance of Irish history, it can be expected that clericalism will modulate to proper clerical-laical relationship later in Ireland than elsewhere.

The evil in that is that Ireland more than any other predominantly Catholic country needs to cherish its Protestant countrymen and their patriotic traditions, for a disproportionate number of Ireland's heroes are drawn from those dissenting heroic ranks, as is also a disproportionate number of its litterary and artistic geniuses. Ireland needs a brave ecumenism until the day of reunion of the Christian churches. What Irish aesthetic and intellectual life needs above all is the leavening influence of a well-to-do Jewish community. Ireland is as free from anti-Semitism as any country in the world, but aside from Cork, the Jewish community is small and not intellectually very potent, even though Ireland provided Israel with its first chief rabbi, and Robert Briscoe became Lord Mayor of Dublin, and David Marcus, literary editor of *The Irish Press*, has done as much (if not more) to encourage contemporary literature in Ireland as any man.

Our essay on exile has not led us as far from the literary path as one might think. What I am arguing is that Ireland and particularly the Catholic church in Ireland, to find its spiritual fulfillment, must respond rapidly and profoundly to the spirit of Vatican II, which sensed the significance of the collapse of the British empire (the paladin of a Protestantism likewise distorted by the demands of nationalism). A true separation of church and state will make the embittered Protestants of the northern counties readier to collaborate with the government at Dublin. The abandonment of the gloomy trappings of Jansenism will free the Irish comic spirit to out-Shaw Shaw and re-Joyce, to use Anthony Burgess's pun.

That done, Ireland, into the Common Market with England, should find herself in a hundred years, being a free and independent nation whole and entire, united to England in a brotherhood of economic and literary exchange which could be extremely fruitful and enlivening for them both. The Irish exile then might well seek fame and fortune in London, Paris, Rome, or Bonn, while the country of his birth remains his home, readily accessible by plane. No longer need poverty and exploitation hold him in isolation (so foreign to the old Celtic wanderers) or a corrupting nationalism which has made the country unbearable far too often for too many of its more sensitive lovers.

For what must be realized as well is that too many artists who have fled their native soil have suffered a diminution of creative talent. That is as true of William Allingham as it is of some writers we must now consider, Dublinish as Joyce and Irish of the Irish, Sean O'Casey, Oliver St. John Gogarty, and Brendan Behan, exiles all. If Joyce escaped their fate of failing fecundity, it was because he carried all Dublin in his head and achieved abroad not so much exile as the isolation the artist needs for the contemplation that precedes the true creation.

From a discussion of exile in the life of the Irish—and we have considered only briefly the millions who have gone around the world and bred generations of writers abroad with the Celtic mark still on them—it is not extraordinary to pass to a discussion of Dublin wit, although we can leave the connection between the two to the psychologists.

From Swift to today, wit in Dublin is a constant. Nor did the martial disasters of 1916–1922 diminish it. One of the giant Dublinesque figures who emerges from this swirl of history— the Easter Rising, the Anglo-Irish war, the Irish civil war—is Oliver St. John Gogarty (1878–1957), physician, poet, playwright, patriot, and supreme wit, who, like Wilde, poured his genius into his life as well as into his writings, but who represents within his glossy idiosyncrasy various conflicting Irish elements. He, too, is one of the exiles who faded in force when he took up residence in the United States and abandoned the pulsating precincts of Dublin. Yet, in the United States as well as in Dublin he established an extraordinary reputation as a wit. Since no history of Dublin and its mastery of words could be written without reference to Irish wit, Gogarty suitably serves as a starting point.

He is, as is well known, the Buck Mulligan whose irreverent presence opens Joyce's *Ulysses*. He and Joyce were friends, but like other Irish friends (Moore and Martyn, for example), fell out as a result of Joyce's portrayal of him. He would thereafter speak of Joyce disparagingly. Gogarty was a medical student at Trinity when Joyce was at the national university, and went on to become a fashionable practitioner in Dublin. He was handsome, erudite, witty, a classicist in his poetry, a Catholic, highly irreverent, and mildly dissolute, in which regard some saw him as Joyce's evil genius. He was made for Joyce to admire. Joyce, whose superb tenor voice helped him earn his livelihood, used to borrow Gogarty's clothes to make his concert appearances. No doubt Joyce also sought to clothe himself in Gogarty's arrogance but the original, however, lacked the bitterness of his imitator.

Gogarty's first book of verse appeared anonymously in 1918. *Secret Springs of Dublin Song* was comedy and parody but later Yeats would reckon him "one of the great lyric poets of our age." When, in 1936, Yeats was asked to edit *The Oxford Book of Modern Verse*, he included seventeen poems by Gogarty, more than he accorded himself or anyone else for that matter. Gogarty was riskily involved in Irish politics, a stout friend of Arthur Griffith and of Michael Collins, and a foe of Eamon de Valera when that statesman was the enemy of the Irish Free State and warring on behalf of a true republic. De Valera's name led some of his enemies to question whether he was Irish. "He's a Hibernian all right," said Gogarty, reflecting on Dev's ungainly figure. "He looks like something uncoiled from the Book of Kells." Gogarty served in the Senate of the Irish Free State from 1922 to 1936 and opposed the I.R.A. During the civil war, they burned down his lovely home in Renvyle in the west of Ireland and thus destroyed some of Joyce's letters. In 1923, his political stance nearly cost him his life. He was seized as a hostage by men of the I.R.A. and threatened with execution. Later Yeats would recount the celebrated story:

> Twelve years ago Oliver Gogarty was captured by his enemies, imprisoned in a deserted house on the edge of the Liffey with every prospect of death. Pleading a natural necessity he got into the garden, plunged under a shower of revolver bullets and as he swam the ice-cold December stream promised it, should it land him in safety, two swans. I was present when he fulfilled that vow. His poetry fits the incident, a gay, stoical—no, I will not withhold the word—heroic song.

In 1924 his book of poetry appeared, *An Offering of Swans*. Several other volumes followed.

His prose works won him equal popularity, and a libel suit; particularly, *As I Was Going Down Sackville Street* and *It Isn't This Time of Year at All*, both autobiographical reflections on a thousand themes. In his fifties he left Ireland for America, a refugee from the political rule he had so vehemently opposed, and abandoned the medical profession for a literary life. It was not wholly successful and he would sometimes in drab New York restaurants hold his head in his hands to regret his declension.

In Ireland he had been a Renaissance man: cyling champion, madcap motorist, aviator, poet, classical scholar, physician and surgeon, conversationalist extraordinary, politician, and revolutionary. Three of his plays were presented pseudonymously at the Abbey. Prime Minister Herbert Asquith once pronounced him the wittiest man in London, and it is for his wit that he is, improperly, most remembered today. He was a heresiarch of mockers in a city whose habituals and sons of habituals are ravenous to mock everyone and everything. Gogarty's witticisms, riotous, ribald, were repeated all over Dublin and he arrived at that eminence where the witticisms of others were attributed to him. He was an antic prankster who set out to restore snakes to Ireland, lured Yeats up in his airplane, asked Lloyd's of London to insure him against his being knighted, and responded when books were banned in Ireland by having his next book surcharged *Forbidden to be Sold in Ireland*.

Ben Lucien Burman, the well-known American writer, was Gogarty's dearest friend at the end and his literary executor. He tells the story of Gogarty's going to the Vatican, an Irish senator, to be received by the Holy Father along with William Cosgrave, then president of the Irish Free State. Medals were prepared for each by the Vatican and when it was discovered that Gogarty by mischance got Cosgrave's and Cosgrave got Gogarty's, a Papal secretary pursued the physician-poet to right the wrong. When he explained, Gogarty declined to relinquish the better medal.

"Did I come to Rome," he said severely, "to have the infallibility of the Pope questioned?"

Even as an undergraduate Gogarty's wit won him preeminence
and prestige and acquaintance with John Pentland Mahaffy
(1839–1919), a maverick scholar who would nonetheless become provost of Trinity, a classicist who had tutored Oscar
Wilde, and a first-rate snob and conversationalist (he wrote a
book, *The Art of Conversation*), and like Gogarty, an athlete
and a wit. Like Gogarty, he spread his interests over too wide
a spectrum. Despite a lisp, which Gogarty mocked in a popular
verse, he was a distinguished talker, but a dull preacher, even
as Gogarty's prose lacked the brilliance of his conversation.
Mahaffy was the man who created an Irish bull about the Irish
bull. "An Irish bull," he said, "is always pregnant." He is
credited with having responded to a lady who asked him the
difference between a man and woman, "Madame, I cannot conceive." Another witty don and contemporary was Robert T.
Tyrrell, who complained of suffering from insomnia in chapel
when Mahaffy stopped preaching. It was he who created the
mot: There is no such thing as a large whisky.

Gogarty's lascivious limericks were as popular with these
scholars as they were in the pubs. Ulick O'Connor, his biographer, himself a Dublin athlete, scholar, talker, and wit in the
Gogarty tradition (and hence today a television star), recounts
that they were quoted by his clerical friends at his graveside in
Renvyle, their metrics mingling sotto voce with the Latin in-
cantations of the officiating priest.

> There was a young man of St. John's
> Who tried to roger the swans,
>   Oh, no, said the porter,
>   Please take my daughter,
> The birds are reserved for the dons.

When George Moore left Ireland for London for good, he regretted most of all leaving Gogarty, whom he called "the author
of all the jokes that enable us to live in Dublin."

Mahaffy, Anglo-Irish and a Unionist, was opposed to the
restoration of Gaelic, which was one language he didn't know.
His mots and aphorisms were widely quoted throughout Dublin.

One remains immortal: In Ireland the inevitable never happens, the unexpected always. His reply, made to an Evangelical who asked him if he was saved, is delightful: To tell you the truth, my dear fellow, I am, but it was by such a narrow squeak that it won't bear discussing.

His definition of an Irish bull was matched by that of Leslie Alexander Montgomery (1873–1961), a banker and playwright (the combination is unusual only outside Dublin) who wrote under the name Lynn Doyle: The Irish bull, he said, is "The saying of a thing in an obscure way to make your meaning clearer than if you had put it in plain language." As Lynn Doyle he wrote some excellent collections of humorous stories dealing with a fictitious town, Ballygullion, which for half a century was as real to readers as Cork.

Books have been written about the Irish comic spirit, Irish wit, and Irish humor, and the Irish gift for repartee and the impromptu molded turn of phrase. Scholars wrangle as to whether the essence lies in the play of words merely or in the clash of concepts. Further distinctions are forever being made between the reaches of Irish wit and Irish humor. It is sufficient for our purposes to think of wit as war and humor as humane; one of the head and the other of the heart; one highly intellectual and the other marked by sentiment. Whether Irish wit is mere word-play or more truly conceptual (and it is most likely both) it roots very deeply in the Celtic fascination with the complicated, the intricate, with the design turning back on itself by the unexpected twist. Significantly, two of the finest works of ancient metallurgy and craftsmanship in Dublin are a brooch and a book, one with a sharp pin, and the other with beautiful convoluted design.

The Dubliner loves logic and, perhaps even more, logic-chopping. In his secret recesses he is more metaphysical than mystical, as is evident in the works of James Joyce. No surprise then that the Irishman turns lawyer and is more eloquent than analytical. Curran and Carson, Grattan and Butt, could be indomitable in verbal passages at arms. When another lawyer, a bully, threatened during a courtroom duel to "put you in my pocket," Grattan replied, "If you do so you will have more law in your pocket than you have in your head."

Curran's reputation as a wit remains after a century and a half. Once a witness became so rattled under Curran's questioning, he blurted out to the judge, "I can't answer . . . Mr. Curran . . . he puts me in a doldrum." The judge inquired, "What's a doldrum, Mr. Curran?" and got the reply: "It's an affection common in witnesses such as this, your honor. A confusion of the head arising from a corruption of the heart."

Dining with Lord Norbury, himself a man of mordant wit, who had a reputation as a hanging judge, Curran was asked by the justice, "Is that hung beef, Mr. Curran?" Curran: "Not yet, my lord, you haven't tried it." Any number of persons, including Lord Byron, reported that they never heard such wit and conversation from any man as they heard from Curran. Curran evidently enjoyed baiting the anti-Irish judges appointed by the crown. To one who said that he saw no difference between the word "also" and the word "likewise," Curran responded that he did not agree. "The distinction is real," he continued. "For many years the great Lord Lifford presided over this court. You also preside over it, but not likewise." Like O'Connell, and Gogarty, and many another Dubliner, he died in exile, heartbroken over the condition of Ireland.

Wit runs through much of Irish politics. This is understandable since the man without a gun facing an armed foe must sharpen his tongue not for victory but mere survival. Even Eamon de Valera, that least humorous of Dubliners, had his moment of verbal glory. Arrested while speaking to a crowd in Ennis, he was jailed for a year, and on release returned to the same platform, and began, "As I was saying before we were interrupted."

In the House of Commons the wit of the Irish enlivened many an otherwise dull scene. T. P. O'Connor, an Irish M.P., is credited with one of the most exquisite of extemporaneous puns, shot off during a debate, in response to a challenge. He was denouncing the absentee landlords of Ireland for impoverishing their tenants when his passion led him into vituperation against the crown.

"Treason!" came the cry from a fellow parliamentarian.

O'Connor, scarcely pausing, replied:

"Treason becomes reason because of the absent *T*!"

In his memoir, *A Penny in the Clouds*, Austin Clarke, the poet, recounts numerous examples of the wit of James Starkey (1879–1958), who, as Seumus O'Sullivan, achieved an eminent reputation as a poet, essayist, and editor, and played a major part in the Irish revival. He even took a turn as an actor, appearing in Yeats's play *On Baile Strand* in the role of a blind man.

Gogarty, sitting in the front rows, called out when O'Sullivan came on stage, "There's the Bard—blind again." O'Sullivan ran a chemist's shop and it would be good to know the exchanges that must have taken place between him and Dr. Gogarty in their professional roles. O'Sullivan also founded *Dublin Magazine* at the height of the Troubles, as the Irish euphemistically called the Anglo-Irish war, and kept it alive, to his friends' astonishment and delight, for three decades. Among his volumes of poetry are *Twilight People, Verses Sacred and Profane, The Earth Lover, Requiem, The Rosses, The Lamplighters*, and others. He wrote in both Irish and English.

A ribald sonnet mimicking Keats's *On First Looking into Chapman's Homer* is attributed sometimes to Gogarty, sometimes to O'Sullivan. It matches Keats's last line,

> Silent, upon a peak in Darien.

With this line,

> Potent, behind a cart with Mary Ann.

O'Sullivan, on a Dublin curb, seeing a load of manure going by, is reported to have said, "I see Paddy Kavanagh is moving. There go his furniture and effects." Paddy, considered by many the greatest Irish poet since Yeats, was reputed by his detractors to have smeared dung on his brogues when visiting Dublin in order to heighten his bucolic image.

On another occasion, hearing, without sympathy, a carpenter who, bristling at fault found with his work, said sullenly, "After all, Christ was a carpenter," O'Sullivan quipped:

"What about the scab who made the Cross?"

Clarke also quotes another Dubliner, James Montgomery, who had the job of film censor, as saying:

"I'm between the Devil and the Holy See."

The wit of Sheridan and Congreve and Farquhar still nourishes audiences wherever their plays are produced. The wit of Shaw and Wilde are everyone's currency. Who doesn't know (and how many have used!) Shaw's reply during a curtain call to a heckler who shouted out that the Shavian production had been terrible: "I agree with you, sir, but who are we against so many?" Wilde's description of an English country gentleman riding to hounds as "the unspeakable in full pursuit of the uneatable," and a hundred of his witticisms have all but come into the language. Among them, for one, "The only way to be rid of temptation is to yield to it." On arriving in the United States, Wilde said, "I have nothing to declare but my genius."

The wisecrack, acid repartee, the impromptu turn of gentle humorous phrase are not confined in Dublin to literati. Ivan Sandrof, urbane New England book editor and himself a wit, purchasing a railway ticket in Ireland after having several other scheduled vehicles come for him tardily, said in exasperation, "I suppose the train will be late." The diminutive ticket agent cocked his head— "You wouldn't want them running ahead of time, would you?" A waiter in a Dublin hotel, asked to bone my sole, presented it first with a flourish and asked, "Would you care to see your sole before I tear it apart?" My mother, Dublin-born, once sent a note from the country, "Please pay my life insurance premium or you'll have to bury me in the garden and the children might dig me up."

That sort of thing is in the air in Dublin. An American newspaperman pushing a reluctant gasoline station attendant to recommend one of two hotels finally got the reply, "Ah, whichever one you choose before the night is half over you'll be wishing to God you had chosen the other." It echoes Mahaffy's definition of an Irish atheist, "A man who wishes to God he could believe in God."

While the pubs are not as full of brilliant talk as the common accounts would have one believe, there's far more in them than one finds in any other city, and, moreover, poets have always been welcome in them to read aloud or sing a verse. Dubliners take their conversation seriously once they get under way (Mahaffy's *The Art of Conversation*) and even their throwaway lines have a special sparkle. Vivian Mercier, the America-based Irish scholar, in his excellent book *The Irish Comic Tradition*, tells of going to the Irish Tourist Board in New York to ask a puckish colleen the cheapest way to get to Ireland. "Swim," she responded. No other travel bureau in the world would provide a prospective visitor with such a reply, but that the Irish girl did can be used as an example of the basic weakness (if weakness is the word) of true wit: everything must be sacrificed to it.

The wit, like any artist, seeks first the perfection of his work, to wit, the witticism. He need not be honest. Congreve once said, "A wit should be no more sincere than a woman constant." The anecdotist has time to consider whether his story may offend any member of a given company or, indeed, on repetition, a distant friend or acquaintance. He can pause, relent, and even alter the story. Not so the wit. The perfection of wit lies in speed of delivery, the instantaneous response, a verbal lightning bolt. When it is done, it cannot be undone; indeed, by the very brevity of its nature, it is easily remembered and easily passed along. As a result, Dublin wit (imagine the Algonquin wits in positions of power in our national capital) has caused a lot of Dublin enmities. This relates not indirectly to Dr. Samuel Johnson's observation that "the Irish are a fair people. They never speak well of one another." He phrased it as an Englishman; an Irishman would have given it more dazzle, saying perhaps, "The Irish are a fair people; they describe themselves as foul." One raises hackles, perhaps; the other raises blisters.

Yeats suffered from Dublin wits. By the yahoos of the streets he was frequently called "Willie the Spooks," because of his interest in the occult; or "The Gland Old Man," because of the rejuvenation surgery he sought. James Joyce said of him that he spoke more like a man of letters than a poet, a jibe that hurt. Professor Dowden of Trinity gave an even meaner cut. Yeats, he said, "was a man born to write the life of Southey." George Moore said of him that he looked "like an umbrella left behind at a picnic." Yeats didn't have the gift of wit, and indeed, one can make the point that it sometimes seems lacking in genius of the highest order. It is important for some geniuses that they take themselves solemnly at all times, at least in public. Joyce's brother, Stanislaus, who would write a book about his famous sibling, resented Gogarty because he feared the doctor's intellectual roistering would keep Joyce from serious work.

George Moore, whose wit was a determinedly cruel cutlass, was given a gentle comeuppance by James Stephens in one of the most delightful of the latter's essays in which he described their meeting. Stephens, however, was too kind to impale. Moore was fortunate that he didn't incur the wrath of Gogarty. His sensuality and the rhymes that ring on his name would have offered the doctor a devastating opportunity. Susan Mitchell (1868–1930) was a Dublin wit and poet who caught Moore with her *bandilleras*. Some men kiss and tell, she remarked, but Moore "tells and doesn't kiss." In a satiric verse, she hit him harder.

> I've puffed the Irish language, and puffed the Irish soap;
> I've used them—on my nephew—with the best results, I hope;
> For with this older, dirtier George, I have no heart to cope.

A friend of AE's and other Dublin intellectuals of her day, she was an Irish Protestant but a Sinn Feiner, which put her on the opposite side of the fence from the Trinity College wits:

Gogarty, Mahaffy, and Tyrrell. Her parody of Rudyard Kipling's "Recessional" in which she lacerated her own Ascendancy, caused a furor. The opening stanza ran:

> God of the Irish Protestant
> Lord of our proud Ascendancy
> Soon there'll be none of us extant
> We want a few plain words with thee,
> Though knows't our hearts are always set
> On what we get, on what we get.

Her first book of humorous verse, *Aids to the Immortality of Certain Persons in Ireland, Charitably Administered*, brought her a measure of immortality.

In the fifteenth century, we are told, more than five hundred years after our legendary poet threatened the Danes with a satire in Dublin, Niall O'Higgin reputedly killed the English Lord Lieutenant of Ireland, Sir John Stanley, with a satirical poem. Most likely it was sung to the accompaniment of a harp. Wit, song, satire, the bitter word, the winging poem, the street ballad, the political lampoon are more a part of literary Dublin than they are of any other English-speaking city.

With all this, we have not touched on the Irish bull itself, which long ago was the subject of an essay by Maria Edgeworth. The bulls of her day were unintentional blunders, semantic confusions that arose on the Gaelic tongue as it struggled to manage English syntax. Today, the Irish bull, like Mahaffy's description of it, is intentional.

"One man is as good as another and often a damn sight better," runs one of modern origin.

We readily see the difference between it and those made by the most notorious of all Irish bull makers, Sir Boyle Roche, who served in the eighteenth-century parliament.

"Half the lies our opponents tell about us aren't true," he once cried out.

On another occasion he cast his vote thus: "I answer in the affirmative with an emphatic no."

He once said meditatively that "the worst of all misfortunes is usually followed by a greater," and declared that in the dim path of the future he could discern "the footprints of an unseen hand."

Dubliners delight in quoting Sir Boyle's comic vagaries to one another. Nothing runs beyond the irreverence of Irish wit, not even Irish wit nor even Ireland's wrongs.

Sir Boyle once remarked that Ireland's cup of sorrows was "overflowing and is not full yet." A modern wag said mockingly that as long as Ireland remains silent, England is deaf to her cries.

The patriotic poem "A Nation Once Again" soon won the response from those who dissented from its principles, "Urination Once Again."

While Gogarty's wit was ebullient, Joyce's was often the wit of gloom. What must be recognized is that *Ulysses* and *Finnegans Wake* are works of supreme wit, wit of the Celtic inheritance where the complexity runs higher than the humor, the riddles and rigmarole of ancient Ireland brought to perfection in the most mellifluous, magical, and mysterious of English prose. We have in Joyce the apotheosis not of the pun, but of paronomasia.

Ever since Oliver Wendell Holmes described the pun as "the lowest form of humor," and then went on to pun incessantly, too many persons dull-wittedly have quoted the observation as a maxim. Actually the pun is but one of the many tropes of paronomasia that is perhaps the most pervasive figure of speech in any language, familiar to the Greeks who named it, and beloved of Shakespeare and all Elizabethans. Paronomasia takes in all forms of word-play, word-shading, word-shaving, puns, parallelisms, the juggling of homonyms, all in the heightening of force or fun. If it would seem at times in Joyce's *Finnegans Wake* to run into paranomia or a real dislocation from sense, something beyond nonce-words and nonsense, that may be his failure or it may be ours. It is not because what is punned should be shunned. In the romantic twilight of our age,

such flights of intellect as the serious pun seem too remote
from passion, but there was a time when Demosthenes in a
most solemn and critical moment in Athenian history could cry
out, in effect, "Carey, you never had a care," and Joyce himself
remarked (and he was not the first) that the Catholic church
was founded on the pun, "Thou are Peter and upon this Rock
I will build My Church."

The tradition of fantastic word-play that Joyce thrust upon
the world and brought all critics (at least those outside Dublin)
to their knees was continued by Brian O'Nuallain, or Brian
Nolan, to give him two of his four names. The others were
Flann O'Brien, under which he wrote novels and plays, and
Myles na gCopaleen, under which, for twenty-nine years, he
wrote a daily column of humor and satire in *The Irish Times*.
In his novel *At Swim-Two-Birds*, Nolan piles parody on fantasy in a manner that set Joyce laughing. The story deals with
an aspiring author who is writing a book about a man who is
writing a book about a group of characters who suddenly get
together to write a book about him. The book, which appeared
in 1939, is an unquestionable classic.

Nolan's most extravagant humor and acerbic satire were reserved for his newspaper column, where he elaborated the
wildest literary puns in anecdotes about two dissolute medical
students named Keats and Chapman. Perhaps one of the stories
might reveal the style of his particular and amusing nonsense.

> Keats and Chapman once called to see a titled friend, and
> after the host had hospitably produced a bottle of whiskey, the
> two visitors were called into consultation regarding the son of
> the house, who had been exhibiting a disquieting redness of face
> and boisterousness of manner at the age of twelve. The father
> was worried, suspecting some dread disease. The youngster was
> produced but the two visitors glass in hand decline to make any
> diagnosis. When leaving the big house, Chapman rubbed his
> hands briskly and remarked on the cold.
>
> "I think it must be freezing and I'm glad of that drink," he

said. "By the way, did you think what I thought about that youngster?"

"There's a nip in the heir," Keats said.

If Nolan continued Joyce's erudite tradition of wit, Brendan Behan (1923–1964) carried on the irreverent tradition of Gogarty but without Gogarty's urbanity, gentility, and grace. Behan was a roisterer, and in the O'Casey tradition without college training, although not reared in poverty as O'Casey was. He was fluent in Irish. Arrested for drunkenness on one occasion, he refused to address the English-speaking Irish judge in anything but Gaelic, which was his right under the law but a bloody inconvenience to the court, as he himself intended. Behan, like Nolan, wrote in Irish as well as in English; but, unlike Nolan, who mightn't turn his head if a friend walked into the room, Behan was an extrovert. His antics in public were frequently those of a clown, but then, in a less boozy way, so were those of Wilde and Shaw and Gogarty, for Behan stood in their tradition—the Irishman out to win, disdain, and even outrage the Sassenach at one and the same time.

Every sword has two sides and so has the Irish tongue. If storytelling—the Celts are the oldest storytelling people in the world—in the Irish is marked by scintillating wit and enchanting conversation, as well as the gift for acting out the narrative, there is the darker side. The Irish wit has been described as a "silver razor" (the phrase was put to the conversation of Ulick O'Connor, the biographer of Gogarty as well as Behan), but it has a serrated edge as well that lacerates an opponent's soul. Although the most famous of Irish wits, Oscar Wilde, is said never to have turned his wit against a person but rather concentrated on institutions of his day, on society's manners and morals, and particularly its hypocrisies, subsequent Irish wits (or earlier ones) have not been so tenderhearted. Indeed, Dublin has perhaps (again that concentrated quality) more literary libel suits than other cities, and more enmities than libel suits, and more alienations than enmities, and more contemptuous evaluations in private than alienations. An interesting volume could be compiled solely of Dublin literary libel suits or court appearances of writers in other actions.

The Irish themselves are well aware of this. "If there were only three Irishmen left in the world," Behan once said, "you'd find two of them in a corner talking about the third. We're a backbiting race." How much pleasanter to remember the wit rather than the calumny, the humor rather than the hurt. There are wit and humor in one of the last remarks Behan made to one of the nuns nursing him during his last illness, "May you live to be the mother of a bishop."

Modern Times

XV

The years from 1916 through 1922 were, in Ireland, years of open warfare, guerrilla warfare, gang warfare, murder, assassination, executions, anarchy, misrule, revolution, and near anarchical upheaval. One disturbance followed another in bewildering sequence or one overlapped the other, or all supervened at once. When it was over (as well as while it was going on) literary life in Dublin was completely altered. Dark Rosaleen had left the dreamy savannahs of romanticized realms, donned a tailored tweed suit, put on stout walking boots, and undertaken to rule her own roost, or at least the larger part of it.

Cathleen ni Houlihan, lustrous in song during the centuries of British rule and abuse, gave way on the Abbey stage, that scrutinizable focal point, to Juno Boyle with her Paycock, and the other plays of a Dublin construction and railway laborer turned genius playwright. Compared to Cathleen ni Houlihan, Juno is equally long-suffering, equally enduring, but her torments come not from British overlords but from the runaway nationalistic, and often narcissistic, passions of puritanical Irishmen.

Under Lennox Robinson, himself a worthy playwright, the Abbey struggled on during the post-Easter Rising period and during the most of the Anglo-Irish war, or the Troubles, as it was euphemistically called by the Irish, but in early 1921, with the actors in tears, it closed its doors. In a way it was fortunate the building was left standing. British guns had rendered rubble the other side of Abbey Street. During 1916, Robinson's *The Dreamer* was performed and his best play, *The Whiteheaded Boy*. During these troublesome times H. Patrick Wilson, St. John Ervine, Fred O'Donovan, and J. Augustus Keogh were in the role of producer, and sometimes playwright. The years were, in more ways than one, desultory.

Robinson describes the years 1918 to 1921 as "full of dread," and gives an example of the tension and excitement under which the Abbey toiled. In February, 1921, it was decided to stage a play, *The Revolutionist*, by Terence J. MacSwiney (1883–1920), another poet-politician-patriot-martyr, who had been mayor of Cork and who had starved to death in a British prison. In 1920 he had been arrested as a result of the Troubles and confined in Brixton prison, where, after going without food for seventy-four days, and exhorting his fellow Irish prisoners to do likewise, he had died. His funeral in Cork had been a major anti-British demonstration. To stage his bold and prophetic play was a daring thing to do. At this time, there were sixty thousand British troops in Ireland at war with the I.R.A. For many citizens, it was difficult to know which faction was fighting whom. Irrational actions, prompted by fanaticism, were the order of the day. Thus when Robinson arrived at the Abbey one day to be confronted by two gunmen he was as much annoyed as surprised, and when they tried to stop him, he brushed them aside and ordered the rehearsal to proceed. As it turned out, the gunmen were intent merely on preventing an English photographer from photographing the rehearsal.

Late in 1921, the Anglo-Irish war ended, and the Abbey resumed. At this moment, its chief problem was finances. The company was all but bankrupt. Three playwrights were to save it: Brinsley MacNamara, a pen name for John Weldon (1890–1963), writer of fiction and plays who would become a director of the Abbey; George Shiels, the invalid Thomas Moore of the Irish theater, and Sean O'Casey (1884–1964), one of the titans of the Irish literary revival and the Irish theater.

Sean O'Casey was born John Casey of an impoverished Protestant Dublin family in slums he despised, and grew up without formal education. At manhood he found work as a laborer, first on construction, and then on railways, but he was often unemployed. The great lockout of 1913 helped forge his political and anticlerical opinions and prompted his first writings. He was consistently anti-Catholic church all his life, and a pledged Communist for the last part of it. The slums into which he was born gave him the substance of the dramas that would make him immortal in the theater, and when he fled Ireland for England, in 1926, his dramatic work diminished in force, a phenomenon already noticed in Moore and Gogarty, although absent in Joyce, Colum, and others.

His first play, *The Shadow of a Gunman*, was produced at the Abbey in 1923. It was followed the next year by *Juno and the Paycock* and two years later by *The Plough and the Stars*. The bitter attacks mounted against this last play drove him from Ireland. The first two plays are credited with having saved the Abbey.

In 1928, Yeats engendered a break with O'Casey because of his rejection of *The Silver Tassie*, a play of O'Casey's dealing with World War I. There was good reason for declining it as the passing years have demonstrated; it was a fall-off from his previous trilogy which, if it had provoked the usual narrow reaction from the pietistic and chauvinistic (again, the heretical nationalism showing through), had won him critical acclaim and an international reputation. O'Casey thought Yeats should have indulged him where he had "lined their pockets." He remained bitter about the rejection and was rude to Lady Gregory years later, she who had early on so befriended him.

All that said of him, it must be added that he was, like many an Irishman, a curious bundle of contradictions. Despite his Communist profession of allegiance, and his description of himself as a rationalist, he was extremely engrossed in religious thought and his language is redolent of the phrases of a man of religion. Brooks Atkinson recounts that near the end of his long life, asked how he felt, O'Casey replied, "Tired, but joyous, praising God for his rightness and the will towards joy in the hearts of men." Despite ulcerated eyes that left him blind at the end, he produced, in his lifetime, a tremendous body of work—twelve full-length plays, fifteen one-act plays, six volumes of autobiography, and four volumes of poems, short stories, reviews, and essays.

His first successful plays, *Juno and the Paycock* and *The Plough and the Stars*, brought him not only fame but his greatest good fortune, his wife, Eileen. She was an Irish girl acting in New York when she read *Juno and the Paycock* and fell in love with the author. She made her way to England, met him, and married him. He was forty-seven at the time and she twenty-two. They would be together thirty-three years, and she would love him and cherish him to the end. They had three children, and the death of one wrenched from O'Casey's heart one of his finest essays. He was a dedicated family man and loved Eileen profoundly. Recently, her autobiography *Sean* gave a charming intimate picture of their lives, including an account of her infidelity, confessed to him when she found herself pregnant. Sean turned white, she recounts, forgave her, arranged an abortion, and all went on as before. Gradually his eyesight failed but not his pen nor his buoyant optimism. He lived out his days in Devon, England, and, still angry at the people of his homeland, refused to have his body returned to Dublin. Her book gives her a place in any history of literary Dublin.

Irish Catholic clergy in America as well as Ireland were consistently opposed to O'Casey's plays at the times of their first productions. In 1934, his play *Within the Gates*, experimental and difficult to mount, was so criticized that O'Casey was again embittered. In it, he had introduced music, song, and dance, as he did also in *Red Roses for Me*, a semi-autobiographical drama that was produced in 1943. *The Plough and the Stars* had created an uproar when it was produced, but the brouhaha that was to alienate O'Casey from Ireland permanently (although he read the Dublin papers to the end) was

Sean O'Casey

the reaction of the Catholic archbishop of Dublin to the play *The Drums of Father Ned*. The play was to be produced along with an adaptation from *Ulysses* at the Dublin International Theatre Festival in 1958, when the archbishop indicated his displeasure sufficiently and both plays were ruled out. O'Casey in righteous indignation barred all his plays from the floors of the Abbey and from the radio waves in Ireland. *The Drums of Father Ned* argues for a more joyous and less puritanical Ireland than a callow nationalism permitted or permits. The clericalism he constantly attacked finally drove him but not his plays out of Ireland, for he remains a favorite with Dubliners and his *The Bishop's Bonfire*, never produced in London, had a six weeks' run in Dublin's largest theater.

If, in leaving Ireland, O'Casey lost touch with the struggling, aspiring, self-deceived, and deceptive characters of the Irish slums whom he knew, loved, and brought to life on the stage, and if his plays fell below the exalted standard of *Juno* and *The Plough and the Stars*, his prose in the six volumes of his autobiography, in which he recounted his fight for place, his antipathy to the psychological tyrannies in Ireland, and his enthusiasm for life, must rank among the best ever put to paper by a Dubliner. It is exuberant, witty, rhetorical, comic, musical, magic, and gay, and if, on occasion, it shades the truth as Sean's memory saw it, he is more honest than George Moore. Was it he or someone else who said of him that if everyone else was concerned with Ireland's honor, he was concerned with its honesty? He portrayed the "poor people of Ireland" as he saw them, human and sinning but heroic and savagely sane.

Through all the long years of O'Casey's life the Abbey Theatre continued to present an array of Irish playwrights. If he and Shiels had saved it from bankruptcy, the Irish government came through with a subsidy that assured its continuance. In 1951, after a performance of *The Plough and the Stars*, an ongoing favorite there, the old theater burned down. St. John Ervine, who was manager during the Easter Rising (when the performances had to be cancelled), had mourned that the old theater had not been rubbled by British guns and "bitterly regretted that I had not come down on Easter Monday and fired the place myself." Now it was gone, and a new one would be built, but not right away. The company performed in the Queens. Ervine himself besides acting as manager (an unpopular one) was the author of numerous plays and novels, was a drama critic, and later a professor of dramatic literature at the Royal Society of Literature. Besides him and the more famous personages—Yeats, Lady Gregory, Robinson, Colum, O'Casey, Shaw, Shiels, and T. C. Murray—there were a score and more of others. Robinson lists Paul Vincent Carroll, Francis Stuart, Frank O'Connor, Hugh Hunt, Andrew Ganly, Frank Carney, Louis D'Alton, Elizabeth O'Connor, Roger Mc-Hugh, Austin Clarke, Robert Farren, Gerard Healy, Joseph Tomelty, Ralph Kennedy, Walter Macken, M. J. Molly, John Coulter, and Seamus Byrne from 1932 to 1950. Such an efflores-cence of playwrights in eighteen years would be extraordinary in the United States with its more than 210 million population. What are we to make of it in a country with a population of little more than three million?

George Fitzmaurice (1878–1963) was a civil servant whose plays were among the first produced by the Abbey. In 1907 his *The Country Dressmaker* was a comedy hit, and he followed it the next year with a one-act tragedy, *The Pie-Dish*. Still other plays followed, and the first remained popular. Like many another writer of his day he was a contributor to Seumus O'Sullivan's *Dublin Magazine*. His play *The Dandy Dolls* is more popular than ever.

In 1932 Yeats organized the Irish Academy of Letters and several of the Abbey playwrights would be elected. Among them was Teresa Deevy (1903–1963), who, all but stone-deaf, was a master of authentic dialogue of poetic beauty. Among her plays were *Temporal Powers* and *The King of Spain's Daughter*.

In the same year, 1932, that *Temporal Powers* was acted, *Things That Are Caesar's* was mounted. The author was Paul

Vincent Carroll (1900–1968), a Dubliner teaching school in Glasgow, Scotland, who was to establish a reputation as one of the outstanding dramatists produced by the Abbey. The year of his appearance, incidentally, was the year De Valera took command of the Dail of the Irish Free State to begin slowly stripping away the remaining connections with England and dissolved the Irish Senate where Yeats and Gogarty had sat as members.

Two years after *Things That Are Caesar's* appeared, Carroll won the Casement Award of the Irish Academy of Letters for his play *Shadow and Substance*, one of the classics educed by the Abbey. That same year Joyce's *Ulysses* was published in New York.

Nor should Gogarty be forgotten as one of the Abbey's contributors. His three plays were produced pseudonymously. The first, *The Blight*, was an attack on slum conditions in Dublin and undoubtedly inspired O'Casey, who acknowledged it as one of the few plays he had seen before his own were produced. The second, *A Serious Thing*, was a satire blistering with sarcasm British rule in Ireland, and the third, *The Enchanted Trousers*, a comedy, produced in 1919.

The terrible years of the Anglo-Irish war and the civil war lay ahead in which Gogarty nearly lost his life, and several Abbey actors and employees found themselves with guns in their hands. One of the stagehands, Peadar Kearney, wrote "A Soldier's Song," which has become the national anthem of the Republic of Ireland. Generally speaking, the years from 1930 to 1935 also were a doldrum for the Abbey and much of the time the company was on tour. In 1935, Frank O'Connor was named to the board of directors and pumped new zeal and new blood into the project.

Through these years the Abbey was not the only theater in Dublin by any means. On other stages popular and more traditional theatrical entertainment was produced, patriotic plays in which the romantic version of Ireland so dear to the hearts of the chauvinists was presented.

In 1928 the Gate Theatre Company was founded in Dublin by Micheál MacLiammóir (1889–   ) and Hilton Edwards, an English actor with a gift for organization. They were fortunate in their own complementary talents.

MacLiammóir is a Renaissance man: actor, monologist, writer, painter, and linguist. The objective of the Gate was to bring international theater to Dublin, and it did. Its directors also discovered new playwriting talent in Ireland. MacLiammóir himself wrote *Ill Met by Moonlight* and *Where Stars Walk*, the last produced in 1961. His autobiographical works reveal him as a writer with style and a raconteur of high humor. The prose works are *All for Hecuba,* which was published in 1946, and *Each Actor on His Ass* in 1957.

The most distinguished playwright developed by the Gate was Dublin-born William Denis Johnston (1901–   ), a lawyer and the son of a lawyer, whose play *The Old Lady Says No* was mounted at the Gate in 1929. Two years later he was made a director. In that year, his play *The Moon on the Yellow River* (produced by the Abbey) was another success. During World War II he served as a war correspondent for the British Broadcasting Company and, like many another Dubliner, remained in virtual exile in England and the United States.

The Gate also can be put down as the discoverer of Mary Manning, author of *Youth's the Season . . . ?,* which some critics deem one of the wittiest plays ever produced at the theater. The play was produced at the Gate in 1931 and from then on the author was a familiar figure in the theater, until in 1935 she married an American lawyer of a distinguished family who, as professor at Harvard Law School, became one of the leading libertarians in the United States. While living in Cambridge, Molly Howe, as she was popularly known, played a leading role in the establishment of the Poets Theater in Cambridge, in the shadow of Harvard University.

Among her other plays are *The Happy Family,* a three-act farce produced at the Gate; *The Saint and Mary Kate,* a tragicomedy adapted for the stage from Frank O'Connor's novel;

and *The Voices of Shem*, a remarkable piece of theater, adapted from Joyce's *Finnegans Wake*. Her prose reminiscences are a delight. Mrs. Howe had three daughters, one of whom, Fanny Howe, married to the black writer Carl Senna, has established in the United States a national reputation with her poetry and her short stories. Mrs. Howe on the death of her husband, himself a distinguished writer as well as a Harvard professor, returned to Dublin to make her home and continue her literary career.

MacLiammóir and Edwards also attracted to their side Edward Arthur Henry Pakenham (1902–1961), the Earl of Longford, a member of one of the writingest families in Ireland. He came onto the board of the Gate in 1931 and continued for the rest of his life not merely as a patron and adviser, but as a playwright, author of *The Melians, Carmilla*, and *Yahoo*, the last based on the life of Swift. He was an accomplished linguist, and his translations of Aeschylus and Sophocles, as well as Molière and Beaumarchais, were also staged.

Without diminishing his concern for the Gate, he formed his own company, Longford Productions, which shared the same theater and, indeed, the same aims.

Longford married an English girl, Christine Patti, who adopted Ireland as her country and Dublin as her home with all her heart. She collaborated with her husband on his translations from the Greek but her literary fame rests on her novels and plays, which made her one of the foremost literary figures in Dublin. On the death of her husband, she took command of the Gate, on which he had lavished his talents and his fortune.

Among her many plays are *Patrick Sarsfield, The Earl of Straw, The Hill of Quirke, Stop the Clock*, and *Stephen Stoney*. Two of her better-known novels are *Printed Cotton* and *Sea Change*.

Frank O'Connor (1903–1966) briefly put new strength into the Abbey Theatre, but he is remembered, of course, as a superb short-story writer. No country in the world in the twentieth century has rivaled Ireland in the number of eminent

Micheál MacLiammóir

masters of the short story. Perhaps, too, this should be no surprise, for the Celtic tradition of the shanachie, the story-teller, is old, respected, even sacred, and as strong as Italy's tradition of opera and tenors. Besides O'Connor, international acclaim has come to Sean O'Faolain (1900–   ), Liam O'Flaherty (1896–   ), Mary Lavin (1912–   ), Nora Hoult (1901–   ), and Bryan MacMahon (1909–   )— to name only six major figures. These are writers whose reputations rest on their short stories, although all have tried their hand at other literary forms.

In turn, any number of Irish writers whose reputations rest on other forms—plays, novels, or poetry—have written successful short stories. One thinks immediately of James Joyce with his *Dubliners*; Seumas O'Kelly (1881–1918) and Brian Friel (1929–   ), playwrights; James Stephens (1882–1950) and George Moore (1852–1933), novelists; and Lennox Robinson (1886–1958), playwright and producer. Then there are minor literary figures whose short stories have distinguished them such as Maurice Walsh (1879–1964) and Michael McLaverty (1907–   ), to say nothing of those writing in Irish who will be considered elsewhere. Nor must we forget Lord Dunsany, who stands at the historic beginning of the short story of utter fantasy, forebear of J. R. R. Tolkien and H. C. Lovecraft.

Three of the six short-story writers first mentioned above were deeply involved in the bitter politics of the early twenties in Ireland, O'Flaherty, O'Connor, and O'Faolain. All three opted against the Free State and for the Republic, serving the I.R.A., and two of them, O'Faolain and O'Connor, were captured and interned. That, for O'Connor, was a piece of good fortune because his education, meager to begin with, was fostered in the camp, and by the time he emerged, he had established himself as a writer with a critical study of Turgenev written in Irish.

O'Connor was born Michael O'Donovan in Cork and received his early education from the Christian Brothers. Another famous Cork writer, Daniel Corkery, influenced him toward the short story and confirmed a desire for a literary life. His dedication to the I.R.A. brought him in touch with Sean O'Faolain, who was slightly older, who had been to the national university, and who became director of publicity for the I.R.A. in 1923. O'Connor was interned, perfected his Irish, broadened his knowledge of literature, and began to write poetry, translating from the Irish to English, and more significantly to write short stories. His diligence won him a post as librarian and his first stories were published by AE in *The Irish Statesman*. O'Connor would become one of the great short-story writers of his day and a leading theoretician of the essentials of the short story, and during his exile in America he lectured widely on literature and became a familiar at various universities, including Harvard and the University of Chicago.

His first collection of stories was published in 1931, *Guests of the Nation*, and bespoke the tragedy of the conflict between Englishmen and Irishmen who, in happier circumstances, would have been friends. It is the theme that runs through Thomas Hardy's poem "The Man I Killed."

In 1932, O'Connor published a novel, *The Saint and Mary Kate* (adapted for the stage by Mary Manning), but although he would write other novels, he returned always to the short story, publishing half a dozen collections before his death, and remaining a steady contributor to *The New Yorker*.

About this time he became associated with the Abbey Theatre and from 1936 to 1939 was a director at Yeats's behest. He wrote two plays that were produced there, *In the Train* (1937) and *Moses' Rock* (1938), but the stage was not his forte. The absurd jingoist censorship that came in with the very government he had supported drove him from Ireland, and he resigned his directorship in the Abbey.

The years he spent in the United States, he remained industriously literary, book following book. Also, he must rank as one of those rare birds, a stout Irish literary critic. His *A Short History of Irish Literature* is a critical appraisal, and an excellent one, rather than a history. He examined the novel at length in *The Mirror in the Roadway* (1957) and the short story in *The Lonely Voice* (1963). In 1952 *The Stories of Frank O'Connor* appeared and in 1954 *More Stories*. His auto-biographical works, *An Only Child* and *My Father's Son*, mingle humor, pathos, and humanistic insights.

In his months of internment, he studied languages diligently and learned something of music, for he had the ear, and he was blessed with a beautiful speaking voice. All this helped with one of his finest books, *Kings, Lords & Commons*, which is an anthology of his translations of Irish poems by poets known and unknown from the seventh century to the nineteenth. The book includes his translation of the ribald, rollicking long narrative poem *The Midnight Court* by Brian Merriman (1740–1805), a schoolmaster, who died in Limerick unsung, and whose famous poem, at which every other Irish poet today tries his hand in translation, was long outlawed by the censorship board in Dublin.

O'Connor was close to Yeats during the last years of the poet's life and wrote amusingly about their friendship. In the very year that O'Connor was interned Yeats received the Nobel prize for literature. The year was one of many significances. It was the year that O'Casey's first play was produced at the Abbey. It was the year that Gogarty published his *An Offering of Swans*. It was the year that AE began publishing *The Irish Statesman* and Seumus O'Sullivan the *Dublin Magazine*. It was also the year in which the Irish Free State at last put down the Republican rump forces and imprisoned Eamon de Velera. The coincidence of Yeats's receipt of the Nobel prize and the emergence after internment of O'Connor and O'Faolain and O'Flaherty (who escaped internment by fleeing to England), like the crossing of two·stars in a magic firmament, can be truly said to exemplify the old hackneyed phrase, the end of an era. Yeats, the supreme Anglo-Irish patriot-artist, was a culmination. The men that emerged were a new Ireland. *Ulysses* had arrived about the same time. The nation that had been wandering for so many years had come home to—what? Its writers are still not sure. While all this is true, and the Nobel prize is said to honor a life work (Shaw and Beckett, Anglo-Irish, would win it later), Yeats was yet to produce some of his greatest poetry in *The Tower* (1928), which came in the same year that the first of *Finnegans Wake* was revealed to the world, and in *The Winding of the Stair* (1933) and *Last Poems* (1936). In 1938 he would make his last public appearance at the Abbey Theatre Festival and the next year he was dead. That same year O'Connor left the Abbey. The cause of his despair was the censorship which, confined for a while to books, began to erode the theater. The raw chauvinism of the new government and the puritanism of the Catholic clergy made them allies instead of counterweights. The arts, as always, suffered, for they represent the free man, the man who feels conformity to the fashion of the hour is treason to a higher principle.

XVI

This became the battleground, and good men fled—Moore, MacNamara, O'Connor, Gogarty, Beckett, and others, while other good men stayed and fought—O'Faolain, Yeats, Peader O'Donnell, and Austin Clarke. This is no attempt to assess blame, one way or the other, for the artist must work where he can, his autonomy rooting in the perfection of his work, but merely to state the historical fact. The writers who remained and opposed, to the best of their ability, the philistinism of the establishment softened it and have somewhat quelled it.

Among these were O'Flaherty (despite his traveling) and O'Faolain. Liam O'Flaherty (1896–   ) was born on Inishmore, the largest of the Aran Islands, and grew up Irish-speaking; he learned English, and at the solicitation of the Holy Ghost fathers began to study for the priesthood, advancing to a seminary in Dublin. Sensing the religious life was not for him, he quit the seminary and entered the university. He left, however, to join the Irish Guards with whom he went to France, where he was wounded. Invalided out, he returned home; then went to Dublin; then to London; then to the United States. His writing career began in Boston, Massachusetts, where he worked as a Western Union messenger and at other odd jobs, including day laborer. At the request of his brother and sister, with whom he lived, he began to record his travel adventures and try his hand at short stories. None of these was successful, but the travel material would ultimately develop into *Two Years* and the brilliant short stories.

He had not merely left the seminary, however, he had left the Catholic church. Disenchanted and bitter, he denounced the church for its indifference to social justice and vowed his Communist sympathies. In 1921 he returned to Ireland to support the Republican cause against Griffith's Free State. The next year with a group of the unemployed he seized and held for three days the Rotunda, a public building, as a protest, until the Free State government threatened armed force to remove them and the red flag they had unfurled. He fled to Cork and then to England, where his first short story appeared in a socialist publication. Three years later he published *The Informer*, which would make him famous. The book is the story of Gypo Nolan, a tragic figure of the slums, who betrays his fellows without losing our compassion. The book is superior to O'Flaherty's two earlier novels, *Thy Neighbour's Wife* and *The Black Soul*, both of which took his native islands for their settings. For *The Informer* he turned to the slums of Dublin.

The title of his first novel, *Thy Neighbour's Wife*, takes on an ironic overtone since in 1926 O'Flaherty eloped with Margaret Barrington, the wife of Edmund Curtis (1881–1943), who was Lecky Professor of History at Trinity College and author of one of the most popular brief histories of the country, as well as other historical studies. O'Flaherty's six years with the former Mrs. Curtis, who became his wife, were among his most productive. Besides a play, written in Irish and published in English, he published two outstanding novels, *Mr. Gilhooley* (1926) and *The Assassin* (1928), and also some of his most distinguished short stories, which some critics rate above those of O'Connor or any other Irish writer. Among his short-story collections are *Spring Sowing* (1924) and *The Tent* (1926) and *The Mountain Tavern and Other Stories* (1929). Synge once said of Aran that there "one is forced to believe in a sympathy between man and nature." This is what marks O'Flaherty's stories, although often nature overwhelms man. The animus, however, is very clear in his stories dealing with animals.

The young Sean O'Faolain

In 1930 O'Flaherty went to Russia but returned disillusioned. A man of contradictions always, he wrote in *I Went to Russia*, "I loathe the multitude, except as a spectacle to be watched, an anthill on the march," although elsewhere he would contend that his one virtue was his love of humanity. After visiting Russia, however, he was suspicious of all political systems.

As his career moved onward, it became evident that despite such novels as *The Assassin* and *Mr. Gilhooley*, his strength lay in the short story and his succeeding collections were to confirm this. In 1952 a collection of the short stories he wrote in Irish was published. William Troy, one of his most perceptive commentators, argued that in *The Mountain Tavern and Other Stories* there was a falling off of his work because of his rage over conditions in Ireland and his railing against the Catholic church. During World War II he was in America, nevertheless, defending Ireland's cause against the British demand for the use of the Irish ports. In recent years, making his home in Ireland, he returned to writing in Irish. He is a familiar figure in Dublin, erect, vigorous, with blue eyes that flash with all the bitterness, bravado, and vehemence that he put into his short stories.

Sean O'Faolain (1900–   ) was born in Dublin and reared in Cork, attended the University College there, and at the age of twenty found himself, like O'Flaherty, in armed insurrection against, first, the British, and then the Irish Free State. He acquired a "savage disillusion at Ireland's ineptitude." At the age of twenty-six he won a fellowship to Harvard University, and left Ireland saying, "I don't care if I never see the bloody place again." He remained in greater Boston for three years (ten miles from where O'Flaherty had worked) and his first short story was published at this time while he was a lecturer in English at Boston College, the Jesuit university in Newton, Massachusetts. During these American years he married an Irish girl Eileen Gould. He returned to Ireland to teach school in Wicklow and publish his first collection of short stories, *Midsummer Night's Madness*, which won immediate critical acclaim. The year was 1932. At this time, O'Faolain, with his rimless glasses, pale eyes, and Mephistophelian beard, looked like a Russian intellectual revolutionary of the nineteenth century. Like O'Flaherty, he also wrote in Irish, but unlike O'Flaherty, had to acquire the language. That bent was interrupted by the civil war and the disillusionment that followed. The disillusionment vanished during the years in America. He returned to Ireland idealistic.

His short-story collection was followed almost immediately by a novel, *A Nest of Simple Folk*, and, in 1936, by another, *Bird Alone*. The following year a play, *She Had to Do Something*, was produced at the Abbey. In 1940, another novel appeared, *Come Back to Erin*, whose theme is exile.

In 1938 he wrote *King of the Beggars: The Life of Daniel O'Connell*, a life of "The Great O'Neill," and then a book on De Valera. There would be other nonfiction, biography, travel, criticism, but the short stories would establish and maintain the reputation, raising him to the pinnacle of Irish authorship. Among the short-story collections were *A Purse of Coppers*; *I Remember! I Remember!*; *The Man Who Invented Sin*; and in 1958 *The Stories of Sean O'Faolain*. His autobiography *Vive Moi* was one of his more popular nonfiction works in America in its year of publication.

One of his greatest services to Irish letters was his work as editor of *The Bell*, a literary magazine published in Dublin. It appeared first in October, 1940, and continued to April, 1948; suspended publication, and revived in November, 1950, to run through December, 1954. The magazine fought the ridiculous censorship and struck at corruption in politics, but was chiefly a literary magazine that stood "for life before any abstraction." It sought to impose nothing but to let Ireland "speak," and so was generous to young writers. The editorials O'Faolain wrote attacking the philistinism of the day and the neurotic censorship were prime features of the magazine. O'Faolain was succeeded as editor by O'Connor. Peader O'Donnell (1893–   ), radical leader and novelist, is perhaps the literary man most associated with *The Bell* because he served as its business manager from 1940 on, and after 1946 as its editor. A distinguished radical and revolutionary in the old Irish tradition, O'Donnell is a fighting literary man. In 1916 he was a labor organizer, and in 1966, at seventy-three, he was marching in protest against America's policies in Vietnam, although ignoring Soviet policy in Czechoslovakia and Hungary. In 1918 he was denouncing conscription, and three years later was fighting for De Valera against the Free State forces. Like MacSwiney, he went on a hunger strike after being sentenced to death, as were too many others, but escaped from jail. He had begun to try his hand at serious writing while imprisoned. For additional political agitation he was jailed again and served more time.

Afterwards, he went to France and joined the agrarian movement, serving so assiduously that in 1930 he presided over the European Peasant Congress, a radical body. Later he was to find De Valera too conservative for his tastes and abandon him. About the same year he had a play produced at the Abbey, *The Wrack*. Indeed, as someone has said, it was almost the mark of a Dublin literary man that he have a play produced at the Abbey.

O'Donnell earlier had written a very popular novel, *The Way It Was with Them*, and many more books were to come, both fiction and nonfiction. In 1934 he told of his prison experiences in *The Gates Flew Open*. Surely no nation has produced more literature in this unusual genre, beginning with John Mitchel and coming down to Brendan Behan's *The Borstal Boy*. O'Donnell's best fiction, some critics believe, lies in *Islanders* and *Adrigaole*. His political writing can be found in *There Will Be Another Day*.

His influence and that of O'Faolain in *The Bell* cannot be overstressed. During the 1940s, nationalistic puritanism was developing to its worst, and the censorship drive headed by

Professor William Magennis of University College was not only
intolerable but close to insane.

Mary Lavin, who is the foremost woman writer in Ireland
today, was born in Massachusetts, in 1912. She was taken to
Ireland by her Irish-born parents as a child, and she remained
there; it is her country. She is, like so many other writers since
1922, while peripatetic, far from nomadic, but a frequent visitor
to the United States, whose publications and publishers have
been her main support, and there lies her largest audience.

She is one of the many writers whose works have added
distinction to that distinguished magazine *The New Yorker*.
While she has written several novels, *The House on Clewe Street*
in 1945 being the first, she recognizes that she is preeminently
a short-story writer and doesn't seek now to go beyond that.
Unlike the usual versatile Irish writer she has done nothing but
fiction, eschewing book reviews, articles, drama, poetry, and
all nonfiction.

Her first collection of short stories appeared in 1942, entitled
Tales from Bective Bridge. The book takes its title from the
neighborhood in which she was reared, and her home in County
Meath is known as Bective Farm. She married, the same year
the collection appeared, a lawyer named William Walsh, but
was soon widowed and left to rear her two children. She made
ends meet with her fiction, but there were lean years. Guggen-
heim Fellowships and then *The New Yorker* kept her going.

In recent years, her own life has taken a turn as romantic
as any of her stories. She married Michael McDonald Scott,
a former Jesuit, whom she had known years before her first
marriage when both were students at University College, Dublin.
After his ordination he was assigned to Australia and worked
in educational ventures of his religious society. He had corresponded with Mary until her marriage, and resumed on the
death of her husband. The note of condolence led to further
correspondence and then to romance and marriage. Scott, re-
leased by Rome from his vows, then journeyed to Ireland to
take a post there as director of a graduate school program for

Mary Lavin

foreign students, and make his home with his bride at Bective Farm. She remains one of the most remarkable of Irish writers, an artist of first rank, whose work was recognized in 1963 when she was given the Katherine Mansfield award.

The first one to give her a leg up had been Lord Dunsany, who wrote the introduction to her first collection of stories. Dunsany was born Edward John Moreton Drax Plunkett near Regent's Park, London, in 1878, the son of the seventeenth Lord Dunsany, an Anglo-Irish peer, and in due time (1899) became the eighteenth Lord Dunsany. His life was in contrast to his writings. After graduating from Sandhurst, the British military academy, he served in the Boer War and in World War I with the Royal Iniskilling Fusiliers and the Coldstream Guards. His first book had appeared between those two encounters. It was *The Gods of Pegana* and came out in 1905, in which, it is fair to say, he anticipated such masters as J. R. R. Tolkien in inventing a weird mythology. The next year he published a second book, *Time and the Gods*. This was all adult fantasy, and many critics rate him as an imaginative genius, and an inspiration to H. P. Lovecraft, that American master of fantasy. Dunsany, as O'Faolain among others acknowledged, was a master of the short story. His foremost collections, besides the two mentioned, are *The Sword of Welleran, A Dreamer's Tale, The Book of Wonder, Fifty-One Tales, Tales of Wonder*, and *Tales of Three Hemispheres*. Later he would write his autobiography, in which he remarked that he had turned to writing novels because he was disappointed at the reception accorded his short stories.

At Yeats's request, he wrote for the Abbey, and the results were published in a book entitled *Five Plays* (1914).

Dunsany, besides being a soldier, was also what might not be expected in view of the world of imagination shown in his stories, a vigorous outdoor man, an athlete, adept at cricket, a hunter of big game, and, more understandably, an assiduous devotee of chess. He too, like many other writers, became disaffected with conditions in Ireland because of the nationalism and its consequent censorship and intimidations which developed with the Free State and intensified under De Valera's government.

Bryan MacMahon (1909–   ) found himself literarily with his contributions to *The Bell*. He was born in Listowel in County Kerry, Ireland, the home of another literary man, John B. Keane, the playwright. MacMahon's first collection, *The Lion-Tamer and Other Stories*, appeared in 1948, and a second book of stories, *The Red Petticoat*, in 1955. In 1952 he published a novel, *Children of the Rainbow*.

Michael McLaverty (1907–   ), another schoolmaster, established his reputation with *The Game Cock and Other Stories* (1949), as well as with his novels. His home is in Northern Ireland, where he was educated. He took his master's degree in science at Queen's University in Belfast.

One of the major influences on both O'Connor and O'Faolain was a schoolmaster in Cork, Daniel Corkery (1878–1964), whose literary work would win him a professorship of English at the university there. He was one of the early enthusiasts for the study of Irish and worked for the Gaelic League. In 1909 he founded the Cork Dramatic Society and his first play was performed there. His intention in part was to set up a Cork literary revival to rival what was going on in Dublin, but Dublin was too much in the minds of men, and too much the center of learning, for his rival school to achieve rank. Indeed, his foremost disciples would make their names in Dublin, as indeed, in a way, did he, for his plays were produced by Robinson at the Abbey—*The Yellow Bittern* in 1920 and *The Labour Leader* in 1919, and others later.

In 1917 *The Threshold of Quiet*, a novel, was published and ran through several printings. Corkery was always more popular in Ireland than outside, which may be due to the lack of rebelliousness in his spirit. Not that he was an anglophile. He wasn't. His lameness kept him from taking arms against British rule, but he was a patriot of individual bent, and one book of his short stories, *The Hounds of Banba*, published in 1920, was of distinct propaganda value. Later he would serve in the Irish Senate. His short stories deserve more of an audience today than they have, and to many of the Irish he is the equal of his famous disciples. Among his collections of short stories are *A Munster Twilight, The Stormy Hills*, and *Earth Out of Earth*. One of his most influential books appeared in 1925. It was *The Hidden Ireland*, a brilliant study of the poets of Munster writing in Irish in the eighteenth century, the purpose of which was to show that, during the darkest hours of the penal laws, a literature of true merit obtained among the people and that the language spoken at the time was no mere patois, but a highly developed one. The impact of the book was distinct and dramatic, for it stimulated more translations of the latter-day Irish writers who had been more or less overlooked when so much attention was being given the ancient pagan tales. Another salient study is his *Synge and Anglo-Irish Literature.*

The ferment in the reading and writing of Irish during these years was immense. The first short stories in Irish were, curiously, a collection of George Moore's translated from the English by an Irish scholar.

The problem of finding a suitable modern idiom and style was defeating for the Gaelic revivalists seeking to construct a twentieth-century Irish literature. Should the writers return to the seventeenth and eighteenth centuries for their styles, or should they adopt the living speech of the Gaeltacht?

From the days of Maria Edgeworth, Dublin has never been without its women novelists, and the tradition continued in the twentieth century. Like the men, some of them fled into exile, some were driven out, some remained in Dublin or close by, and some found their books banned, much to their astonishment, but not necessarily to their dismay. Two Dublin-born distinguished novelists of Anglo-Irish lineage, both of whom went to live in England, are Elizabeth Bowen (1899–1973) and Iris Murdoch (1919–   ), both of whom fall into the tradition of Irish writers who have become ornaments of an almost strictly English tradition.

Miss Bowen, the daughter of an Irish lawyer, was educated in England, married Alan C. Cameron in 1923, and settled near Oxford, but several of her books take Ireland for their scene. Her first novel, *The Hotel*, appeared in 1927, and dealt with the postwar situation in England, but in 1929 she published *Last September*, the story of an Anglo-Irish girl set in the troubled times that followed the war in Ireland and preceded the treaty of 1922. From then on, her reputation was secure, and she came to be recognized as one of the outstanding novelists of the first half of the century.

Her subsequent novels confirmed her place: *Friends and Relations* (1931), *The House in Paris* (1935), *The Death of the Heart* (1938), and *The Heat of the Day* (1949), which dealt with the second world war in London, and the bombardment. In 1942 she published *Bowen's Court*, the story of her Cork family, and the same year, *Seven Winters*, which told of her Dublin girlhood. She also published several volumes of short stories.

She was one of the great figures of modern Anglo-Irish literature. Because of her detached irony, her wit, and her somewhat convoluted style, she has been compared to Henry James, Virginia Woolf, and Maria Edgeworth. Her novels deal with the upper classes.

Iris Murdoch's withdrawal from her Irish beginnings has been more pronounced. She too was educated in England and lives there still. She began her career as a teacher of philosophy and published a study of Sartre, but not until 1956 did she bring out her first novel, *Under the Net*. Her strength of style would first appear in *The Flight From the Enchanter* and attain its epitome of wit and weirdness, tenderness and farce, and brilliant imaginative reality in *The Bell*, which was published in 1958. The novel displays the comic spirit at its shrewdest. While she never has had the wider appeal of Miss Bowen, she is deemed one of the outstanding novelists of our day, complex, mixing the fantastic and the real, somewhat coldly detached, a novelist with purpose, highly organized, highly gifted. In one of her novels, *The Red and the Green*, she too took the 1916–1923 period to examine the problems of the Anglo-Irish in Ireland.

A current literary sensation in England is Edna O'Brien (1932–   ), who has elected to make her home in London. Edna O'Brien was educated in Ireland and took up the study of pharmacy in Dublin. In 1958, she moved to London, some years after her marriage, and her first novel, *The Country Girls*, was published there in 1960. This was almost immediately followed by *The Lonely Girl*, which was highly successful as the film *The Girl with Green Eyes*. In 1964 she published *Girls in Their Married Bliss*, the next year *August Is a Wicked Month*, and the next year *Casualties of Peace*. All three were promptly banned by the censorship board in Ireland.

Edna O'Brien's novels, although basically Christian one might say, dealing with the adolescence of young girls in Ireland, or Irish girls in London, are strongly oriented toward sex. Kate O'Brien (1897–   ), her namesake and predecessor, had one of her novels banned for a single reference in it, one line, dealing with homosexuality. The novel was *The Land of Spices*, published in 1941, and thought by many critics the finest Catholic novel published in Ireland in decades.

Kate O'Brien was born in Limerick in 1897 and educated at University College, Dublin. She took a job as a governess which took her to Spain, where she acquired not only an interest in Spanish literature, but a broader Catholic view than one usually finds in a graduate of the UCD. In 1931, her novel *Without My Cloak* won the Hawthornden prize in England, where she had already had a play produced. The Hawthornden prize, however, established her as an important literary figure. She continued to write plays and novels.

In 1936, her novel *Mary Lavelle*, Catholic in spirit, was banned under the censorship act. *The Land of Spices* dealt with her convent life in Ireland, where she had the good fortune to study under a group of French nuns, and the book contrasts the civility of the nuns with the turmoil of adolescence in the students. The banning of the book brought such a wave of protest that the censors unbanned it.

They had done this first, however, in the case of *The Tailor and Ansty* by Eric Cross (1905–   ), which illuminates the hysterical censorship crisis in Ireland. The book was a series of sketches drawn from the life and talk of a crippled, self-retired tailor named Timothy Murphy and his wife Anastasia, called Ansty. They were, to the countryside around, "The Tailor and Ansty," who lived, as the Tailor styled it, "in the townland of Garrynapeaka in the district of Inchigeela, in the parish of Iveleary, in the barony of West Muskerry, in the county of Cork, in the province of Munster." They were pleasant, earthy people, with the wisdom of the soil in their blood and bones, and their cunning exceeded by far by their charity, their loving acceptance of life and their fellowman. The book was promptly banned under the Censorship of Publications Act.

This act and its subsequent administration is one of the best examples of Catholicism grown implicitly heretical. F. S. L. Lyons (1923–   ), a graduate of Trinity College and a fellow there, before going to a professorship in England, in his *Ireland Since the Famine: 1850 to the Present*, tells the story with insight. As early as 1926, he points out, a committee was set up by the government to exclude lascivious magazines from entering Ireland from England.

But when, three years later, the Censorship of Publications Act was passed, it went much further than striking at the gutter press and at salacious paperbacks. Not only did the Act contain a section designed to banish from Ireland any publication advocating birth control, but it also set up a Censorship Board with the responsibility of recommending to the Ministers of Justice the banning of books which they considered to be indecent or obscene. The censorship thus imposed was, it must be emphasized, motivated neither by political nor religious intolerance.

It was, indeed, reinforced by the argument that neither art nor literature had any rights against God and the censorship at its inception and afterwards had strong clerical approval.

Innocuous at first, it became silly during the 1940s and vindictive during the 1950s. During the 1940s Sean O'Faolain's *The Bell*, as well as the Irish Association for Civil Liberties in the fifties, wrought a change in public opinion and in the operation of the censorship board. What the board and the act sought was to keep Ireland not only independent but clear of interdependence (which was impossible) and free of corrupting foreign influences (particularly English) and thoroughly Celtic and Catholic (which was likewise impossible). They sought, Lyons points out, "to translate into reality the puritanism that often goes with revolution, to establish, so far as laws could establish it, that the new Ireland should shine like a good deed in a naughty world."

To read *The Tailor and Ansty* today and the bucolic innocence of its ribaldry (and that not too much) is to wonder by what logic the censors came to ban it, just as a reading of *The Shewing-Up of Blanco Posnet* leaves one astonished at the state of mind of the English censors in dealing with that play. When a Protestant member of the Dail sought to have the ban on *The Tailor and Ansty* lifted, a debate followed ranging over a four-day period, the animadversions expressed in which leave one with the sense of moving through a sort of nightmare.

Frank O'Connor writes in *A Short History of Irish Literature*:

> The debate that raged about *The Tailor and Ansty* is an indispensable document for any student of our literature because it shows better than anything that I can say to what depths the intellectual life of the country had sunk. Sir John Keane insisted on reading the passages from the book that had been objected to, but the Senate retorted by having all quotations stricken from the record, so that, as its spokesmen quite seriously argued, pornographers could not buy the House reports for the purpose of reading indecency.

Although the Catholic bishops never openly called for the enforcement of the censorship laws, they never opposed them, and any number of the minor clergy showed their Manichaean enthusiasm for them. Three of these, motivated by their Lord alone knows what sort of apostolic zeal, descended on the Tailor one day, forced him down on his knees, and made him burn the book. He bore this as he bore his own disfigurement, he crippled in leg, others crippled in soul. The incident shocked all but the dim-witted in Dublin, but didn't diminish the dedication of the politicians to the value of censorship. They applied the laws with what can only be deemed vindictiveness against the writers who criticized them.

The zealous censors were ultimately finessed out of their positions. A farsighted Minister of Justice, Brian Lenihan, appointed liberals to the board whose attitudes drove the conservatives to resignation. The censorship continued but on a more sensible basis. Nevertheless, between 1960 and 1965 some nineteen hundred books were banned, an average of thirty a month. Although the vast majority were junk, and all can be purchased by mail from London or the United States, the nagging fact is that the censorship remains in Ireland long after the Catholic church (the analogy is not exact) itself has abandoned the Index Librorum Prohibitorium. It is amusing to think of *The Tailor and Ansty* being banned by representatives of Rome, which never saw fit to ban Rabelais. The Latin nature takes a broader view of ribaldry. The Tailor happily was honored in death because the sculptor Seamus Murphy (whose autobiographical study of the stonecutters of Ireland, *Stone Mad*, deserves a place in any literary history of Dublin) carved his monument.

XVII

The spirit of Vatican Council II, undoubtedly, will in its turn reorder the conscience of the Irish puritan as surely as it is regularizing the liturgy in the Catholic churches of the United States despite the intransigence of aging Irish pastors who relinquish the practices of their youth begrudgingly.

Edna O'Brien's novels, meanwhile, remain on the censor's list in Dublin although they are sold there, and despite the acclaim given her by Catholic critics in England. Monica Dickens, one of England's better-known women novelists and critics, now removed to the United States, has hailed Miss O'Brien as "one of the most exciting writers in England today."

The clerical censorship—for such it was—is not the only way in which the rampant effete latter-day nationalism of the arriviste Irish Republic expressed its convictions. Some libraries, it is charged, were long intimidated from buying books unacceptable to the "true Irish spirit." *Protest in Arms*, by Edgar Holt, with an introduction by Cathal O'Shannon, an Irish labor leader, was barred from the Longford County libraries as pro-English. Worse still, you can scour the shelves of many an Irish library and not find the works of some of the country's most celebrated authors. Since the purchase of library copies is often the main source of income to a writer, it is easy to see why one after another has left Ireland for England or the United States.

Charles J. Haughey, one of the more forward looking statesmen in Ireland today, in his determination to rectify the literary situation, brought into the law of the land the exemption from taxes for artists and writers on the income they receive from their artistic work. The government has a trump card in that it could conceivably deem a writer's work not worthy, but to date no applicant has been barred on that ground. Indeed, within Ireland there are authors who are receiving income on works banned by the board of censors and not having to pay taxes on that income. All too recently, however, John MacGahern (1935–   ), a Dublin-born schoolteacher, whose first novel, *The Barracks*, won the AE Memorial Award, was driven from his teaching post in Dublin because of his second novel, *The Dark*, published in 1965, which dealt with masturbation. His situation was complicated by his marriage outside the Catholic church. He fled to London.

Through these years, the Abbey Theatre and the Gate struggled on. But the whole theater movement in the Irish revival has one central, curious figure. If genius is the infinite capacity for taking pains, literary Dublin has a genius unrivaled among diarists, curiously unsung, although called upon by every student of the Irish theater to fill out a thesis. He is Joseph Holloway (1861–1944), a devotee of the theater without peer, who, beginning in the 1880s and without stop until his death in 1944, attended every opening in his native city, diligently recording it all in 221 hand-written volumes totaling an estimated 25 million words!

He is, although no one I know has said so, the rival of Joyce, doing for half a century what Joyce did for twenty-four hours. One cannot, of course, compare the imaginative creation with the chronicle, but each has its voice, and Holloway's, like that of Joyce, is unrivaled. He outdoes arithmetically Samuel Pepys in London or William Bentley in Salem, Massachusetts. Pepys has been well praised and is at last getting a definitive edition. Bentley has been too much neglected but was saluted in an editorial in the Boston *Globe* as "The Immortal Footnote," because of the reliance of historians of his period on his diary.

That sobriquet might well be applied to Holloway and yet the only extracts of his work that I know have been published are those done by the Proscenium Press in Newark, Delaware, which has brought out several slim volumes of excerpts from his monumental work. They are *Joseph Holloway's Abbey Theatre*, and *Joseph Holloway's Irish Theatre*, Vol. I, 1926–1931, Vol. II, 1932–1937, and Volume III, 1938–1944.

What insights he gives into the whole period! What vignettes of the dominant figures! Yeats ambling down the street, peering into the displays in the shop windows. AE hurrying along the street, pipe clinched in his teeth, beard outthrust, coattails flying. The swank and excitement of the first nights. Meeting Frank Fay on the streetcar going home; disclosing to us the envy in the man and the resentment at the Abbey he had left. Holloway's friendship with T. C. Murray and his revelations about the playwright's disappointments at the rejection of a play. Yeats's gloom on hearing that stink bombs had been thrown in the Abbey by the yahoos. Holloway's enthusiasms for Yeats's Noh plays, based on the Japanese models. His distaste for the intransigence of Sean O'Casey. His own disclosures of his own limitations and prejudices.

Holloway was an architect by profession and was called upon to make over the old Mechanics Institute when Miss Horniman, devoted still to Yeats, put up the money to give him a theater. No theater ever had a more earnest goer than the Abbey's architect. His diary records not merely theater and his critiques of various plays, various performances, and his observations of all the great and near-great actors and actresses, but is filled with fascinating comments and conversations relating to thousands of persons.

For instance on June 14, 1938, he wrote:

Richard Best called in the afternoon, and we had a long chat— Eileen was present—chiefly about Mr. Best meeting with Synge in Paris, and also about James Joyce. Best never thought much of Synge as a writer; he couldn't spell, and his writing was very bad—almost illegible. He was told of Synge's coming to Paris, and soon after Synge called on him. Synge used to write reviews for some papers. He had been to Aran when Best met him first and had the script of a book with him. Best advised him to buy a cheap typewriter and transcribe his Ms which he did, and Best corrected for him. Synge at the time wore a wig made of his own hair. His hair grew again. Best spoke of tearing up Synge's letters and the day after meeting W. B. Yeats who was full of the new genius he had discovered, who was Synge. Best never thought much of Joyce's writing either. He never read through *Ulysses*, but only looked up passages said to refer to himself. . . . He met Joyce when he came from Trieste and started the first [motion] picture house in Dublin. Joyce was a great one to touch one at the time, but one day he asked Best to have luncheon with him and took out from his breast pocket a bundle of notes, held them up, and replaced them. Meaning there would be no touching about the transaction. . . . When Joyce disapproved of a person or thing he usually haw-hawed under his breath in a most uncanny way. Someone said, "Standish O'Grady is a good writer," and Joyce haw-hawed in a most irritating way. Best destroyed the many letters he had from Joyce thinking he would never become famous. Now he keeps everything in the hopes some may turn up trumps. . . .

On another day he tells of going into a bookstore and seeing Paddy Kavanagh, the poet,

with his left elbow resting on a shelf. He was hatless as usual. And he told me he was looking for some of Carleton's novels— *Valentine McClutchy, The Black Baronet*—or any others that he could pick up. They were very rarely to be had now. He was the greatest writer of Irish novels in Kavanagh's estimation. It was a pity in his later work he became so anti-Catholic in outlook to please his publishers. . . .

Holloway and Kavanagh go on together to mourn the absence of good playwrights at the Abbey.

"Oh, if only the dramatists were equal to the players," Kavanagh exclaimed.

Holloway knew Kavanagh, of course. After all his years moving around the theatrical and literary circles of Dublin, he knew everybody. It is interesting to picture the two of them in a Dublin bookstore chatting about the Dublin literary scene, for Kavanagh is the major figure in any discussion of post-Yeatsian Dublin poetry.

Let's observe Holloway at another first night in his own words:

> Monday, May 19, 1941—The Abbey was packed for the first night of the new play, *The Lady In the Twilight* in three acts by Mervyn Wall, but I saw only a few I knew going in. The play proved a formless thing of empty talk, leading nowhere and rarely if ever gripping the attention, as the author had little to say or expressed it in such a crude way through his characters who made their entrances and exits in the most haphazard way or sat around awaiting their turn to put in their say. "It was as full of words and as empty of ideas as the literary page of the *Irish Times*," said a young man who sat next to me on the balcony and who left in the middle of the second act. . . .

The playwright who that night suffered the disdain of the young man in the balcony is a leading Dublin author, Mervyn Wall (1908–   ), much appreciated on the European continent, who made his reputation in the 1940s with both his novels and his short stories. Besides *The Lady in the Twilight*, two other of his plays produced at the Abbey are *Alarm Among the Clerks* and *The Shadow*. His novel *The Unfortunate Fursey* was made into a musical show. Wall has a gift of satire.

Holloway gives us a marvelous glimpse of Yeats and Mrs. Patrick Campbell, that formidable actress, on the Abbey stage.

> Wednesday, April 10—I saw by *The Evening Herald* that Mrs. Pat Campbell died at Paris, France. . . . I was present at a rehearsal of *Deirdre* when Yeats was on the stage with Mrs. Pat and the company. He was gesticulating wildly within a yard of where Mrs. Pat stood and stopping the progress of the rehearsal at every moment to explain, until at last the great actress laughed outright and said, "Oh, Mr. Yeats, you are too funny, and I fear you must get off the stage if I am to proceed with rehearsal." Yeats got off.

The names of novelists and playwrights are on almost every page of his journal. We find him praising Ria Mooney's performance in a production of Elizabeth Connor's play *Mount Prospect*, adapted from her novel of the same name which had been banned by the Irish Free State; dismissing Nora Mac-Adam's play, *Birth of a Giant*; mourning the death at the age of thirty of another Abbey playwright, Maeve O'Callaghan; complaining about the false accents in *Marrowbone Lane* by Dr. Robert Collis; and shaking his head over a play by Frank O'Connor and feeling that it was only O'Connor's egotism that led him to write for the Abbey.

When he died *The Irish Times* wrote:

Mr. Joseph Holloway, the Abbey Theatre's most consistent "first-nighter" since he designed it in 1904, died yesterday at the age of 83. Mr. Holloway has become one of the best-loved personalities in Dublin theatrical life, but his name will live through the memoirs of Dublin that he had been writing for 50 years. Bound in manuscript volumes covering a quarter of a year, these memoirs have been presented to the National Library where they are housed in a special room. They are a complete record of Dublin life, with emphasis on theatrical matters. For over 60 years he lived at 21 Northumberland road, and the house in later years was merely a case for his collection of pictures, theater programmes, manuscripts, and other articles connected with his collection of historical material about Dublin. It was a contemporary museum of Irish art, and the manuscript of his memoirs was deemed so valuable that Dr. Best, of the National Library, arranged for its removal to the library where Mr. Holloway used to work on it afterwards.

Mr. Holloway was interested in the cinema from its first appearance, and became deputy film censor for a time. He also became a governor of the National Art Gallery, and played a part in the founding of the Academy of Christian Art, while other cultural associations profited by his membership. After each performance that he witnessed in a theater he wrote about 800 words of comment, and did the same for art exhibitions. He was born in Camden street, and was educated at Castleknock

College, learned to draw at the School of Art, and, after quali-
fying as an architect, the first building he worked on was the
O'Brien Institute.

T. C. Murray, his friend of long standing, wrote of him:

> I found him a great soul, honest as the sun, and clean of mind
> and heart as a St. Francis . . . as a critic I never knew a man
> of such complete integrity. He was utterly unmoved by the
> catch-cries of fashionable literary coteries. He spoke out of the
> promptings of his heart and was incapable of giving utterance
> to a thought that was not his own. . . .

Holloway did not live to see the Abbey Theatre rebuilt after
the fire. That did not come, indeed, until 1966, when the Irish
government appropriated 250,000 pounds for the rebuilding,
and in July, 1966, the new Abbey Theatre was formally opened
by President Eamon de Valera. Between the death of Holloway
and the reconstruction of the new theater, the Abbey suffered
a decline. Seamus Kelly, the dramatic critic of *The Irish Times*,
and one of Dublin's outstanding journalists in the high tradition, puts onus for the decline on the shoulders of Ernest Blythe,
"a former politician," he writes, "who gained what amounted
to absolute control of the theater in 1941 and subsequently
ousted directors like Frank O'Connor, who were trying to maintain the Yeats tradition." Lennox Robinson had his weaknesses
also.

This showed in the rejection of *The White Steed* by Paul
Vincent Carroll in 1938, which prompted one of those lively
literary exchanges so common in Dublin. In 1939, the New
York Drama Critics Circle pronounced the play the best foreign
play of the year. In response to innuendoes and criticisms made
against him, Carroll, in a letter in *The Irish Times*, laid into
both Blythe and Robinson.

> Blythe [he wrote] is apparently one of those Protestants who is
> so obsessed with the fear of being called a bigot that he urgently
> appears to agree at all costs with the merely pious utterances
> of any given Catholic nonentity. As for Mr. Robinson, he seems

to have considered *The White Steed* brutal and raw, but recently he was, I understand, chiefly instrumental in having accepted by the Board a notoriously poor play which he insisted was a "really lovely delicate little thing" until the Abbey audience in no uncertain terms showed both him and the play where they both got off.

His worst barb was saved for O'Connor.

> Mr. Frank O'Connor in a personal letter asked me to suppress *The White Steed* for the sake of my reputation. While respecting his acidulous opinion, I feel myself wishing that he had had the critical sense and strength to suppress all of his plays for the sake of his reputation as a writer.

He was, of course, quite right about O'Connor's plays. The success of O'Connor's material on the stage would have to await the ingenuity of Mary Manning Howe, who would adapt his novel *The Saint and Mary Kate*.

For fifteen years the Abbey was housed in the Queen's Theatre. During this period, also, the Dublin Verse-Speaking Society was founded, with the poet Austin Clarke as the moving spirit. It carried on Yeats's dream of poetry on the stage, which the Abbey had forgotten. Clarke's own plays were produced at the Abbey, but his fame rests on his poetry, for, he is, with Kavanagh, one of the major figures to appear since Yeats.

Despite the vicissitudes of the theater, and the decline of the Abbey's strength, Irish playwrights continue to emerge from Dublin and enchant both Broadway and London. *Philadelphia, Here I Come* by Brian Friel (1929–   ), who taught school until he was thirty-one, and then relied on his short stories and plays for his livelihood. His first play was performed in Belfast, where he had studied at St. Joseph's Training College, but in 1962 *The Enemy Within* was produced at the Abbey. He was made a shareholder at the Abbey in 1965, the year after his *Philadelphia, Here I Come* captured Dublin and then went on to capture London and New York. In 1966, his *The Loves of Cass Maguire* was performed in Dublin but missed success in Boston and New York, despite a brilliant performance by Ruth

Gordon, who "loved the play, and enjoyed the role." Possibly the play was too Irish in its essence for American audiences; it deserves revival.

Friel is one of the Irish dramatists who has remained in Ireland, rejecting the exile of Beckett or rustication in London. Others who have followed Friel's style of life are Eugene McCabe (1930–   ), who lives in the north of Ireland, but whose play *The King of the Castle* was a triumph of the 1964 Dublin Theatre Festival. He it was who said of the Abbey of the fifties and sixties, "a lovely new chassis, same old engine backfiring now for over thirty years and in no danger whatsoever of exploding." Drama critic Seamus Kelly of *The Irish Times*, however, is hopeful of the future.

One of the figures of hope, accomplishment, and promise is John B. Keane (1928–   ). Born in Listowel, he worked until he saved enough money to buy a pub in his native town, where he still ministers to the thirst of his fellows. In 1959 he found himself a successful playwright with *Sive* and has followed it with one success after another, although his critical acclaim lags behind his popularity. He has written several prose works, among them an amusing self-portrait which begins, "I was born on the 21st of July, 1928, in the town of Listowel, in County Kerry. Apart from my birth, it was an uneventful year, free of plague, war and famine."

Thomas Murphy (1936–   ) and Hugh Leonard, a pen name for John Keyes Byrne (1928–   ), are two Irish playwrights who have left Ireland for the lure of England and the prosperity promised those who write for English television. Murphy's major play, *Whistle in the Dark*, dealt with Irish immigrants in England and was a sensation in Dublin and London. A later play, *The Fooleen*, takes its setting in rural Ireland.

Leonard's *The Poker Session* and *Stephen D.*, the latter an adaptation of Joyce's *Portrait of the Artist as a Young Man*, and *Mick and Mick* give him high literary cachet in Dublin while he makes his headquarters abroad. His themes remain Irish.

That is far from exhausting the list. There is Seamus De Burce, one of six sons of P. J. Bourke, a former manager of the Queen's Theatre. His adaptations of Kickham's *Knocknagow* and Lever's *Handy Andy* have been as popular as his original work, *Limpid River* and *The End of Mrs. Oblong*. Seamus Byrne (1904–1968) was a drama critic, lawyer, and revolutionary who had three plays done by the Abbey. Like the playwright-mayor MacSwiney, Byrne too undertook a hunger strike in a British jail. James Douglas (1929–   ), besides work for Irish television, has had three successful plays in the last decade. Michael J. Molloy, author of *The King of Friday's Men* and other plays, is another leading figure.

The two most celebrated Dublin playwrights of the mid-twentieth century are Brendan Behan (1923–1964) and Samuel Beckett (1906–   ), two men of astonishing contrasts, who, between them, span all the force and faults of Ireland, and to understand them is to understand not only the country, but the hope for its future. There is paradox in Ireland which deceives the superficial observer.

In Behan we have the ancient culture of Ireland, the uproarious, boisterous mixture of paganism and Catholicism, the latter subduing the barbarity but not the ribaldry of the former. In Behan we have the Irishman who, while peripatetic, never abandoned Ireland; who spoke its aboriginal tongue; and wrote English with an exuberance denied its native speakers.

In Beckett we have the Anglo-Irish intrusion, but, whatever the determinations of his forebears, annealed into an Irishman, and thus, forever, as Irish as Behan, inextricably, thoroughly, perdurably Irish, but, as Behan, in rebellion. Rebellion in man operates on at least four levels, just as literary criticism operates on four levels. Beckett left Dublin, and, indeed, left the English language, and now writes in French. Even as Beckett is able to move back and forth between French and English, Behan moved back and forth between Irish and English. But even as Behan is a rambunctious figure, rooted in Dublin vulgarities, Beckett is attenuated, etiolated, the Anglo-Irishman extruded by history past Shaw and past Yeats, without surrendering his Irishness, whose successors must return to the nourishment of Irish soil or die.

Behan was born Francis Brendan Behan, on February 9, 1923, in Dublin, the first child of Mr. and Mrs. Stephen Behan. It was his mother's second marriage, his father's first. Brendan (the Francis was forgotten, perhaps even by him) was educated by the nuns and the Christian Brothers. He was not a slum child like Sean O'Casey or James Stephens, but a son of the middle class. When he was thirteen years old he went to a day school to learn the trade of house painting, and when he was sixteen he was arrested in Liverpool as an agent of the I.R.A., armed with explosives, intent on damaging British shipping. He was sentenced to a reform school, one of several taking its name from an English penologist of advanced ideas, and called a Borstal school. From that experience would come *Borstal Boy*, a brilliant autobiographical account of his incarceration.

On his release he was deported to Ireland. He had not been long home when he became involved in a ridiculous shooting outside Glasnevin Cemetery, was arrested and sentenced to fourteen years' imprisonment. He was probably drunk at the time; but he served four years before he was paroled.

Back at his trade of house painter (he did the kitchen at the Hotel Gresham), he became an apprentice writer. In 1942, the year he was sentenced, he had had a piece published in *The Bell*, but it was not until 1953 that *The Scarperer* appeared, serially in *The Irish Times* and under a pen name, and to complete which he betook himself to the Aran Islands, far from the temptations of Dublin's stout congeniality. *The Scarperer* is a novella and if not his best work, nonetheless a commendable effort. He now turned newspaperman and for a couple of years wrote for *The Irish Times*. His heart was set, however, on becoming a playwright, and in Gaelic he wrote a play, which, taking its cue from Douglas Hyde's *The Twisting of the Rope*, called itself *The Twisting of Another Rope*. The play was rejected by the Abbey (twice) and by the Gate but was at last produced by the Pike Theatre under the title *The Quare Fellow*. The year was 1954 and the next year he married Beatrice ffrench-Salkeld, daughter of a distinguished Irish painter.

The next year, *The Quare Fellow* was produced in London and acclaimed. Kenneth Tynan praised it in ordinately and rhapsodized, "It is Ireland's sacred duty to send over every few years a playwright who will save the English theatre from inarticulate dumbness." In 1958 *An Giall*, the Gaelic play that would be Englished as *The Hostage*, was produced in Dublin, and Brendan was whisked off to Sweden to do the English translation. This was the year *Borstal Boy* was completed and published. The next year, 1959, *The Hostage* was a hit in London and prepared for translation in half a dozen languages for the continent. Unfortunately, success was spoiling Behan, and he was drunk more often than sober.

An amusing courtroom incident is recounted in which he insisted on being heard in Irish (his constitutional privilege) after being arrested for drunkenness in Bray, south of Dublin. While it is expected that every civil servant in Ireland be bilingual with Irish and English, not too many are fluent in Irish. Brendan was, and he was out to embarrass the court and the prosecuting officers. The judge's Gaelic was limited to "Sit Down," which he used not too effectively on Behan, who, nevertheless, ended up paying a small fine. In 1960, *The Hostage* opened on Broadway, and Behan carried on with his customary antics, evidently as thirsty for publicity or public performance as he was for alcohol. In 1963, his daughter was born, and in 1964 he was dead, a suicide of sorts, having utterly disregarded the warnings of doctors that to drink was to die. The I.R.A. honored him at his funeral, as did the Republic of Ireland. Critics saw his life as a sad waste of enormous talent. He himself saw all his critical acclaim as a sort of joke; and no doubt the artist was simply unable to adjust to voracious commercialism.

Flann O'Brien, his fellow Dubliner, journalist, playwright, novelist, and "man of letters" (which was how Behan thought of himself), wrote as follows:

> Brendan will not be replaced in a hurry, or not at all. There has been no Irishman quite like him, and his playwriting, which I personally found in parts both crude and offensive as well as entertaining, was only a fraction of his peculiarly complicated personality. He is in fact much more a player than a playwright, or, to use a Dublin saying, "He was as good as a play." One can detect some affinity in him with O'Casey, but the pervasive error lies in ranking a delightful rowdy, a wit, a man of action in many dangerous undertakings where he thought his duty lay, a reckless drinker, a fearless denouncer of humbug and pretence and so a proprietor of the biggest heart that has beaten in Ireland for the past forty years. I know it is only foolishness in my own head, but there are streets in Dublin which seem strangely silent tonight. The noisy one-time son has gone home this time for good.

One paradox is that the man who drank in the ebullience of despair, and so lived the tragedy he should have given us, wrote the literature of optimism just as surely as the British soldier shot and killed in *The Hostage* rises from the dead to demand of death where is its "sting-a-ling—aling," whereas the Irishman in exile, wrapped in the asceticism of the Protestant mystics, writes the literature of despair while living in hope without ebullience. If Behan is the heir of Gogarty, Beckett is the heir of the puritans Shaw and Joyce, whose secretary, for a while, he was, and mostly Joyce indeed. He has been further tinctured by the continent's postwar miasma of existentialism. When Beckett's play *Waiting for Godot* in the mid-fifties won him international acclaim, Sean O'Casey was once again in dissent. Writing in *Encore*, which had become the outstanding Dublin literary magazine, he proclaimed:

Beckett? I have nothing to do with Beckett. He isn't in me; nor am I in him. I am not waiting for Godot to bring me life; I am out after life myself, even at the age I've reached. What have any of you to do with Godot? There is more life than Godot can give in the life of the least of us. That Beckett is a clever writer, and that he has written a rotting and remarkable play, there is no doubt; but his philosophy isn't my philosophy, for within him there is no hazard of hope; no desire for it; nothing in it but a lust for despair, and a crying of woe, not in a wilderness, but in a garden.

Beckett, however, had known the wilderness. He had been born in Dublin in 1906, grew up in the city, and attended Trinity College, where he played cricket. In 1928 he was a lecturer in English at the École Normale Supérieure, Paris, and began his writing career there. In 1930 he returned to Trinity as a lecturer in French. In 1932 he went to the continent and traveled until 1937, when he returned to Paris to make it his home since. He served as an occasional secretary to Joyce, and began to write in French as well as English. His first book was *Whoroscope*, a poem, written in English and published in 1930. His first novel was *Murphy*, published in 1938, to be followed by *Watt* in 1944, and *Molloy*, which was to make his reputation, in 1951.

In 1940 he was in Paris when the Nazis occupied the city. At first, as an Irishman, he sought to maintain the same neutrality that was elected by Prime Minister de Valera for Ireland, but the savagery with which the Nazis treated the Jews drove Beckett into the underground. He became a part of a transmission belt for information for the Allies. As a result, he and his wife were sought by the Gestapo and had to flee the occupied zone. He lived as a laborer in an obscure village in the Pyrenees, and it was there he wrote *Watt*, a comic tale of Dublin country.

Molloy came after the war; and was followed by *Malone meurt* in 1952 and *Unnamable* in 1953. He had now adopted French as his first language, and in the winter of 1952 in the Babylone Theatre on the Boulevard Raspail in Paris, *En At-*

tendant Godot was first performed. Described as a tragicomedy in two acts, it is, indeed, comic with the attar of despair rising from it. The English translation and American productions (one with an all black cast giving it added significance) won him international fame. Other plays, equally bleak with comic lightning flashes, followed.

He said of *Waiting for Godot* that it was a play striving to avoid definition, and has said again that the pertinent word for all his plays is "perhaps." As early as 1930 he had had a French play, *Le Kid*, presented at the Peacock Theatre in Dublin, twenty-two years before *Godot*. It was a literary exercise. Not until 1955 was *Godot* acted in London and in Dublin, and the next year, in New York. Less than fifteen years later, in 1969, he was awarded the Nobel prize for literature. Shaw had got it in 1925; Yeats in 1938. There is more or less general agreement that Joyce would have had it had he lived.

Bernard F. Dukore, who directs the Ph.D. program in theater at the City University of New York, has written a book, *Bernard Shaw, Director*, to show the tremendous command Shaw had over the practical exigencies and demands of the stage. Beckett has the same gift and takes like care that every turn of phrase and every movement on the stage, indeed, every rise and fall of the lights, be done exactly as he wishes.

All this is revealed in a preeminent study of Beckett by a fellow Dubliner, Alec Reid, also a graduate of Trinity, who has written extensively on Beckett. His book, *All I Can Manage, More Than I Could: An Approach to the Plays of Samuel Beckett*, is a brief, but, to my mind, the best introduction, and more, to the plays.

Beckett's links with Dublin have remained close always. He frequently returned from the continent to visit his mother, particularly during her last days. In 1937 we find him testifying in a suit against Oliver St. John Gogarty on behalf of a plaintiff who claimed to have been libeled by Gogarty in *As I Was Going Down Sackville Street*. Dublin produced *Waiting for Godot* as soon as Beckett translated it, but, like O'Casey, he would quarrel with Dublin's producers and censors and illiterate self-appointed critics. *Waiting for Godot* was produced at the Pike Theatre, whose brief history (1953–1959) underscores again the quicksand of censorship over which producers and writers must tread their way. Besides producing *Waiting for Godot*, Alan Simpson and his wife Caroline Swift, two young enthusiasts who founded the Pike (in an old garage), brought *The Quare Fellow* to Dublin audiences and built up a theater ticket club of three thousand members. There, Dublin, for the first time, saw the Theater of the Absurd as well as other modern foreign importations. Tennessee Williams's *The Rose Tattoo* brought about the downfall. An anonymous letter to the police, alleging obscenity, closed the show and involved the Simpsons in a legal action that foundered their enterprise.

In the same year Beckett became involved in a row with the Dublin Drama Festival, as had O'Casey, and withdrew three short plays he had offered, cancelled a projected performance of *Endgame* at the Pike, and banned all his plays from Dublin showings. The next year his alma mater, Trinity College, gave him an honorary D. Litt. Resuming in 1962, various Dublin producers brought his works to the stage, and in 1966 he himself joined with his brothers and the late Irish actor Jack Mac-Gowran in making the superb recording, *MacGowran Speaking Beckett*. The recording was made by Claddagh Records, which must be saluted as one of the sophisticated cultural forces in Dublin today. In 1971 MacGowran brought his Beckett show to New York City and made several memorable television appearances.

Beckett's Irishness cleaves to the heart of Irishness even more truly than Behan's, or at least as truly, for it can be said that he is, like Wilde, Mahaffy, Gogarty, Behan, and Shaw, the master of grand talk. Almost all his characters appear to have nothing to live for except to talk, to talk interminably at times, comically at times, poetically at times, but to talk. One gets the feeling that if at last his woman buried in sand to her neck and left no action but to stare at her vanity possessions and to talk were to disappear entirely in the sand, submerged in the help-lessness of man's position, her talk would go on, in the air, above the desolation. One can see Beckett's work then as a thesis running parallel on the track with Irish history, for the Irish have known centuries where there was left to them nothing but talk, no professions, things that should have been theirs manipulated by someone else, and Godot daily expected but daily absent; expected without a true sense of anticipation. For had the anticipation been there as well as expectation, nation-alism would not have blemished the cultural life of the country the way it has.

I don't believe Beckett is seeking to write any parable about Irish history, indeed, we know from his own words that he is not. He is writing, as he says, about what other authors have rejected as subject matter, "ignorance and impotence," and the way people suffer under them. Beckett knows, of course, that Ireland has suffered from both, although in inverted order: from impotence for centuries, from ignorance, or, the aestheti-cally ignorant, for too many decades.

XVIII

Ireland has been called the land of saints and scholars, but actually in recent years, the canonization process of the Catholic church has found no one there worthy of notice. That it is the land of sinners and singers is a statement that many of its churchmen would acknowledge, for they have been at pains to condemn many of the writers and statesmen, but no one will dispute that it produces more than its share of poets. The poetic voice of Ireland may at the moment sound subdued but that is only because of the pervasive quality of the great voices that have been recently stilled. After Yeats, the poetry of Dublin sounded thin indeed, but it was only by contrast.

The three major post-Yeatsian names are Austin Clarke (1896–   ), Patrick Kavanagh (1905–1967), and Thomas Kinsella (1928–   ). Through their careers we can mark the progression of Irish poetry since Yeats. Clarke began his poetic career drawing on the Gaelic myths which had inspired Yeats. Kavanagh rejected Yeats, the myths, and the revival of Gaelic, which he referred to contemptuously, as "the Irish thing." Kinsella, heir to all three men, has freed himself from all three, both as to influence and reaction, and, if, on occasion, somewhat obscure because of the modern manner and the age's preoccupation with introspection, has become nevertheless the figure of the present-day Dublin poet.

Clarke brought out his first volume of poetry in 1917, the

year after the Easter Rising, when Yeats was moving into his most distinguished period. England still ruled Ireland, the Irish Republic was years away. He was, at the time, a lecturer in English at University College, Dublin, where he had succeeded Thomas MacDonagh, executed following the Easter Rising. MacDonagh (1878–1916) had published three volumes of verse by the time of his death, and a play of his had been produced at the Abbey. His *Literature in Ireland*, published posthumously, had an introduction by Padraic Colum. Clarke had succeeded him as lecturer and was influenced, as were many others, by his scholarship and verve. In *Literature in Ireland*, he wrote, "We are the children of a race that, through need or choice, turned from Irish to English. We have now so well mastered this language of our adoption that we use it with a freshness and power that the English of these days rarely have. But now also we have begun to turn back to the old language, not old to us."

Clarke was born in Dublin and educated there, at Belvedere College and University College. When he succeeded MacDonagh lecturing, he remained three years, until 1921. Then for seventeen years he lived in London as a professional writer, critic, editor, a familiar figure in Fleet Street, and a typical Irish exile seeking a livelihood on foreign shores. He is, however, one of those figures who saw that his resources lay in Ireland, whatever his dissent from its politicians and prelates, and he returned. When the Abbey drifted from its role as a theater of poetry, he organized one in Dublin. From his pen poured novels of medieval Ireland, among them *The Bright Temptation* and *The Singing Men of Cashel*; plays, many in verse; innumerable essays and criticisms; and autobiographical reminiscences, *Twice Round the Black Church* and *A Penny in the Clouds*. But always, the poetry, and it is as a poet (not to depreciate his delightful memoirs) that he has his reputation, generally acknowledged, as the dean of Irish poets since Yeats, having won that title, to follow Gogarty's distinction, from Time and not Age. Throughout his literary career, he has been a stout foe of the institutional practices of the Catholic church in Ireland, with a lively detestation for the pharisaical manners nationalism has developed. In 1921 he published *The Sword of the West* and in 1925 *The Cattle-drive in Connaught and Other Poems*. For a while he had his own press, to turn out his own and the worthy material of others. Two volumes of his poetry appeared in the sixties, *Mnemosyne Lay in the Dust* being the more recent, and his *Collected Plays* were published in 1963. His critical work abounds in periodicals and deserves collection.

When he was writing in the years that Yeats was alive, it must be remembered that Dublin thronged with poets. Gogarty and AE were still writing first-rate poetry, and James Stephens, Padraic Colum, and Joseph Campbell were at work. There was Monk Gibbon (1896–   ), who came back from the war in France in 1918 to become a teacher and a literary figure, poet and novelist, and the first Dublin man to express his resentment against Yeats because of the latter's overweening vanity. The book is *The Masterpiece and the Man: Yeats as I Knew Him*. Gibbon's novels have been mostly autobiographical. His collected poetry was published in 1951 under the title *This Insubstantial Pageant*.

The first woman's magazine in Dublin (short-lived) was founded by the poet Frederick R. Higgins (1898–1941), who turned from labor organizing to literature; he co-edited a poetry magazine with Yeats and became one of the founders of the Irish Academy of Letters. His first book of poetry, *Salt Air*, published in 1924, took its inspiration from the same folk songs and poems of Connacht that Douglas Hyde had translated with such success. Other volumes followed: *Island Blood, The Dark Breed, Arable Holdings*, and *The Gap of Brightness*, the last in the year before his death. His play, *A Deuce of Jacks*, was mounted at the Abbey. His most famous poem is an elegy for Padraic O'Conaire, one of the most celebrated modern writers in Irish.

Nor are these men the only ones who were writing creditable

poetry in those years. Clarke spanned the decades and soon
found as his major rival Patrick Kavanagh, familiarly known
as Paddy, one of the most vibrant and cantankerous figures in
modern Dublin's literary life, but, to many, the greatest Irish
poet since Yeats.

Kavanagh was born on an Irish farm, the son of an Irish
cobbler, and reared there, in Monaghan County, and he looms
in the history of Dublin literature as one of those mythic Pro-
tean creatures Yeats dreamed of, only half emerged from the
soil, as knotty as trees, somehow slightly primordial. Yet he is
not the natural man shouting into the wind, but rather a per-
fectionist at his verse, working meticulously.

His first book, *Ploughman and Other Poems*, appeared in
1936 and he soon followed it into Dublin to try his hand as a
free-lance writer. He wrote the Irish equivalent of a gossip
column and some motion picture criticism for Dublin papers,
and in 1938 published *The Green Fool*, an autobiographical
novel. His reputation was made however with *The Great Hunger*,
which appeared in 1942.

In 1947 he published *A Soul for Sale*, and the next year a
novel, *Tarry Flynn*, dealing poignantly with the Irish rural
scene. In 1960 another collection of poems, *Come Dance with
Kitty Stobling*, confirmed the strength of his earlier poetic work.
Kavanagh, unlike Clarke or Kinsella, declined to leave Ireland
either to work or teach abroad, and his critical position has
suffered somewhat because of the ignorance of his work in
England and America. His *Collected Poems*, published in 1964,
by Devin Garrity, a long-time New York publisher and enthu-
siast for Irish literature, deserved a far wider readership than
it received. The tragic quality of American higher education and
American publishing assures interminable Ph.D. theses and subsequent books on every possible aspect of Joyce and Yeats (and
now Synge) and a neglect of practically all other figures.

This computerized sterility of American scholarship was
pinned like a butterfly under glass by Kavanagh in his poem
"Who Killed James Joyce?"

Patrick Kavanagh

Who killed James Joyce?
I, said the commentator,
I killed James Joyce
For my graduation.

What weapon was used
To slay mighty Ulysses?
The weapon that was used
Was a Harvard thesis.

How did you bury Joyce?
In a broadcast symposium.

And did you get high marks,
The Ph.D.?
I got the B. Litt.
And my master's degree.

Kavanagh, because of the lack of a degree, might have had more difficulty in finding a place on an English university faculty or an American faculty than other Irish poets. But in any event, he clung to Dublin after he left his Monaghan farm.

"On many occasions," he wrote of himself, "I literally starved in Dublin. I often borrowed a 'shilling for the gas' when in fact I wanted the coin to buy a chop. During the war, in Dublin, I did a column of gossip for a newspaper at four guineas a week."

Kavanagh enjoyed the prestige and place that he won as a poet. He could be troublesome, an antagonistic man in a pub, and he could be a troublesome house guest. James O'Toole, the late Irish journalist in exile, could recount for hours stories of Kavanagh's invasion of his home as a guest with a persistence to match *The Man Who Came to Dinner*.

Kinsella, who has succeeded Kavanagh as the paradigm of a poet in Dublin, has been careful to retain his connection with Irish soil and sustenance while holding professorships at American universities, like many another Irishman a welcome figure on various campuses. He was born in 1928 in Dublin and had his education there. He went from University College, Dublin, into the Irish civil service and worked for the department of finance until 1965. In that year he went to Southern Illinois University in the United States, a large state university known widely for its publishing house, and remained there until 1970, when he became a professor of English at Temple University in Pennsylvania. Among his books are *Poems* (1956), *Another September* (1968), *Downstream* (1962), *Nightwalker and Other Poems* (1968), and *Notes from the Land of the Dead* (1971).

Unlike his predecessors Yeats and Kavanagh, however, he is knowledgeable in Irish. He is a figure of reconciliation in more ways than one. He does not, like Yeats, reject Ireland's Christian heritage; he does not, like Kavanagh, reject Ireland's pagan mythology. He becomes for us, indeed, the figure of the future; sophisticated, erudite, contemporary, not isolated from the mainstream of literature as Kavanagh seemed to be; and not isolated from Ireland's mainstream as Yeats struggled not to be. Kinsella is a man at home in many worlds.

One of his finest contributions, beyond the scope of Yeats or Kavanagh, is his translation of the *Tain Bo Cuailnge*, described as "the centre-piece of the eighth-century Ulster cycle of heroic tales," by Liam Miller, the distinguished Dublin publisher who brought out the translation. Miller, proprietor of The Dolmen Press in Dublin, deserves special mention among Dublin publishers not only for the high quality of the typography of his works, his beautiful book building, but for the incessant, sacrificial encouragement he has given to Irish poets.

The Dolmen Press brought out Kinsella's *The Tain* in 1969, and could well claim that it was "the first attempt to present 'a living version' of the story, complete and unbowdlerized." In his introduction, Kinsella says it was the work of fifteen years, off and on; that while there had been numerous "retellings," there have been no more than half a dozen translations. He found Lady Gregory's paraphrase, *Cuchulain of Muirthemne*, one of the truest, but "lacking in some important ways, refining away the coarse elements, and rationalizing the monstrous and the grotesque. . . ." Irish epics, unlike those of Greece, are for the most part in prose, and Kinsella brings over *The Tain* in prose and poetry. The result is a triumph.

To confine a discussion of contemporary poetry in Dublin to Clarke, Kavanagh, and Kinsella would be a travesty. They are used because they point if not a direction, then several directions, all Irish, however conflicting; a growth, an adventure, a development. They are, not incuriously, better known on the European continent than they are in the United States, I believe, and the future of the Common Market may make this first a trend and then a tradition.

Neither exiles nor expatriates, Valentin Iremonger (1918–) and Denis Devlin (1908–1959) were distinguished by their work in the Irish foreign service, but even more by their poetry. Devlin was Ireland's ambassador to Italy when he died. In 1937 he published his first book of poetry, *Intercessions*, the year before he was sent to Washington, D.C., to serve in the Irish embassy there, where he remained until 1946. His collected poems were published after his death by the American poets Allen Tate and Robert Penn Warren, who were admirers. He is bracketed with Iremonger, because the latter also has served Ireland's foreign office, as ambassador to several Scandinavian countries, while taking an active part in Dublin's literary life.

Iremonger was born in Dublin in 1918, and spent a good many years in the theater, at both the Abbey and the Gate. In 1946, the year after he won the AE Memorial Award for his poetry, he entered the foreign service. He too, as is asked of the Irish civil service, has a command of Irish that enables him to translate from the Irish.

Robert Farren (in Irish, O Farachain) (1909–), a director of the Abbey Theatre and an official of Radio Eireann, has written several volumes of poetry; Desmond O'Grady (1935–), who taught for a while in the United States and is now a resident foreign correspondent in Rome, is primarily a poet; and Eavan Boland (1944–), daughter of an Irish diplomat, has written poetry that puts her in the first rank of Dublin poets today. Anthony Cronin (1926–), who worked on *The*

Bell, has been active in several literary publications, including the *Dublin Magazine*, and has published impressive poetry. Maurice Craig (1919–   ) has published two books of poetry although he is perhaps better known for his local history and particularly his delightful *Dublin 1660–1860*, which because of his position as inspector of Georgian buildings has a unique architectural appeal. Donagh MacDonagh (1912–   ) is a judge and the son of the Irish patriot-martyr of 1916, but has made his name with verse plays as well as poetry. Nor must an observer overlook Padraic Fallon (1906–   ), whose verse plays have been sensational on Radio Eireann; John Montague (1929–   ), like Kinsella, a peripatetic lecturer in America and England and a powerful modern voice; and Richard Murphy (1927–   ), whose home is in Connemara, who was educated in England and Paris and stands as one of Ireland's major modern voices.

Brendan Kennelly (1930–   ), a Trinity College don, who is married to an American, and in 1970–71 served as poet-in-residence in Swarthmore College in Pennsylvania, is another example of the new breed of Irish economic exile who quickly retreats from the "outside world," as the Irish used to call it, to his native haunts to replenish the fires of his imagination. Kennelly is among the foremost of the young poets and author of nine books of poetry; and I shall look at the list no longer lest I find another omission, say, Seamus Heaney, as much of Dublin as of his native County Derry in the north, and a major poet. The omissions in any cursory list, such as the above, leaves any chronicler uncomfortable.

Sufficient to the story of literary Dublin is the knowledge that it continues to buoy poet after poet to the surface of its swirling waters.

XIX

To discuss the contemporary novelists in Dublin reimposes the sense of inadequacy one must feel in describing or exploring the inchoate, vibrant, turbulent current Irish literary scene. To dissect the dead is not difficult; the taxonomic task is comparatively easy; for the dead lie still. To classify the living properly is impossible because they squirm away under the knife and metamorphose before you, appearing at one moment poet, one moment novelist, one moment critic, and then playwright, biographer, humorist, or master of the short story; or they suddenly retire from the field in which they shone or began to shine.

One of the phenomena of Dublin writing is the versatility of the writer. He is not readily categorized because he performs too well in various roles and genres. The causes of this quality in him are in great part economic. While the people of Dublin buy more books per capita than those of any city in the United States, the small size of the country itself means fewer books are sold in the entire Republic than are sold in greater Boston, which has a population double that of Dublin. The Irish novelist then cannot expect that his novels, unless they appeal to the "outside world," will support him or even be profitably published. The Dublin writer has to write with one eye on England and one on the United States. Even then he has to be a utility man.

Let us cite the case of Paddy Kavanagh, who is sometimes credited with being the finest Irish poet since Yeats. During

World War II, he was a writer for *The Irish Press*, turning out a column called City Commentary and signed Piers Ploughman, in which he wrote as he pleased, sometimes in verse. At the same time, he brought out his most famous poem, *The Great Hunger*, and wrote his novel *Tarry Flynn*, which, when it was published, had the singular honor of being banned by the board of censors on Monday and unbanned by the censorship appeals board before the week had run.

Another reason for such versatility (besides the economic) is the Dublin Dimension, the intensity of intellectual exchange in the city, where writers more easily commingle with friends and foes alike, and have the high-mindedness of national concerns pressed on them, and find the itch of competitiveness and obligation more nagging than would be the case elsewhere. To give a trifling example of this: During the years of World War II, when Ireland stood neutral, much to England's annoyance, Sir John Maffey was the British representative to Ireland. His public information officer was John Betjeman, the English poet, who quite naturally soon found himself a member of a circle of Dublin wits, including Paddy Kavanagh, Brian O'Nolan, Emm-Jay MacManus, and others. Very soon, Sir John was a member of it as well. One can imagine the spirited exchanges, the literary quality of the conversation, and, at times, the intensity of emotion.

For other Dublin writers, the facility they have in a second language, Irish, and the access it gives them to the subtleties and nuances of the body of Irish literature prompt them to try their hands at surprising forms or to draw strength from an intimacy with its classics. Brendan Behan's poetry in Irish is an example, and a side of him unknown to his readers in America or England. Behan thought of himself as a writer and man of letters, and it is that gentle appellation, as Georgian as the best architecture in Dublin, that applies. In Dublin, it has no pejorative connotation.

By the end of the nineteenth century, the title man of letters, we are assured by John Gross in his book *The Rise and Fall*

of the Man of Letters had become passé. The chief reason for
its passing may have been the determination of specialization
that gripped writers. H. G. Wells, G. K. Chesterton, J. B.
Priestley, and Hilaire Belloc were throwbacks of versatility; for
the twentieth century has apotheosized the writer of one genre.
Evelyn Waugh, Iris Murdoch, P. G. Wodehouse were novelists;
John Betjeman and Philip Larkin, poets. The same was true
of the United States, perhaps more so. Robert Frost, Robinson
Jeffers, and Edwin Arlington Robinson were poets; Pearl Buck,
William Faulkner, John Steinbeck, novelists. There were and
are exceptions, of course—Robert Penn Warren, say, and the
late Edmund Wilson—but the general delineation is clear. In
Dublin, the literary life aligns itself oppositely; the specialist is
the exception. From Thomas Moore to W. B. Yeats, the Irish
poets have committed to paper a great deal of prose; and more
prose writers have composed poetry than not; playwrights have
been politicians, and storytellers, playwrights.

Thus a discussion of Dublin novelists necessarily becomes an
astigmatic view of the Irish man of letters. If you were to ask
David Marcus, literary editor of *The Irish Press* (and himself
author of a novel), who was the foremost literary critic in
Dublin, he would more than likely reply, "Terence De Vere
White," as he did to me. But White, Marcus's counterpart on
a rival paper, *The Irish Times*, would generally be thought of
as one of Ireland's foremost novelists, and Denis Donaghue,
the foremost critic. Certainly, White is the most urbane of Irish
novelists, and if his moderate political views and pro-English
bias win him the disdain and denunciation of nationalists, dis-
passionate criticism must put him in the front rank of Anglo-
Irish novelists, except that in his case the "Anglo-" has become
not merely unnecessary or a desiccated vestigial prefix, but
incorrect.

We have here a central point and White becomes, for purposes of understanding, a key figure. Many of the original Irish
patriots wrote in English and had English ancestry and therefore were called Anglo-Irish. Because of historical exigencies

they were necessarily Protestant. It has fallen to modern times outside Ireland to use the term "Anglo-Irish" carelessly to refer to any Protestant in Ireland who happens to be a writer. This has become in the twentieth century a semantic misfortune, divisive for Ireland, and awkward there and elsewhere not only for the aims of the irenic ecumenism that is moving through the Christian world, but for an American understanding of Irish literature. No one would think of calling Sean O'Casey, Protestant that he was, Anglo-Irish, and Douglas Hyde would have abhorred the term. The same follows for White, who, a Catholic by tradition, writes in what can lazily be called the Anglo-Irish stream.

When the last British soldier sensibly has been withdrawn from Irish soil, White will then be seen as a figure of reconciliation, a Dubliner who has absorbed the Anglo-Irish strain of the Irish heritage, who has deprecated Ireland's chauvinist claims, but who has spurned the flight to some modern Tir-na-nOg such as Golden London. White has not only remained in Dublin and helped intensify the Dublin Dimension, he abandoned a lucrative law career to declare himself solely a literary man and has continued to write his novels for a small, perceptive Irish and English audience. For him, it would have been an easy matter to have sought and have become, like Edna O'Brien, a literary sensation in London or the United States, by grafting onto his witty, satiric, and sometimes hilarious comedies of manners the sexual extrapolations that have become almost rountine. He has clung to a more cultivated presentation of the world around him, proclaiming, if only covertly, the autonomy of Ireland, and his reputation is certain to grow after his death or with the final expulsion of British occupying troops, whichever comes first.

White was born in 1912 and educated at St. Stephen's Green School in Dublin and at Trinity College, where he read law, and became a solitictor in 1933. In 1941 he married Mary O'Farrell and four years later published his first book, *The Road of Excess*, an excellent biography of the genial Isaac Butt, the moderate Irish leader who gave way to Parnell. This was followed three years later by a biography of Kevin O'Higgins (1892–1927), who was minister for justice and for external affairs in the first cabinet of the Irish Free State and was assassinated by members of the I.R.A. on his way to mass. An example of the serrated side of the Irish satiric tongue is the retort one literary Dubliner of opposite political views to White, and ready to derogate his biography of O'Higgins, made on a television talk show. "Who killed Kevin O'Higgins?" the show master innocently asked, and got the reply, "Who killed Kevin O'Higgins? Terence De Vere White."

White followed that book with *The Story of the Royal Dublin Society*, and then with the autobiographical novel *A Fretful Midge*.

Not until 1959 did his first novel appear, *An Affair With the Moon*, taking its title from Irish-born Laurence Sterne, which was hailed by critics in England as well as Ireland, compared to the work of Evelyn Waugh, and praised for its delineation of "delightfully horrible Anglo-Irish types." Since 1959, he has written seven novels: *Prenez Garde* (1962), *The Remainder Man* (1963), *Lucifer Falling* (1965), *Tara* (1967), *The Lambert Mile* (1969), *The March Hare* (1970), and *Mr. Stephen* (1971).

The attention given White in this history is not because of any putative superiority of his novels over those of his contemporaries but rather his signal position. None of his novels, for example, rivals *At Swim-Two-Birds* by Flann O'Brien, who wrote an erudite humor column, Cruiskeen Lawn, side by side with White under the pseudonym Myles na gCopaleen, but who was born Brian O'Nolan (1911–1966). He maintained the column for twenty-seven years, writing it first in Irish, then in Irish one day and English the next, and finally in English only (although with Irish and Latin jokes). After his death, the column was continued under the heading The Best of Myles, and a collection under that title was published in book form in 1968, a Dublin classic. O'Nolan is another one who, despite

Terence De Vere White

preeminent talent, elected to remain in Dublin challenging the pomposity, the obscurantism, and the faults and foibles of Irish society. To support himself, however, his writings were not always sufficient and he worked many years as a civil servant. His play *Faustus Kelly* was produced at the Abbey, and another novel, *The Dalkey Archives*, was dramatized for the stage. Two other novels of his are *The Hard Life* and *The Third Policeman*. Neither has the supreme force of *At Swim-Two-Birds* which many critics rate the greatest Irish novel since *Ulysses, Finnegans Wake* remaining the most unread masterpiece of the century, a transcendent masterpiece and indisputably Irish.

Because of the Irish lust for talking, more novels are talked about than written, and many a writer has produced only one. Michael Farrell (1900–1962) won posthumous fame with *Thy Tears Might Cease*, a novel put together by Monk Gibbon (1896–   ) from a jumble of manuscript left at the death of the procrastinating Farrell. *The Riddle of the Sands* was the only novel by Erskine Childers (1870–1922) and *On Another Man's Wound*, a reminiscence sold widely in the United States as *Army Without Banners*, was the sole work of another Irish patriot, Ernest O'Malley (1898–1957), whose life matched Gogarty's or Childers's for the drama of his experiences. O'Malley was wounded by the Free State soldiers, left paraplegic and imprisoned, but recovered and wrote his classic autobiographical account of the war.

There is no way to point up the fecundity of Dublin as a city of novelists without sounding like a catalogue. David Marcus (1926–   ), who for some years edited *Irish Writing*, one of the best of Dublin's literary magazines, has written one novel, *To Next Year in Jerusalem*. Bryan MacMahon (1909–   ), celebrated for his short stories, had a major success with his novel *Children of the Rainbow*. Christy Brown (1933–   ), one of twenty-two children reared in a Dublin slum, crippled and paralyzed, without the use of his hands, able to type with one toe only, had a Book-of-the-Month Club selection in his novel *Down All the Days*. James Plunkett Kelly (1920–   ), who drops the Kelly to form his pen name, is also the author of a single novel, *Strumpet City*, which made him an international reputation. The novel takes its title from a line in a play by Denis Johnston and deals with the famous strike or lockout of 1913. Another novelist-poet is Anthony Cronin (1926–   ), whose novel *The Life of Riley* is one of the more rollicking Dublin narratives of the century, but Cronin's true niche may be as a poet. Both he and Plunkett display the versatility that marks the Dubliner. Cronin's work as editor of a literary magazine has gone hand in hand with his poetry and his prose. Plunkett first established his reputation as a playwright and author of short stories. Among his radio plays are *Homecoming* and *Farewell Harper,* and his radio work led him to the post of executive producer at Telefis/Eireann. The Abbey produced his play *The Risen People*, and his short stories in two collections won him an audience abroad before *Strumpet City*. The short-story collections are *The Eagles and the Trumpets* and *The Trusting and the Maimed.* He could become Ireland's foremost novelist.

Any chapter on Irish novels must include Peader O'Donnell (1893–   ), the veteran revolutionary and to many the dean of Irish letters, who was long associated with *The Bell*, which made his literary influence immense; Liam O'Flaherty (1896–   ), equally famous for his short stories; Monk Gibbon (1896–   ), more celebrated for his poetry; William Trevor (1928–   ), whose full name is William Trevor Cox, better known on the European continent in translations than in the United States; John Broderick (1927–   ), a businessman; Benedict Kiely (1919–   ), better known in the United States for his short stories in *The New Yorker* and his literary criticism, a man of such versatility that he might well be a chapter in himself to exemplify the talent; Robert Louis Constantine Fitz-Gibbon (1919–   ), who was born in Lenox, Massachusetts, educated in England, has served in both the British and the United States armies, and now makes his home in Dublin; Bryan Walter Guinness (1905–   ), who bears the title Lord Moyne,

is a member of the famous brewing family as well as a patron
of the arts, and also a distinguished poet and playwright, and
author of children's stories; Mervyn Wall (1908–   ), secretary and treasurer of the Irish Academy of Letters, who has
written also short stories and plays of distinction; and Brian
Cleve (1921–   ), like Mary Lavin and Constantine Fitz-
Gibbon, born abroad, a journalist of first rank, well-known
because of his radio and television work as well as his exciting
novels; Bernard Share (1930–   ), also born abroad, who
has taught abroad after attending Trinity College, but who is
now resident in Dublin and exhibiting a unique Irish literary
talent.

Two aspects of the careers of Irish novelists have marked
and will mark them, and can be exemplified by considering two
of them, Walter Macken (1915–1967) and Francis Stuart
(1902–   ). Certain Irish writers win American audiences;
and some do not. The fact must not be taken as a measure of
their worth or lack of it. Our catalogue of Irish poets and novelists currently writing in Dublin for the most part lists names
not widely known in the United States. Macken won an American audience; Stuart has not. Yet many consider Stuart the
superior writer. In brief, to know and appreciate the literature
of Dublin, it is necessary to get behind the exigencies and dis-
tortions of the American market.

Walter Macken began his career as an actor at the Abbey
but turned to novels and short stories to win his reputation:
*Quench the Moon, I Am Alone, Rain on the Wind, The Scorch-
ing Wind*, and others. Virtually unknown in the United States,
Stuart early won the praise of Yeats and others for his poetry.
Like Macken, he too had his plays produced at the Abbey,
but found his forte in the novel. He was only eighteen when
he married Maud Gonne's daughter, Iseult, and still in his
twenties when he published his first novel, *Women and God*.
When World War II exploded, he was working in Berlin and
continued to live there, which, while it gave him material for
some later novels, won him denunciation in some quarters as

being pro-Nazi. Among his novels are *Try the Sky, The Coloured Dome, and Pigeon Irish.* Sir Compton Mackenzie considered him a genius and his work of "the most profound spiritual importance to the modern world." High praise indeed. L. A. G. Strong (1896–1958), who himself belongs to the story of literary Dublin, also regarded Stuart very highly. Strong, born in England of Irish parents and a frequent visitor to Ireland from childhood until his death, wrote some of his best novels about Dublin. He is the author also of the familiar quatrain about the Abbey Theatre:

> In this theater they has plays
> On us, and high-up people comes
> And pay to see things playing here
> They'd run like hell from in the slums.

Some Irish writers still run like hell from certain subjects in print. No doubt the censorship, waning in force though it is, still has an inhibiting effect on many a novelist.

A recurring subject for discussion for Dublin writers—more heightened there than elsewhere—is whether the writer has an obligation to revolt or simply to report, to render, or to reform. Actually, both types have, in the past, had their works banned. Such banning has never made acquisition of a book more than time-consuming, and has, no doubt, increased popular interest that might otherwise lie fallow.

John MacGahern is one of the writers who stand, more or less, in the Joycean tradition. Others who share that influence, again, to a greater or less degree, are Aiden O'Higgins (1927–), in his *Langrishe, Go Down*; Anthony Cronin (1926–), in his *The Life of Riley*; Bernard Share in *Inish*; Michael Farrell, in *Thy Tears Might Cease*; and of course Flann O'Brien in *At Swim-Two-Birds*. Writing about provincial life are Benedict Kiely, one of the most versatile of Dublin writers, and John Broderick. Brian Cleeve delves into modern political life in Dublin as well as providing first-rate thrillers.

A unique figure is American-born James Patrick Donleavy

(1926–), whose novels are signed J. P. Donleavy. He was born in Brooklyn but was educated at Trinity College, and makes his home in Bective, County Meath, where Mary Lavin has her farm. His first novel, *The Ginger Man*, glamorized, for American campuses, the anti-hero. Donleavy shares the Dublin gift for satiric and wild comedy, and his protagonists seek to escape some of their personal loneliness or alienation with inventive antic gestures. His books have too ribald a sexual element for the Irish censors, and his audience is chiefly in England and America, where he has had a wide appeal. The stage adaptation of *The Ginger Man* was a Broadway success and a restaurant taking the name is operated successfully in New York by the star of the original production. *The Ginger Man* was published, even as *Ulysses*, in Paris. The year was 1955. Donleavy is also the author of *Fairy Tales of New York, Meet My Maker, the Mad Molecule, The Saddest Summer of Samuel S.*, and *The Beastly Beatitudes of Balthazar B*. He has, as many more may in the future, found Ireland, with its tax exemptions for artists, a nourishing haven, and it is interesting that the tax office grants this privilege to authors whose works are banned by the Dublin censors. Minister Charles Haughey's tax incentives may yet make Ireland again a colony of scholars.

X X

The most unique feature of Dublin's literary world must be, of course, the presence of a current, modern, vigorous Irish literature; that is, a literature written in the indigenous language of Ireland, and written, as it must be, not with an eye on England or America, but for Irish-reading (even if not Irish-speaking) Irishmen and Irishwomen.

To strangers, the Irish are deprecatingly defensive about their Irish language and its literature or as boastful as Strabo, the ancient Roman historian, long ago found the Celts to be. They need be neither, and, naturally, the most knowledgeable are not.

Many of the young are defensive because of their lack of command of the language that they have studied in school but failed to master, coming away with not too much more knowledge of Irish than the average American high school graduate after four years of study acquires of French, German, or Spanish. Thirty to forty years ago, a near hysteria filled many young Irish to learn the language of Keating, Raftery, O'Fahilly, O'Sullivan, and Merriman. Now too many young people are loathe to acknowledge how much or little of the language they know while the newspapers bristle with letters contending for and against the compulsory teaching of the language. Almost everyone, however, agrees that the complete loss of it as a living idiom would be a cultural tragedy.

The revival of Irish as a national language is unlikely; the preservation of it as a practical second language is possible. As Thomas Davis said of it, "It is the badge of nationhood; a surer fortress than mountain or river." The movement to maintain it will be greatly helped by the body of literature in Irish which is now being written in Dublin today. As that corpus grows, assisted by state funds, the future will find not merely delight in it, but the mystic sustenance that flows to any people through the tubes that run to its racial roots.

The story of modern Irish writing, not enough of which has been brought over into English, could be said to begin with priests, poets, and a pornographer, although the last word is chosen merely for alliteration. Brian Merriman (1740–1805), or to give him his Irish name, Brian MacGiolla Meidhre, was a schoolmaster in the west of Ireland, whose reputation rests on one Rabelaisian poem, and that a most remarkable one, *Cuirt an Mheadhon-Oidhche* (The Midnight Court), first published in foreign translation in German in 1904, and since translated several times in English. The poem runs over one thousand lines and is, in the original Irish, full of technical brilliance, exquisite rhythm, and ribald wit.

Three of the chief translators are Frank O'Connor, David Marcus, and Arland Ussher (1897–   ), another Dubliner, known chiefly for his philosophical commentary, but a most versatile scholar and writer as well. More recently a Merriman (sometimes more aptly spelled Merryman) festival has been organized on an annual basis, and the Limerick schoolteacher, so long disregarded, has his deserts at last. His poem presents a dialogue between a young lady mourning the lack of passionate men to make her a husband, and an old man discoursing on the frailties of women. The debate takes place in the court of Aeval, a faery queen, a battle of the sexes which ends with the men condemned for their lack of rampant virility. Queen Aeval passes judgment on them. The whole is happily Rabelaisian in tone, full of wit and irony, and offering, among other insights, a prophecy that Rome will soon let the clergy marry. That the censors once banned its translation, and that now an annual literary festival honors the author, indicates the Republic's maturity.

Long before Merriman turned out his vigorous, lusty lines, the Reverend Geoffrey Keating, D.D. (1570–1644), the priest-historian, wrote his monumental history of Ireland to set the basic style of modern Irish. Seanthrun Ceitinn, to give him his Irish name, was educated in France, a man of such scholarship, sanctity, and charm that Irish Protestants (in a bitter age) contributed to the building of his chapel.

Of the Irish language which he did so much for with his work (saving any number of words from oblivion), he wrote in verse (here badly translated decades back):

> The Irish is a language completely sweet
> In aid of which no foreign e'er did meet;
> A copious, free, keen and extending voice,
> And mellifluent, brief; for mirth most choice;
> Although the Hebrew language be the first
> And that, for learning, Latin be the best,
> Yet still, from them, the Irish ne'er was found
> One word to borrow, to make its proper sound.

Keating died in 1644 and for almost two centuries thereafter the Irish language labored under tremendous disabilities. When those diabilities were lifted, other causes delivered a mortal blow to it. If a priest was the last scholar of the seventeenth century to write the language as a learned man, a priest was the first to revive it and give it a twentieth-century style. Before we turn, however, to Father Peadar O Laoghaire (Peter O'Leary) (1839–1920) let us list some of the Irish writers from the earliest days who have left us something of their work.

The list would include Mael Isu Ua Brolchain (1000–1086), Donnchadh Mor O Dalaigh (1170–1244), Muireadhach Albanach O Dalaigh (1180–1250), Giolla Brighde Albanach MacConmidhe (1180–1260), Gearoid MacGearailt (?   – 1398), Maghnas O Domhnaill (?   –1563), Tadhg Dall O hUiginn (1550–1591), Flaithrie O Maoil Chonaire (1560–

1629), and Eoghan Ruadh Mac an Bhaird (1540–1591). These were some of the Irish writers before Keating.

Some who came after him were Aodhagan O Rathaille (1670–1726), Niall MacMhuirich (1637–1726), Tomas O Casoide (1710–1770), Seamus MacCuarta (1647–1732), Toirdhealbhach O Cearbhallain (1670–1738), Sean Clarach MacDomhnaill (1691–1754), Eibhlin Dubh ni Chonaill (1750–1800), Brian MacGiolla Meidhre (1740–1805), and Antoine O Reachtabhra (1784–1834). Some of the dates are perforce approximations. Concealed in the thicket of Irish orthography are the names of Brian Merriman and Anthony Raftery, known as Blind Raftery (the title, by the way, of a novel by Donn Byrne), and Turlough O'Carolan, often called the last of the Irish bards.

The names of these Irish writers are invoked or cited to indicate that the continuity of Irish writing was disrupted but not discontinued until the most tragic break of the nineteenth century, and then not irrevocably. There is no way of knowing how much of their work has been lost. The poems of Raftery would have been lost entirely had it not been for the diligence of Douglas Hyde, the first president of the Irish Republic. What masterpieces may have perished with the men who created and recited them but were able to write them down no more than their unlettered auditors.

What must be observed is that the Reverend Peter O'Leary (1839–1920) was born only five years after the death of Raftery. Father Peter, as he was known, more than anyone else determined the course for revived Irish, pointing out that it should take its literary style not from the archaic grace of the old masters with their linguistic complexities, but from such demotic Irish as remained in the various parts of the country. He it was who first wrote and published a collection of short stories in Irish, and he was even ahead of Douglas Hyde with a play in Irish which was produced by an amateur group in Cork at the turn of the century.

His other works, written in the Irish dialect of Cork, included devotional essays, a folk novel *Seadna*, dealing again with the sale of a soul, and renderings of many of the Irish classics into simpler Irish diction (with some unfortunate bowdlerizing), as well as translations of the Bible and Latin and Greek masterworks into Irish. A result of his bellwethering led many to write the living speech of their own districts. Later a standard was to emerge.

In 1936 in Eyre Square in Galway, Eamon de Valera unveiled an extraordinary and appealing statue of a small man in a business suit and a felt hat, seated, about to tell or write a story.

The statue honors Padraig O Conaire (1883–1928), a native of Galway, and hails him as The Story Teller. O Conaire was reared in an Irish-speaking community but went to London to earn a living. While working there as a British civil servant, he read of a Gaelic League competition for writings in Irish, penned an essay, and won first prize. Later his short stories and sketches would win other prizes.

Among his collections of short stories are *Seacht mBuraidh an Eirghe Amach* (1918), *An Grann Geagach* (1919), and *Siol Eabhan* (1922). His work took its tenor from writers on the continent and showed a felicitous urbanity quite extraordinary for a young man from rural Ireland, and a happy contrast to the starchier work of Father O'Leary.

As might be expected, the first Irish writers in the twentieth-century revival came from outside Dublin. The inspiration for the revival, however, came from the activity of the Gaelic League or the earlier Society for the Preservation of the Irish Language founded in 1876. Both had their headquarters in the capital city. The audience those first writers had was pretty much created by the league, which was formed in 1893. While the native speakers made their salient contributions, urban scholars worked busily in Dublin. Among them was another priest-pioneer, the Reverend Patrick Dineen (1860–1934), who prepared the first modern dictionary and wrote the first attempt at a modern novel, *Cormac O Conaill*, if we deny the cognomen to Father O'Leary's *Seadna*. The dictionary was English-Irish.

The first Irish-Irish dictionary has yet, I believe, to be compiled. Father Dineen's dictionary was his paramount contribution, a mine of Irish learning, and is still in use in Irish households. It helps to place these men in history if we remember that the type for Father Dineen's book was destroyed in the Easter Rising of 1916 and the whole work necessarily reconstituted.

Of the rebels of 1916, the men who became the heroes of the Rising, the one most determined to revive the Irish language was Padraic MacPiarais (Padraic Pearse), who started his school, St. Enda's, with that purpose in view. He himself wrote poetry of worth in Irish, which stands besides the work of Douglas Hyde, and short stories of idyllic charm. From these initial efforts the body of Irish writing began to evolve.

One early result was three extraordinary autobiographical works, all from the Blasket Islands. They were *An tOileanach* by Tomas O Criomhthain, *Fiche Blian ag Fas* by Muiris O Suilleabhain, and *Peig* and *Machtnamh Seana-Mhna* by Peig Sayers, all published in the 1920s and the 1930s. O Criomhthain's *An tOileanach* was the first published, written in 1926, and translated into English as *The Islandman*, and then widely translated into other languages. The Blaskets stand off the southwest coast of Ireland and still harbor Gaelic-speakers. It is interesting to note that O Criomhthain could read and write English but had to be taught how to write Irish in order to put his spoken reminiscences on paper. Muiris O Suilleabhain's autobiography won popularity in the United States under the title *Twenty Years A-Growing*. Other books, more or less autobiographical, although not of such literary worth, came out of the countryside. As late as 1969, Sean O Criomhthain, son of the Islandman, wrote *La Dar Saol*.

Since Douglas Hyde's *The Twisting of the Rope* was performed in the Abbey, Dublin has had a lively theater in Irish (there are three in all in Ireland) with such contributing dramatists as Padraic Pearse, Micheál MacLiammóir, Brendan Behan, Seamus O'Neill, Mairead Ni Ghrada, Sean O Tuama, Criostoir O Floinn, and Eoghan O Tuainse. Other landmarks in the revival of Irish have been the formation of the School of Celtic Studies in the Dublin Institute for Advanced Studies by Dr. Osborn Bergin, the establishment of the monthly journals *Comhar* and *Feasta*, the founding of Gum (no Russian department store), a government publishing bureau, a private publishing house specializing in Irish books, and several anthologies featuring the work of a variety of writers, among them, Maire Mhac an X tSaoi, Maire MacEntee O'Brien (the wife of Conor Cruise O'Brien), Sean O Riordain, Mairtin O Direain, and Seamus O'Neill.

The last man, Seamus O'Neill, has worked in several genres in Irish (in typical Dublin fashion) and his novel *Tonn Tuile*, the first book published by Sairseal agus Dill, the publishing house given over to works in Irish, was regarded as marking an important development in Gaelic literature. His *Maire Nic Artain* is a sensitive examination of the tragic division in the north of Ireland.

Modern Irish writers whose critical acclaim runs high are Seamus O Grianna and his brother, Seosamh MacGrianna, and Mairtin O Cadhain. O Cadhain's novel, *Cre na Cille*, published in 1949, is perhaps the best of modern novels in Irish and has not yet been translated into English, mainly because it would be too difficult a task, such was O Cadhain's gift with Gaelic. Among the best novels in Irish are *Caisleain Oir*, published in the twenties by Seamus O Grianna, *Padhraic Mhaire Bhan* by Sean O Ruadhain, and *Ceol na nGiolcach* by Padraig O Conaire, *Dianmhuilte De* and *Caoin Thu Fein* by Diarmuid O Suilleabhain, and *Bride Bhan* by Padraig Ua Maoileoin.

Some excellent work is being done in the field of biography, and Sean O Luing's *Life of Arthur Griffith*, to give it its English title, is by far the principal study to appear on the founder of the new Irish state and is likely to remain the chief source of information on Griffith for some while.

Most of these men have done something in the short story as well, and, as we have seen, Liam O'Flaherty has also made a contribution there. Seamus O Grianna, who signed himself

Maire, and Seosamh both distinguished themselves with their short stories. A collection of George Moore's, by the way, did very well translated into Irish. Other names that could be added are Tarlack O hUid, Tomas Bairead, Donchadh O Ceileachair, and Criostoir O Floinn. Nor are the movie, drama, poetry, and the short story the only interests of Irish writers. Leon O Broin is one of several who has written notable volumes of history and biography in Irish, which, translated into English, were well received in America and England.

Three elements are thus involved in the struggle of Irish to survive as a living language in a shrinking commercial world: the Gaeltacht, that is, the small number of persons, perhaps one percent of the Irish people, who use Irish as their sole language; the scholars and creative artists in the country who are working to expand the body of literature; and the slowly growing body of educated persons sufficiently bilingual and so able to enjoy Irish literature, including a small but growing group in the United States. Meanwhile the discussion continues all over Ireland as to the best method of preserving Irish. The whole is, one can readily judge, a unique factor in the Dublin Dimension.

EPILOGUE

This book is, to the best of my knowledge, the first literary history of Dublin. The idea was conceived by the late Richard Taplinger, the publisher, founder of the firm that bears his name, a frequent visitor to the British Isles and the Republic of Ireland, an informal ambassador of goodwill, blessed with an easy gift of friendship. Dublin fascinated him and he sensed the inadequacy of acquaintance those outside the Pale have with the ancient capital. He wanted to acquaint the public with the literature that has been produced because that city is what it is, a city for which, from the literary point of view, fecund seems an adjective of understatement. I have attempted to relate the literature to the history of the place, for in that country more than anywhere else, it seems, the two are inextricably intertwined. All the more reason for not subsuming Irish literature under English literature.

Literature on the island began before the introduction of the English language, and now proceeds in two languages. I have attempted to tell about those in different balance than has been done in other literary studies of literature in Ireland, for the literary history of Dublin is not the same thing as the literary history of Ireland, and non-Irish interests differ from Irish interests. I have tried to account for the proliferation of literary activity in Dublin by describing a confluence of conditions which engenders an ambiance that I have called the Dublin Dimension.

The influence of exile and expatriation I have sought to deal with as briefly as possible, for it is a book in itself; and just as briefly, I have tried to indicate those factors that exist in the city and are sufficiently European in character to be alien to American thinking on the one hand and English on the other.

The role of the Catholic church, or better, the Irish Catholic church, not only in the development of nationhood, in the struggle for independence, in the weakening of the place of the Irish language, in the opposition to artistic freedom, and in providing those inspirations and tensions without which a literature can become jejune, I have dealt with several times. I regard Catholicism as central to the idiosyncrasy of Ireland, but wounded there in the long struggle to survive English persecutions, and by its ambivalence toward foreign domination, with the lower clergy often with the rabble in arms and bishops thundering anathemas against them. Yet there is always a danger of Catholicism becoming a test of Irish nationalism with the result that Irish Protestants and others may feel a sense of isolation. The recent disestablishment of the Catholic church in Ireland from its legal position of preferment should help minimize that danger.

The ignorance of Irish history, Irish politics, and Irish literature outside Ireland is vast, even among Irish Americans. Catholic colleges founded by Irish Americans, for example, and staffed in part by Americans of Irish descent have subsumed Irish literature under English literature. They rarely offer courses in the Irish language or in Irish history, and are no better in any of these regards than state, secular, or Protestant universities. I was able to spend four years at a Jesuit college in Irish Catholic Boston and never hear the name of William Carleton, read a poem by Samuel Ferguson, or explore the Celtic mythology. Such I had to discover on my own. As in other universities, Yeats, Joyce, O'Casey, and Shaw were allowed to veil all others in the aureole of their incredible luminosity. I do not think the situation has altered much in forty years. I am told the situation in England is no different.

A literary history of Dublin thus makes sense for a number

of reasons. There are very few literary histories of Ireland. A stranger dipping into that by Douglas Hyde will find no one who wrote in English, for, as Hyde himself said, he was really writing a history of Irish literature. Others give an exaggerated amount of space to writers of Irish, at least from the outsider's point of view. Frank O'Connor's work on Ireland's literary history is a critical evaluation of some Irish writers, and, as might be expected, a work of brilliant insights. It does not present the legions of Irish writers in any sort of narration or perspective. The overall story of Dublin and the writers it has bred, fostered, encouraged, or stimulated has remained untold.

Now as both England and Ireland have entered the Common Market, and as Ireland finds itself an independent if truncated nation, facing the second half of its first century of independence and freedom, the time has certainly come to separate its literary history from that of England, allowing, of course, for the symbiotic relationship.

In a way, our literary history of Dublin ends as it began with the Irish language struggling to assert itself and the Richard Stanyhursts deprecating its presence. One thousand years have turned the world topsy-turvy in every other regard. Instead of being an Ultima Thule, Ireland is one of the four corners of the air-minded world. Its ancient foe remains its best customer but now they deal as equals. Its emigrants can return as they wish; its exiles are reconciled expatriates. Violence of an insane savagery still disfigures the northeastern corner of the island because the English cannot or will not extricate themselves from a doomed enclave. The peripatetic scholars no longer languish in foreign monasteries or universities unless they so desire, for they can return to lecture in their own academic halls or retire on a government pension. Ireland, no longer an occupied country, nevertheless writhes to find itself.

Out of the lecture halls is coming a new literature, a new Irish examination of Ireland, an examination that is not written with one eye on England, or on America, or on Europe, but only on the perfection of the work. To be sure, much is still being written for the English market or the American market, and there are creative Irish writers who could not survive without those markets, for every so often there is a recrudescence of the waning formal or informal censorship. American shops sparkle with entertaining books about Ireland—travel books, political books, sociological books, cookbooks, picture books, ingenious books, cordial books, all of them discussing all of Ireland's problems, aspects, people, and salmon fishing in one swoop. Meanwhile a mass of scholarly Irish studies that rarely reach the American or English market are emerging from the Irish universities.

While American university scholars—the sort pinioned by Paddy Kavanagh in his poem—make a business out of contorted, convoluted, tortuous studies of three or four Irish writers, letting a thousand go unmentioned, Irish scholars are writing with insight and verve on their minor figures for the illumination of us all, redeeming many from undeserved oblivion.

Irish critics—always a small elite—may today turn their attention to American or English writers but it is less to catch an audience than to say what they have to say. The first of the great Irish critics, Edmund Malone (1741–1812), turned to Shakespeare to find a subject worthy of his talents and was the first major critic to do so. Ernest Boyd interpreted Irish writing for American audiences in the 1920s. Conor Cruise O'Brien was concerned with literary criticism before national and international politics caught up his energies. Denis O'Donoghue, a University College don, has examined American poets as well as Yeats, and, it is a pity, has withdrawn from doing the definitive life of Yeats. Too often Irish critics have left their literary giants to foreign critics, although John Eglinton was one of the first to write on Joyce. Criticism traditionally has been the work of wealthy aristocrats or university scholars and Ireland is just moving into its own in that regard, but there are few Dublin writers who have not contributed something to literary criticism. I have a compilation of their insights that make a pretty book.

Meanwhile the literary life in Dublin continues, feeds on itself, flourishes, and is raked by self-criticism. Writers mourn the absence of writers, meaning giants, and ignore one another. Critics scan the horizon for the successor to Yeats or Synge or Kavanagh, forgetting that, usually, we can have only one Titan at a time.

The Dublin Dimension remains in full force like a magnetic field. The winds of exchange and incitement can fan any spark to flame. As the spirit lists, it flies. Beyond the ancient Pale, the Dublin Dimension works like a whirlpool sucking the out-landers into its vortex. Yet, dramatists like John B. Keane and poets like Richard Murphy, one based in Listowel, the other in the fishing village of Cleggan, need not flee their villages today to find the world, or to have available to them the resources of their origin and the facilities of the national capital at the same time. Travel is quick and easy.

Stationed wherever they may be, American transplants like J. P. Donleavy, Richard Condon, J. F. Powers, and John Philip Cohane, to name but four, can benefit from the Dublin Dimension, from the resonances and emphases it sets up, and from the reverberations of history and hope which merge in it. In brief, Dublin is likely to continue to spawn literary men writing in English in a greater incidence to the general population than any other English-speaking city. Its advantages are many; its tradition is established; its idiosyncrasy unique and strong. The Irish language remains, curiously, a trump card, a singular factor in a singular city, and can impart to Irish writing in English a strength of its own. England's strength during its burgeoning decades and its great days came from cross-fertiliza-tion: the superior Latin culture moving in on the rough Anglo-Saxon culture, dominating it and melding with it to produce the greatest empire since the Pax Romana. So too Ireland can benefit from cross-fertilization if it can persuade its educated class to secure to itself the country's aboriginal language as a second language and even a secret language, and, indeed, make it perhaps the language of the drawing room.

On the other hand, Dublin must never surrender, and it is supremely unlikely that it will or can, the English tongue that was thrust upon it, for it is the best of languages, and through it Ireland spoke at last to the world, as did India. Equally tragic as the loss of English or Irish would be Dublin's repulsion, through native bigotry, clerical obtuseness, or a misbegotten political exclusivity, of those Christians or dissidents whose creeds contradict the tenets of the majority. Ireland needs, for example, the civility that ran through the Anglo-Irish inheritance and it needs the *"cortesia"* of Francis of Assisi, which so insisted on the dignity of every man.

As for the differences among the Christian sects, the ecumenical movement will reduce them in time if charity—in the fiery term of Saint Paul—can be the first rule of Irish life. Were a true irenicism achieved, Ireland might again become the prime civilizing influence in a disintegrating society. Even if such a profound destiny never again returns to its people, Dublin has within its grasp to continue to provide some of the world's best literature.

SELECTED BIBLIOGRAPHY

Bence-Jones, Mark. *The Remarkable Irish*. New York: David McKay, 1966.

Bowen, Elizabeth. *Bowen's Court*. New York: Alfred A. Knopf, 1942.

Bowers, Claude G. *The Irish Orators*. Indianapolis: Bobbs-Merrill, 1916.

Boyd, Ernest A. *The Contemporary Drama of Ireland*. Dublin: Talbot Press.

————. *Ireland's Literary Renaissance*. Rev. ed. New York: Barnes & Noble, 1968.

Boyle, Ted E. *Brendan Behan*. New York: Twayne Publishers, 1969.

Brooke, Stopford A., Rolleston, T. W., et al., eds. *A Treasury of Irish Poetry in the English Tongue*. Rev. ed. 1931. Reprint. St. Clair Shores, Mich.: Scholarly Press, 1971.

Brown, Malcolm. *The Politics of Irish Literature*. Seattle: University of Washington Press, 1972.

Cleeve, Brian. *Dictionary of Irish Writers*. 2 vols. Cork: Mercier, 1967. New York: British Book Center, 1971.

Cohane, John P. *The Indestructible Irish*. New York: Hawthorn Books, 1969.

Colum, Mary, and Colum, Padraic. *Our Friend James Joyce*. 1958. Reprint. Gloucester, Mass.: Peter Smith, 1961.

Colum, Padraic. *A Treasury of Irish Folklore*. 2d rev. ed. New York: Crown Publishers, 1967.

Corkery, Daniel. *The Hidden Ireland*. Dublin: Gill & Macmillan, 1970.

————. *Synge and Anglo-Irish Literature*. 1931. Reprint. New York: Russell & Russell, 1965.

Craig, M. J. *Dublin, 1660–1860*. Dublin: Allen Figgis; New York: Coward-McCann, 1952.

Curtis, Edmund. *A History of Ireland*. 6th rev. ed. London: Methuen, 1950. New York: Barnes & Noble, 1951.

de Blacam, Aodh. *A First Book of Irish Literature*. Dublin: Talbot Press, 1940. Port Washington, N.Y.: Kennikat Press, 1970.

Duffy, Sir Charles Gavan. *The Rivival of Irish Literature*. London: 1894.

Ellis-Fermor, Una. *The Irish Dramatic Movement*. 2d ed. London: Methuen; New York: Barnes & Noble, 1967.

Ellmann, Richard. *Yeats: The Man and the Masks*. New York: Dutton Paperbacks, 1958.

————. *James Joyce*. London and New York: Oxford University Press, 1959.

Evans, E. Estyn. *Irish Folk Ways*. London: Routledge & Kegan Paul; Old Greenwich, Conn.: Devin-Adair, 1957.

Flanagan, Thomas J. *The Irish Novelists, 1800–1850*. New York: Columbia University Press, 1959.

Greene, David H., and Stephens, Edward M. *J. M. Synge, 1871–1909*. New York: Crowell Collier and Macmillan, 1959.

Gregory, Isabella Augusta, Lady. *Journals 1916–1930*. Edited by Lennox Robinson. London: Putnam, 1946. New York: Macmillan, 1947.

————. *Our Irish Theatre*. 1914. Reprint. New York: G. P. Putnam's, Capricorn Books, 1965.

Hogan, Robert. *Dion Boucicault*. New York: Twayne Publishers, 1969.

Holloway, Joseph. *Joseph Holloway's Abbey Theatre*. Edited by Robert Hogan and Michael J. O'Neill. Carbondale, Ill.: Southern Illinois University Press, 1967.

————. Holloway Papers, unpublished journal "Impressions of a Dublin Playgoer." (National Library of Ireland, Dublin.)

Hyde, Douglas. *Literary History of Ireland*. 1889. Reprint. New York: Barnes & Noble, 1967.

Kain, Richard M. *Dublin in the Age of William Butler Yeats and James Joyce*. Norman: University of Oklahoma Press, 1962.

Kavanagh, Patrick. *Collected Poems*. Old Greenwich, Conn.: Devin-Adair, 1964.

Keanne, John B. *Self-Portrait*. Cork: Mercier, 1964.

Kennelly, Brendan, ed. *The Penguin Book of Irish Verse*. London and Baltimore: Penguin Books, 1970.

Kiely, Benedict. *Poor Scholar: A Study of the Works and Days of William Carleton 1794–1869*. New York: Sheed & Ward, 1948.

Lecky, William W. H. *A History of Ireland in the Eighteenth Century*. 5 vols. London: 1892; New York: Appleton.

Lyons, F. S. *Ireland Since the Famine*. New York: Charles Scribner's, 1971.

MacDonagh, Thomas. *Literature in Ireland*. 1916 ed. Reprint. (Irish Culture and History Series.) Port Washington, N.Y.: Kennikat Press, 1970.

Meally, Victor, ed. *Encyclopedia of Ireland*. Dublin: Allen Figgis, 1973.

Mercier, Vivian. *The Irish Comic Tradition*. London and New York: Oxford University Press, 1962.

Moore, George, *Hail and Farewell*. 3 vols. New York: Appleton, 1911–14. London: Heinemann, 1933.

Murphy, Gerald. *Tales from Ireland*. Buffalo, N.Y.: Desmond & Stapleton, 1947.

O Broin, Leon. *Dublin Castle and the 1916 Rising*. New York: New York University Press, 1971.

————. *Fenian Fever*. New York: New York University Press, 1971.

O'Casey, Sean. *Autobiography*. 6 vols. London and New York: Macmillan.
  I Knock at the Door (1939)
  Pictures in the Hallway (1942)
  Drums Under the Window (1945)
  Inishfallen, Fare Thee Well (1949)
  Rose and Crown (1952)
  Sunset and Evening Star (1954)

O'Connor, Frank. *A Short History of Irish Literature: A Backward Look*. New York: G. P. Putnam's, 1967.

O'Connor, Ulick. *Brendan*. Englewood Cliffs, N.J.: Prentice-Hall, 1971.

————. *Oliver St. John Gogarty.* London: Jonathan Cape, 1968.

O'Faolain, Sean. *The Irish: A Character Study.* Old Greenwich, Conn.: Devin-Adair, 1949.

Power, Patrick C. *A Literary History of Ireland.* Cork: Mercier, 1969. New York: British Book Center, 1971.

Pyle, Hilary. *Jack B. Yeats.* London: Routledge & Kegan Paul, 1970.

Sheehy, Michael. *Is Ireland Dying: Culture and the Church in Modern Ireland.* New York: Taplinger, 1969.

Stanford, W. B., and McDowell, R. B. *Mahaffy.* London: Routledge & Kegan Paul, 1971.

Starkie, Walter. *Scholars and Gypsies: An Autobiography.* Berkeley and Los Angeles: University of California Press, 1963.

Synge, John M. *Letters to Molly: John Millington Synge to Maire O'Neill.* Edited by Ann Saddlemyer. Cambridge, Mass.: Harvard University Press, 1971.

————. *The Writings of J. M. Synge.* Edited by Robin Skelton. Indianapolis: Bobbs-Merrill, 1971.

White, Terence De Vere. *Ireland.* New York: Walker & Co., 1968.

Yeats, William B. *Collected Plays.* Rev. ed. New York: Macmillan, 1953.

————. *Collected Poems.* Definitive 2d ed. New York: Macmillan, 1956.

————. *Dramatis Personae 1896–1902.* Dublin: Cuala, 1935. New York: Macmillan, 1936.

————. *Letters to the New Island.* Edited by Horace Reynolds. 1934. Reprint. Cambridge, Mass.: Harvard University Press, 1970.

————. *Memoirs.* Edited by Denis Donoghue. New York: Macmillan, 1973.

INDEX